The 1984
Olympic Scientific
Congress
Proceedings
Volume 10

Sport for Children and Youths

Series Editors:

Jan Broekhoff, PhD
Michael J. Ellis, PhD
Dan G. Tripps, PhD

University of Oregon
Eugene, Oregon

The 1984
Olympic Scientific
Congress
Proceedings
Volume 10

Sport for Children and Youths

Maureen R. Weiss and Daniel Gould
Editors

Human Kinetics Publishers, Inc.
Champaign, Illinois

Library of Congress Cataloging-in-Publication Data

Olympic Scientific Congress (1984 : Eugene, Or.)
    Sport for children and youths.

    (1984 Olympic Scientific Congress proceedings ;
v. 10)
    Bibliography: p.
    1. Sports for children—Congresses.   2. Running
for children—Congresses.   I. Weiss, Maureen, R.,
1952—   .   II. Gould, Daniel, 1952-   .
III. Title.   IV. Series: Olympic Scientific Congress
(1984 : Eugene, Or.).   1984 Olympic Scientific
Congress proceedings ; v. 10.
GV565.O46 1984 vol. 10   796 s   85-18111
[GV709.2]   [796'.01'922]
ISBN 0-87322-009-9

Managing Editor: Susan Wilmoth, PhD
Developmental Editor: Gwen Steigelman, PhD
Production Director: Sara Chilton
Copyeditor: Olga Murphy
Typesetter: Karl Taira and Theresa Bear
Text Layout: Cyndy Barnes
Cover Design and Layout: Jack Davis
Printed By: Braun-Brumfield, Inc.

ISBN: 0-87322-006-4   (10 Volume Set)
ISBN: 0-87322-009-9

Printed in the United States of America

10 9 8 7 6 5 4 3 2 1

Human Kinetics Publishers, Inc.
Box 5076, Champaign, IL 61820

Figure 1 on p. 47 is adapted from "Nature and meaning of readiness for
school" *Merrill-Palmer Quarterly*, **3**, (1957) by A. Brenner by permission of the
Wayne State University Press.

Contents

Series Acknowledgments

The Congress organizers realize that an event as large and complex as the 1984 Olympic Scientific Congress could not have come to fruition without the help of literally hundreds of organizations and individuals. Under the patronage of UNESCO, the Congress united in sponsorship and cooperation no fewer than 64 national and international associations and organizations. Some 50 representatives of associations helped with the organization of the scientific and associative programs by coordinating individual sessions. The cities of Eugene and Springfield yielded more than 400 volunteers who donated their time to make certain that the multitude of Congress functions would progress without major mishaps. To all these organizations and individuals, the organizers express their gratitude.

A special word of thanks must also be directed to the major sponsors of the Congress: the International Council of Sport Science and Physical Education (ICSSPE), the United States Olympic Committee (USOC), the International Council on Health, Physical Education and Recreation (ICHPER), and the American Alliance for Health, Physical Education, Recreation and Dance (AAHPERD). Last but not least, the organizers wish to acknowledge the invaluable assistance of the International Olympic Committee (IOC) and its president, Honorable Juan Antonio Samaranch. President Samaranch made Congress history by his official opening address in Eugene on July 19, 1984. The IOC further helped the Congress with a generous donation toward the publication of the Congress papers. Without this donation it would have been impossible to make the proceedings available in this form.

Finally, the series editors wish to express their thanks to the volume editors who selected and edited the papers from each program of the Congress. Special thanks go to Maureen R. Weiss of the University of Oregon and Daniel Gould of the University of Illinois for their work on this volume.

Jan Broekhoff,
Michael J. Ellis, and
Dan G. Tripps

Series Editors

Series Preface

Sport for Children and Youths contains selected proceedings from this inter-disciplinary program of the 1984 Olympic Scientific Congress, which was held at the University of Oregon in Eugene, Oregon, preceding the Olympic Games in Los Angeles. The Congress was organized by the College of Human Development and Performance of the University of Oregon in collaboration with the cities of Eugene and Springfield. This was the first time in the history of the Congress that the event was organized by a group of private individuals, unaided by a federal government. The fact that the Congress was attended by more than 2,200 participants from more than 100 different nations is but one indication of its success.

The Congress program focused on the theme of Sport, Health, and Well-Being and was organized in three parts. The mornings of the eight-day event were devoted to disciplinary sessions, which brought together specialists in various subdisciplines of sport science such as sport medicine, biomechanics, sport psychology, sport sociology, and sport philosophy. For the first time in the Congress' history, these disciplinary sessions were sponsored by the national and international organizations representing the various subdisciplines. In the afternoons, the emphasis shifted toward interdisciplinary themes in which scholars and researchers from the subdisciplines attempted to contribute to crossdisciplinary understanding. In addition, three evenings were devoted to keynote addresses and presentations, broadly related to the theme of Sport, Health, and Well-Being.

In addition to the scientific programs, the Congress also featured a number of associative programs with topics determined by their sponsoring organizations. Well over 1,200 papers were presented in the various sessions of the Congress at large. It stands to reason, therefore, that publishing the proceedings of the event presented a major problem to the organizers. It was decided to limit proceedings initially to interdisciplinary sessions which drew substantial interest from Congress participants and attracted a critical number of high-quality presentations. Human Kinetics Publishers, Inc. of Champaign, Illinois, was selected to produce these proceedings. After considerable deliberation, the following interdisciplinary themes were selected for publication: Competitive Sport for Children and Youths; Human Genetics and Sport; Sport and Aging; Sport and Disabled Individuals; Sport and Elite Performers; Sport, Health, and Nutrition; and Sport and Politics. The 10-volume set published by Human Kinetics Publishers is rounded out by the disciplinary proceedings of Kinanthropometry, Sport Pedagogy, and the associative program on the Scientific Aspects of Dance.

Jan Broekhoff,
Michael J. Ellis, and
Dan G. Tripps,

Series Editors

Preface

The Olympic Games signify the pursuit of excellence and the opportunity to test human potential. The pursuit of excellence is not experienced exclusively by Olympic athletes, however. Millions of young athletes develop and compare both physical and mental skills on tracks and playing fields and in gymnasiums and natatoriums around the world. Sport provides ample opportunities for children to test their skills and experience the joy of participation, whether swimming a personal record in the 100 m sprint medley, learning how to catch a long pass in American football, or scoring a goal in soccer. Sport for children and youth, then, is an important topic of concern for anyone interested in more fully understanding the Olympic spirit.

There are a number of reasons why sport for children and youth was selected as a major theme for the 1984 Olympic Scientific Congress. First, a tremendous number of children are involved in organized sport programs around the world. Second, many of these children do not just participate in sport, but are intensely involved in these activities. In fact, recent studies have shown that children rated sport participation as one of the most important activities in their lives. Third, children participate in sport during the crucial and formative years of their lives. These early sport experiences can often have important long-term consequences on their physical growth, socialization, and psychological development. Finally, it has been recognized that sport participation for children is *not automatically* beneficial or detrimental. Rather, the *quality* of experience children receive in these programs has been identified as the critical variable determining the beneficial or detrimental effects of participation.

It is the task of the youth sport researcher to identify those sport experiences which are beneficial as well as those experiences which are detrimental to the physical and psychological health and development of young athletes. Unfortunately, few forums have been available for the world's sport scientists to interact and discuss their findings regarding this important topic. Moreover, efforts to disseminate research findings to those working with young athletes have been limited. This volume of the 1984 Olympic Scientific Congress Proceedings is an attempt to fill this void. Leading youth sport researchers from around the world were invited to address the critical scientific and practical issues in the area.

The volume is divided into seven parts with each part focusing on a different issue of theoretical and/or practical importance. In Part I the focus is on the practical topic of determining the status of youth sport and youth sport research around the world. Experts from selected countries address a series of common issues. Further, problems common to all, as well as areas requiring additional study are identified. In Part II the controversial question of when children should begin competing is discussed from an interdisciplinary perspective. The focus in Part III and IV is on the important psychological topics of perceived competence and perceptions of stress. Both sections include papers summarizing original research from which practical implications are derived.

Parts V and VI turn to the issue of protecting the health and safety of child athletes. Specifically, in Part V injuries in youth sport with particular emphasis placed on overuse and epiphyseal disorders are examined. Then from a multidisciplinary perspective, the practical issue of sport and game modification to protect children's health and foster their optimal growth and development is discussed. Lastly, in Part VII of the volume, the results of a unique interdisciplinary study of the elite young runner are summarized. This longitudinal study involves over 35 investigators from a variety of disciplines and is the only one of its kind in the world.

The contribution of this volume, thus, lies in its timely theme and its attempt to address critical issues and questions posed by youth sport researchers and practitioners. It is hoped that the information present in this volume provides a clearer understanding of youth sport and will generate increased interest in the area for years to come.

Maureen R. Weiss
Daniel Gould
Editors

The 1984
Olympic Scientific
Congress
Proceedings
Volume 10

Sport for Children and Youths

PART I

Youth Sport Around the World

A major problem facing those interested in youth sport is the lack of available information in the area. In most countries, systematic research efforts have only begun within the last decade, and demographic data regarding program size, organization, and funding are often lacking.

Not only is youth sport information lacking within individual countries, but youth sport leaders and researchers have few methods of acquiring and sharing knowledge about programs and policies in other lands. This is unfortunate because much could be learned by examining the common problems and concerns that span youth sport programs in different countries around the world, as well as the unique characteristics of youth sport within individual countries. In addition, youth sport researchers could greatly expand their knowledge by comparing research questions, methods, and findings across cultures. By sharing information from an international perspective, youth sport researchers can begin bridging gaps in our knowledge base.

The papers presented in the first part of this volume provide basic information about youth sport as it presently exists in six different countries. Specifically, Ian Robertson writes about Australia; Maria Beatriz Rocha Ferreira speaks about Brazil; Terry Valeriote and Lori Hansen discuss Canada; Sue Campbell adds insights from the United Kingdom; Rainer Martens examines youth sport in the United States; and Stephen Jefferies reports on the USSR.

To facilitate the process of making multi-country comparisons, each author was asked to address the following five themes which provide the major sections of each paper:

1. The scope of youth sport participation (e.g., number of children involved, the age at which children begin participation, most popular sports, gender differences in participation patterns).

2 . The organization of youth sport (e.g., local and national organization, funding).
3 . The education of youth sport coaches (e.g., sport specific, technique, sport science, and medicine education).
4 . The status of youth sport research (e.g., research history, scope, and current status of research, major questions being studied, injury data in youth sport, most pressing research questions needing study).
5 . Major strengths and areas in need of improvement.

1

Youth Sport in Australia

Ian Robertson
SOUTH AUSTRALIA COLLEGE OF ADVANCED EDUCATION
SALISBURY, SOUTH AUSTRALIA, AUSTRALIA

> Organized sport looms large in the lives of many Australian children because it is so inescapably a part of the adult culture. The pressure to participate, or to back up a decision not to, is there both at school and outside it (*The National Times,* Feb. 3-9, 1984, p. 20).

The sporting life of Australians is in part mythology and in part reality. The mythology evolves from the media coverage and mass consumption of the performances of elite athletes; the reality comes from the many Australians, particularly those between the ages of 4 to 18, who actually physically participate in organized sport during most of the year. Perhaps one of the most visible social phenomenons of contemporary Australian sporting society is the organization of children and youth into competitive sport by volunteer adults: This manuscript will report on this phenomenon.

The Scope and Organization of Youth Sports

A decade ago, Norman (1975) provided the results of a survey of youth that examined involvement in sport (see Table 1). Using these figures to generalize to the total population, it is reasonable to assume that well over 1 million children between the ages of 9 and 14 are presently involved in organized competitive sport in Australia.

Although each state in Australia has its uniqueness in regards to the organization of youth sport, all have much in common. Unfortunately, few studies have been conducted, and national statistics are not available regarding the scope and organization of youth sport in Australia. Therefore, for the purpose of this particular paper, statistics from the state of South Australia (population 1,353,000) and, in particular, the city of Adelaide (population 800,000), will be provided as a case study.

Table 1. Responses to a survey of youth involvement in sport

	"I often chose to do"	Male %	Female %
Play competitive sport	12-14 years	60	52
or team sports	15-17 years	41	39
	18-20 years	44	33
Play casual sports	12-14 years	49	45
	15-17 years	38	31
	18-20	39	37

Note. From *Youth Say Report: The Recreational Priorities of Australian Young People.* (pp. 49-51) by M.J. Norman, 1975, Canberra: Australian Government Publishing Service. Reprinted with Permission.

Extent of School and Community Sport

In the Adelaide region, sport involvement is the most preferred leisure activity of preadolescents with 75% of boys and 67% of girls participating in at least one organized sport. Youth sport involvement is either organized by the community or school systems (state or independent) with children playing within one or both organizations. The community sport agencies are usually specific sport clubs or multisport community service or religious organizations. The system is not without problems as stated in Schools Discussion Paper No. 4 (1978).

> There is no common pattern for sport organization in schools. Some sports are offered as after-school activities, others are catered for on Saturday mornings. Frequent conflicts have occurred between school authorities and local clubs. Students have often become the 'meat in the sandwich' between the schools and the clubs competing for the services of students with sporting ability. (p. 13)

Funding

The facilities and equipment essential for school sport are usually provided from government funds supplemented by school fundraising, sponsorship, or minimal payment by parents. Community sport organizations need to be more resourceful in obtaining financial support via membership fees, in fundraising, and, possibly, in seeking commercial sponsorship or government grants.

Sport Institutes

The Australian Institute of Sport was established in Canberra in 1981 to give young Australians the opportunity to pursue excellence in sport to the highest level. Educational and career training opportunities are currently given to 190 athletes who are on scholarships. Specialist coaching is available to these athletes in eight sports (basketball, gymnastics, netball, soccer, swimming, tennis, track and field, and weight lifting), as well as access to world-class facilities and competition, and sport science and sport medicine support. In addition, two state-based institutions of sport (in South Australia and Western Australia) also provide help to a wide range of sports on an advisory and technical support basis.

Table 2. The favorite sport of children in the Adelaide metropolitan area

Sport	Boys 1979 (N = 663) %	Boys 1980 (N = 515) %	Sport	Girls 1979 (N = 624) %	Girls 1980 (N = 464) %
Australian football	21.1	37.1	Australian football	1.6	2.8
Athletics	1.2	2.3	Athletics	2.9	3.0
Baseball	4.2	0.8			
Basketball	2.4	2.7	Basketball	6.7	5.4
			Calisthenics	0.8	1.1
Cricket	15.2	7.6	Cricket	2.4	1.1
Fishing	1.8	.0			
Gymnastics	0.2	1.4	Gymnastics	1.8	3.9
Hockey	3.6	2.3	Hockey	2.4	4.5
Lacrosse	1.1	1.2	Horse riding	3.2	1.3
Motorcycles	1.4	0.6	Netball	25.2	33.8
Rugby union	2.3	0.8	Rollerskating	2.7	0.4
Soccer	17.8	18.6	Soccer	2.6	3.7
			Softball	12.0	10.8
Swimming	4.1	4.7	Swimming	9.1	6.9
Tennis	6.3	3.3	Tennis	11.7	5.6
			Volleyball	2.2	1.1
Other sports	11.4	6.7	Other sports	7.6	7.1
No response	5.9	9.9	No response	5.1	7.5
	100%	100%		100%	100%

Note. From *Children's Perceived Satisfaction and Stresses in Sport*, by I.D. Robertson (1981), Melbourne.

Most Popular Sports in Adelaide

The most popular sports for 12- to 14-year-olds are illustrated in Table 2. Inspection of this table reveals that Australian football, soccer, and cricket are the most popular sports for boys, whereas netball, softball, and swimming are the most popular sports for girls.

Gender and Sport

Competition in sport is predominantly single sex, although in recent years, girls have become involved in collision sports such as Australian football and rugby (but not always without opposition from male coaches and administrators). According to participation figures, girls are underrepresented in sport (Marsh, 1980).

Dropout Rate

Unfortunately, the dropout rate, like those of other Western countries such as Canada and the United States, is about 60% with over half the dropouts citing the stress imposed by the programming and the behavior of adults as reasons for discontinuing. Of those who dropped out, only half indicated that they intended to play that sport again, while approximately 75% of both sexes indicated that they would like to learn a new sport (Robertson, 1981).

The Education of Youth Sport Coaches

The education of many youth sport coaches, unfortunately, has taken place informally by the "hidden curriculum" of sport in Australian society. That is, coaches have had to learn to coach from their own player or spectator experiences or vicariously through the observation of professional coaches viewed via the mass media.

Australian coaches no longer must learn to coach on their own, however. A three-level National Coaching Accreditation Scheme (NCAS) has been developed and formal coaching education is now provided by 67 sport organizations affiliated with the NCAS. Of the 23,000 coaches taking part in this program, approximately 80% have completed the Level 1 course.

Although the NCAS has been successful in educating a large number of coaches, a major problem confronting the coordinators of the NCAS is the finding that only a small minority (approximately 10%) of Australian youth sport coaches have attained a Level 1 coaching certificate, and an even smaller number would be interested in undertaking the full 14-hour course (Robertson, 1983). Because of this, some sport organizations have modified their Level 1 curriculum from a theoretical sport-specific and science-information lecture base to a more practical "hands on" approach. Others have offered a less demanding and intermediate course of 4 to 6 hours to attract youth coaches who may be apprehensive about the Level 1 course.

Finally, during the late 1970s and early 1980s, a considerable amount of sport-specific material has become available, much of it promoted by the national magazine *Sports Coach*, produced by the Department of Youth, Sport, and Recreation in Western Australia. This department has also produced a series of eight videotapes supported by workbooks relevant to the needs of the volunteer youth sport coach. Other materials recently produced include modified sport booklets on a number of sports (e.g., Australian football, hockey, netball, cricket, rugby, and baseball); a joint policy paper prepared with the Australian Sport Medicine Federation; a brochure, "Developing Children and Youth Through Sport," produced jointly by the Australian Council for Health, Physical Education, and Recreation (ACHPER) and the Youth Sport Institute, Salisbury, South Australia; and many sport-specific manuals produced by individual sport organizations.

The Status of Youth Sport Research

In the past, little research has been conducted in the area of youth sport in Australia. Therefore, Australians have greatly depended on North American research with the implications for change being considered relevant to the Australian situation. The most significant Australian research has been associated with the presence of the graduate programs at the Universities of Western Australia and Queensland. Reports by Willie (1973), Bloomfield (1975), Coles (1975), Watson (1978), Winter (1980), Mutton (1981), Thompson (1982), and Sunders and Jobling (1983), have stimulated sport coaching and innovative programs considerably.

Sports Injuries

One of the areas least researched is that on the incidence and severity of youth sport injuries. The only available evidence at this point appears to be either anecdotal or that sensationalized by the mass media. Fortunately, the Australian Sport Medicine Federation has recently called for applications for research projects to investigate specific issues in this area.

Future Research

A $100,000 federal government innovative program that encouraged proposals from individuals and then advertised for researchers interested in specific projects stimulated the scope for future research considerably. The most significant questions being considered are in the areas of elite performances, talent identification, social problems in youth sport, and the most desirable modifications of sport for children.

Major Strengths and Areas Needing Improvement

In Australia, as in North America, the issues concerning the outcome of children's involvement in organized sport tend to be polarized into two distinct schools of thought. In one school are the proponents of children's sport who have observed children being made into leaders, turning away from delinquency, developing a variety of desirable character traits, and, eventually, becoming well-rounded individuals. On the other hand, the opponents of children's sport cite countless examples of coaches and parents becoming highly emotional, children being made neurotic, and the occurrence of a wide range of physical injuries caused by the overuse of various body parts. Unfortunately, there is not enough objective information concerning the long-term consequence of sport participation to substantiate the superiority of either of these viewpoints.

One of the earliest critics, Henry Pang (1974), felt that school sport was a heresy. Pang's argument stated in essence that "junior competitive sport was a cultural process acting on human society causing maladaption" (p. 12). To demonstrate the "maladaptions" of this cultural process, Pang presented statistics which revealed that the dropout rate of junior players from the sport of rugby was as high as 60 to 70% of all those registered.

Later, Nettleton (1979) reconsidered Pang's statistics, and by using the same dropout percentages, reached the following alternative conclusion:

> Looking at this data another way presents an entirely different perspective. There are very few organizations . . . that can retain the interest of 25-30% of their clientele over a period of ten years . . . What is it about the sporting experience that appeals to so many for so long? (pp. 1-2)

Certainly any confict between these two positions can be resolved by removing those stresses Pang emphasized and discovering and fostering the satisfactions that Nettleton suggested. Not only is it necessary to identify sources of stress and satisfaction, but it is also necessary to determine whether or not they exists equally for all children and, if so, their relative magnitude in different sport programs. Once these things are known, then we must ask, How do we influence the behavior of the adults who impose those stresses? An evaluation of coaching education programs in affecting change in coaches is also badly needed.

References

Bloomfield, J. (1975). *The role, scope and development of recreation in Australia.* Canberra: Australian Government Publishing Service.

Blundell, N. (1984). Superior coaching. *Sports Coach,* **27** (7, 4), 49-53.

Coles, A.J. (1975). *Report of the Australian sports institute study group.* Canaberra: Australian Government Publishing Service.

Marsh, K. (1980). *Girls and PE: Missed messages? R-12 physical education bulletin.* Adelaide: Education Department of South Australia.

Mutton, N. (1981). *Physical education and sport in south Australian schools.* Adelaide: Department of Education.

The *National Times* (1984, February 3-9). p. 20.

Nettleton, B. (1979, June). *The social institution of sport today and tomorrow.* Paper presented at the Sport Today: Health or Disability Seminar. Lincoln Institute of Health Sciences, Australia.

Norman, M.J. (1975). *Youth say report: The recreational priorities of Australian young people.* Canberra: Australian Government Publishing Service.

Pang, J. (1974). *School sport and heresy.* Paper presented at the XXth World Congress in Sports Medicine, Melbourne, Australia.

Pyke, F.S. (Ed.). (1980). *Towards better coaching: The art and science of coaching.* Canberra: Australian Government Publishing Service.

Robertson, I.D. (1981). *Children's perceived satisfaction and stresses in sport.* Paper presented at XIII ACHPER Biennial Conference, Melbourne, Australia.

Robertson, I.D. (1983). *The attitudes, values and educational needs of adults in primary school sport.* Salisbury: Youth Sport Institute.

Saunders, J.E. & Jobling, I.F. (1983). *Sport in education.* Kingswood, South Australia: ACHPER Publications.

Schools Discussion Paper No. 4 (1978). *Physical education and sport.* Adelaide. Adelaide Education Department.

Thompson, M.W. (1982). *Sports research in Australia, equipment, facility and personnel directory—1982.* Kingswood: ACHPER Publications.

Watson, G. (1978). *Little athletics and childhood socialization.* A report presented to the Community Recreation Council of Western Australia.

Willie, A.W. (1973). *Australian youth fitness survey—1971.* Commonwealth Council for National Fitness, Canberra: Australian Government Publishing Service.

Winter, G. (1980). *A child is not a little adult: Modified approaches to sport for Australian children.* Hobart Department of Education.

2

Youth Sport in Brazil

Maria Beatriz Rocha Ferreira
UNIVERSITY OF TEXAS
AUSTIN, TEXAS, USA

For many years sport in Brazil has been encouraged at different state capitals such as São Paulo, Rio de Janeiro, Belo Horizonte, Porto Alegre, Fortaleza, and Manaus. However, it was only after World War II that the sport movement began to spread into other cities throughout the country, increasing the numbers of programs available to children and youth. This increased interest in sport took place in a number of settings that included both public and private schools, sport centers, and sport clubs (J.P. Vale, Junior, personal communication, July 1984).

The schools are central to Brazilian youth sport because it is here that all youth have an opportunity to participate in the traditional sports of volleyball, basketball, soccer, European handball, rhythmic gymnastics, gymnastics, swimming, and track and field (Ministério de Educãçao e Cultura, 1983a). In addition, it has been mandated that physical education be given two times per week during the first 4 grades and three times per week after that (Ministério de Educãçao e Cultura, 1982). All private schools have instituted this mandate. Public schools, however, have not been able to follow the mandate because of limited financial resources. Specifically, the lack of financial support has limited the construction of facilities for all grades and impaired the payment of physical education specialists for the first 4 grades. Therefore, classes are taught by the elementary school teacher, the majority of whom do not have a background in physical education. Some schools offer an extramural sport program, but only after the fourth grade (Lierge, 1981). In other words, the problem of physical education in Brazil is still at the mercy of private initiative and the random availability of school facilities.

It is estimated that 18 million children between the ages of 7 and 18 participate in Brazilian school sport, with 2.8 million of these children involved in the extramural school sport program (Lierge, 1981). Although the official age for the initiation of school physical education and sport programs is 7 years, participation in gymnastics and swimming has been initiated at an earlier age in private and specialized schools.

The official age for the start of competition also varies among sports (Departamento de Educação e Cultura, 1984). The earliest age is 6 years in swimming, soccer, and gymnastics. While some children are selected at this early age, the majority are selected after the fifth grade (by age 11). This selection is supervised by the secretary of sport and culture of the state (e.g., São Paulo) who schedules 13 competitions per year for youth of school age. From these competitions, promising athletes are directed into private club programs (C.A. D'Avila, personal communication, July 1984).

Private clubs play an important role in the Brazilian sport organization (Nogueira, 1965). In general, they have better facilities, financial support, and opportunities to develop sport programs than do the schools. However, clubs have had significant internal political problems which influence sport opportunities. The emphasis on social or sport activities also varies with the objectives of the board of directors of each club. In general, the boards are not interested in education, but rather, in competition. Competition is important for a club because competitive success results in visibility and status which in turn encourages greater membership and increased financial support. The best players are, therefore, encouraged to participate in club sports, while the less skilled children are quickly eliminated. Thus, the best opportunities are reserved for relatively few individuals, while the remaining children are left with limited programs and facilities offered by schools and neighborhood associations.

In Brazilian society, team sports are more popular than individual sports. Soccer is practiced primarily by males and is played locally on fields, in the streets or squares, and in gymnasiums. The most popular sport for females is volleyball. Besides these two team sports, basketball and European handball are commonly practiced. Individual sports have been more popular at private clubs than in the schools because of the expensive facilities and equipment required. The most popular individual sports for both sexes are swimming, tennis, track and field, and gymnastics (M.P. Vale, Junior, personal communications, July 1984).

The Organization of Youth Sports

The two main sport governing bodies in Brazil include the National Council of Sports (NCS) and the Brazilian Olympic Committee (Ministério de Educaçao e Cultura, 1983b). The NCS is part of the Ministry of Education and is the normative and disciplinary institution for national sport. Its purpose is to encourage, orient, and control all sport activities in the country. The NCS is given its power from the national congress and president of the republic, who are ultimately responsible for mandating Brazilian sport policy. In contrast to the NCS, the Brazilian Olympic Committee is a civic association with independence and autonomy. It is responsible for organizing and directing all activities related to the Olympic Games and other international competitions.

The national sport system of Brazil is comprised of a number of organizations. These consist of community sport groups (club and neighborhood associations), school-sport groups (elementary-secondary and university), military sport groups, and work-related sport groups. School and club sport organizations will be given the greatest emphasis in this chapter because they are the organizations most heavily involved in sport for children and youth (Ministério de Educação e Cultura, 1974).

The NCS governs club sports. Clubs are united in leagues at the municipal level and linked to federations at the state or provincial level. The various state federations, then, constitute sport organizations at the national level (Ministério de Educação e Cultura, 1982).

School sport (both at the primary and secondary level) is supervised by a specialized sector of the Ministry of Physical Education and Sport. Specifically, a secretary of sports is designated at the federal, state, and municipal level and is responsible for organization and administration of sport in the areas of his or her jurisdiction (Ministério de Educação e Cultura, 1982).

Finally, financial support for school and club sport is generated in a number of ways. These include, but are not restricted to, the National Fund for Education Development, the National Fund for Social Development (sport lottery), property income tax, endowments, and private support (Ministério de Educação e Cultura, 1982).

The Education of Youth Sport Coaches

Coaching education programs are offered to Brazilian physical education majors, either as a specialization after graduation or, in the case of some private colleges, during the senior year of college. For sports such as tennis and soccer, however, many classes are taught by former athletes who do not have formal training in coaching. Similarly, in the least privileged areas of the country, formal education of coaches is almost nonexistent.

Some sport medicine education is available for physicians through 1-year programs taught in university departments of physical education. Unfortunately, few universities in Brazil offer such programs.

The Status of Youth Sport Research

Despite the efforts of the federal government since 1970 (Ministério de Educação e Cultura, 1974), very little youth sport research has been conducted in Brazil. Significant programs can only be found in the states of São Paulo, Rio de Janeiro, Rio Grande do Sul, Minas Gerais, Paraná, and Amazonas. In these states, research has focused on the areas of motor ability, anthropometry, exercise physiology and, to a lesser degree, on nutrition, biochemistry, and psychology. Outside of these areas, little research is being conducted.

While youth sport research has been limited in the past, recent events have increased the probability that more research will be conducted in the future. Most notably, the Sport Science Brazilian College has been founded and has already stimulated additional physical education and sport research. It has also organized scientific events and courses and has published a quarterly journal (Oliveira, 1983).

Given this increased emphasis on research, several recommendations seem warranted. To begin with, youth sport studies should be conducted throughout the country and not just in the urban areas of the states already mentioned. Similarly, more emphasis should be placed on developing research which can be conducted with inexpensive materials. Study groups should also be encouraged and their studies on youth sport published. Translations of youth sport research books from other languages to Portuguese is also an important step in this process. Finally, research should be conducted examining the young athlete as a whole, as opposed to studying specific isolated aspects of the child (e.g., physiological, nutritional aspects only).

Major Strengths and Areas Needing Improvement in Youth Sport in Brazil

A major strength of Brazilian youth sport is the growing popularity of sport in the country. The number of participants in sport for all ages has increased, especially sport for children and youth.

A second strength is the development of the physical education profession in Brazil. In many cities physical education departments were founded at public and private universities. In 1963 there were 9 departments and in 1980 there was 95: 2 in the north, 13 in the northeast, 5 in the centerwest, 51 in the southeast, and 24 in the south (Caram, 1983). In general, 100 students enroll each year and an average of 70% of them graduate. Physical education curricula have been adapted to the local reality. In addition, research laboratories have been established in many universities.

Improvements are needed in the school-sponsored sport and physical education programs. Specifically, greater financial support is needed, especially for the development of physical education programs for the preschool child. Currently, these are nonexistent. Students should also become more involved in the sport organization and should be encouraged to organize competitions for themselves.

Although the secretaries of sport and culture organize many competitions during the year in order to encourage sport and to select the best athletes, other programs must be developed (C.A. D'Avila, personal communication, July 1984). Specifically, competitions for children of all ability levels should be established. Activities and sport from the folk culture, especially from the Indians, should also be encouraged, and the government should not only support the traditional sports, which are often incompatible with the daily realities of underdeveloped countries, but nontraditional ones as well. Finally, sport for girls and women must also be given more emphasis and recognition from both a financial and psychological standpoint.

References

Caram, E. (1983). Considerações sobre o desenvolvimento da educação física no ensino superior [Considerations of the development of the physical education departments]. *Revista Brasileira de Ciencias do Esporte*, 5(1), 9-11.

Departamento de Educação Fisica e Desportos. (1984). *Lei n. 6251.* [Law n. 6251]. São Paulo, Brazil: DEFE.

Lierge, A.V. (1981). *Le sport parascolaire. Etude comparative dans 25 pays, realisée en collaboration avec L'L.S.F.* [Extramural sports. Comparative studies in 25 countries, under the collaboration of L'L.S.F.]. Lisboa, Brazil: Direção Geral dos Desportos.

Ministério de Educação e Cultura (1974). *Plano nacional de educação física. Educação física e desporto estudantil* [National plan for physical education. Physical education and student sport]. Brasilia, Brazil: MEC.

Ministério de Educação e Cultura, Conselho Nacional de Desportos. (1982). *Deliberação 08/82* [.Deliberation 08/82] Brasilia, Brazil: MEC.

Ministério de Educação e Cultura, Secretaria de Educação Física e Desportos. (1983a). *III Cebs avaliação desportos coletivos e individuais.* [III. Evaluation of collective and individual sports)]. Brasilia, Brazil: MEC.

Ministério de Educação e Cultura, Secretaria de Educação Física e Desportos. (1983b). *Legislação desportiva* [Sport legislation]. Brasilia, Brazil: MEC.

Nogueira, P. (1965). *Clubes Esportivos* [Sport clubs]. Brasilia, Brazil: Cia Brasil Editõra.

Oliveira, O. (1983). Colégio Brasileiro de Ciências do Esporte [Sport Science Brazilian College]. *Boletim Brasileiro de Ciências do Esporte*, 5(3), 2-15.

3

Youth Sport in Canada

Terry A. Valeriote
COACHING ASSOCIATION OF CANADA
OTTAWA, ONTARIO, CANADA

Lori Hansen
UNIVERSITY OF OTTAWA
OTTAWA, ONTARIO, CANADA

Youth sport in Canada is fairly new in terms of organization. Nevertheless, the demand by Canadian youth for additional streams of participation, improved coaching, and increased organization at all levels—local, provincial, and national—continues to increase. Accordingly, most sport associations are in the process of modifying the form of their programs.

Because very little research on Canadian youth in sport has been conducted, a questionnaire was developed and distributed to 27 major national sport associations. In Table 1 is a list of sports surveyed, categorized by team or individual sports and Olympic or non-Olympic sports.

The results support the assumption that Canadian sport still lacks consistent direction. Developmental programs leading into an established training program for elite athletes exist, but only in some sports. Associations should be more aware of their counterparts and of what else is going on in Canadian sport than they have been.

This brief report on the status of youth sport in Canada confirms what federal administrators, national and local coaches, and athletes themselves have known for a long time: Canadian youth sport needs a common base, a consistent development model, and standardized programs for both developmental/recreational and elite/competitive participants.

Participation in Youth Sports

Approximately 2.5 million Canadian youths between the ages of 6 and 18 participate in Olympic and non-Olympic team and individual sports. Team sports

Table 1. Sports included in national sport association survey

Olympic sports		Non-Olympic sports	
Team *n* = 6	Individual *n* = 13	Team *n* = 6	Individual *n* = 2
Basketball	Alpine Ski	Baseball	Rhythmic Gymnastics
Field Hockey	Badminton	Ringette	Tennis
Hockey	Boxing	Rugby	
Soccer	Canoe	Softball	
Volleyball	Cross-Country Ski	Football	
Water Polo	Fencing	Lacrosse	
	Figure Skating		
	Gymnastics		
	Rowing		
	Speed Skating		
	Swimming		
	Track & Field		
	Wrestling		

are more popular than individual ones. The 10 favorite sports of Canadian youth are hockey, soccer, baseball, softball, figure skating, football, basketball, lacrosse, volleyball, and swimming.

Seventy-three percent, or 1.8 million, of these youths are male. The male participation rate in team sports is twice as great as that of females, but females participate in individual sports at a rate 50% greater than males. Sixty percent of youth participation is in Olympic sports; 40% is in non-Olympic sports.

The average age of beginning competitors is 9, although the age of entry ranges from 6 to 16. The average age of entry in non-Olympic sports is 8, but it is 10 1/2 in Olympic sports. This difference is easily accounted for: In the non-Olympic sports, instruction and skill development are the areas emphasized in programs for 8- to 10-year olds.

The age range of Canadian youth in national competition is 15 to 18. Sixty percent of the sports surveyed offer competition at the provincial and regional level for youths 11 or older; 9- and 10-year-olds are usually offered only local competition for fun. However, 12% of the sports surveyed offer 6- to 8-year olds provincial competitions, and 32% offer it to 9- and 10-years-olds.

Funding of Youth Sport

Funding for competition from the local to the national levels comes from various sources: government, private sponsorship, fund raising, and registration fees are the major sources. The sources of funding for the three levels of sport are summarized in Table 2.

Ninety-five percent of the national associations receive 50% or more of their funding from the federal government. By contrast, at the provincial level, the provincial government accounts for 30% of financial support. The next largest source of funding is sponsorship: 45% of the national associations and 20%

Table 2. Percent contribution of local, provincial, and national sport funding sources

Source	Local	Provincial	National
Government	4.6	57.0	59.0
Sponsorship	21.6	11.7	16.6
Fund raising	35.1	11.7	10.6
Registration fees	32.9	15.0	6.2
Other sources	5.8	4.3	6.8
Total	100.0	100.0	100.0

of the provincial associations receive 15% or more of their total funding from this source.

At the local level, fund-raising activities and registration fees generate more than half of total monies, and government provides only minimal support.

The Status of Research on Youth Sport

Sixty-four percent of the Olympic sports have conducted research that has focused on equipment safety and modification, the development of Mini-Sport and skill awards programs, and physiological and psychological testing and training.

Research conducted in hockey and football has provided significant published data on injuries in contact sport as well as information on how to reduce or eliminate these injuries with safer equipment and modified rules. Volleyball, soccer, lacrosse, rugby, and basketball have implemented Mini-Sport programs in varying degrees. These programs introduce youth to the sport and develop youth within the sport. Skill awards programs accompany these Mini-Sport programs; however, most associations without a Mini-Sport program offer a skill awards program.

Considerable research is currently being done on skill awards programs, on systems for the identification of talent, on the dropout problem, on equipment modification, and on the expansion of youth programs via integration with the schools' programs. In the near future, all sports should have incorporated the results of this research into their youth programs.

Olympic sport research now focuses on the long-term effects of training and competition, whereas non-Olympic sport research emphasizes how to increase participation by the masses and, therefore, develop a broader base. Each group has indicated a desire to study the other's research interest: That is, Olympic sports would like to know how to increase participation among the younger age groups, and the non-Olympic sports would like to determine the long-term effect of training and competition on youth.

Safety in sport is constantly under review. All sport associations are aware of the need for safe, appropriately sized equipment for all youth. According to the vast majority of sport associations, the most effective way of eliminating injuries is by having qualified, certified coaches teach participants proper technique.

The Education of Youth Sport Coaches

Since 1974, Canada has had a coaching certification program for coaches in all sports across the country. The program has five levels, the first 3 of which have a separate theory, technical, and practical component. At Levels 4 and 5, the national and international levels, the theory and technical components are combined.

To date, 150,000 coaches have participated in the program. Furthermore, certification is more frequently expected of coaches at all levels of competition.

Strengths and Areas Needing Improvement

A wide variety of competitive and recreational programs exist across Canada. The programs, especially those in the Olympic sports, enable the youth participants of Canada to select a sport suited to their needs.

However, the involvement of all Canadian youth is far from a reality. The overemphasis at all age levels on winning contributes to the high dropout rate from competitive programs among those in their mid-to-late teens. Recognition of this fact indicates that the sport associations are becoming aware of their weaknesses and are taking steps to correct them.

Another recognized problem is violence in sport, and research on safety and equipment modification is the means of finding solutions. Also, increased parental awareness of the role of sport for youth and the continuation of the National Coaching Certification Program will help improve coaching standards and create an appropriate and positive attitude toward participation in youth sport.

However, Canada still needs a common base. Certified coaches of standardized, consistent programs will help create such a base, as will the integration of these programs into school programs. Once completed, development models should provide each sport with a set of guidelines with which to plan its programs. Organization at the base of youth sport will not only ensure enjoyable growth experiences for youth, but will also enable elite sport in Canada to move forward and achieve its goal of international success.

The involvement of youth in sport is a compelling issue. Ongoing evaluation of the areas identified above will generate recommendations on important issues, such as the optimal age of entry into competition, the most appropriate training programs for elite athletes, the safest ways to play sport, and the most appropriate program for developmental sport at the younger age levels.

4

Youth Sport in the United Kingdom

Sue C. Campbell
THE NATIONAL COACHING FOUNDATION
LEEDS, ENGLAND

Sport has a long and rich history in the United Kingdom, and today it remains as one of the country's most popular leisure-time pursuits. Sport plays an especially important role in the lives of Britain's children, a great many of whom engage in a wide variety of sport. This review will examine the status of youth sport in the United Kingdom. Specifically the scope, organization, and funding of youth sport will be discussed, as well as the education of youth sport coaches, research in youth sport, and major strengths and areas needing improvement.

The Scope of Youth Sport Participation

The most recent figures available show that in 1979, 7.5 million children between the ages of 5 and 15 years participated in organized youth sport in the United Kingdom (Martin & Mason 1981). In addition, interpolations based on these figures reveal that 6.3 million children will participate in 1985, reflecting the decline in birth rate which occurred in the country during the 1970s. It is of further interest to note that when the total number of children in the population are considered, 78.2% participated in 1979, whereas 79.1% are estimated to do so in 1985. Thus, participation has increased slightly.

Age Children Begin Participation

Organized sporting activities begin at the primary school level (ages 7 to 11) and include an introduction to the fundamental activities of games, swimming, gymnastics, and dance. Children in primary schools are taught by their classroom teachers who are not "specialists" in physical education. When children later enter secondary schools (ages 11 to 18), they undertake a full physical education program taught by a specialized staff.

Nonschool sport occurs in local clubs and associations under the guidance of leaders or coaches. Participants in these clubs vary in age according to the nature of the activity, and both recreative and competitive opportunities exist. There has been a growing concern about when children should enter competition, and some sports (e.g., swimming) have raised the minimum age for competition in efforts to protect the well-being of the child.

Available Sports and Their Popularity

An enormous range of sports are available throughout the United Kingdom with well over 100 sport-governing bodies in existence. These national governing bodies offer opportunities through various clubs and associations to people of all ages. The major activities in secondary schools are soccer (men), rugby-football (men), cricket (men), field hockey (women), netball (women), athletics (men and women), and lawn tennis (men and women). Swimming, gymnastics, and dance are also major components of the school timetable. Also, the range of opportunities in school and nonschool sport has grown enormously over the last decade. This has reflected the need for new approaches to education and recreation brought about by changing patterns of leisure and, more recently, the dramatic growth in unemployment. The popularity of sport for the young is also subject to the strong influences of the media and fashion.

Gender Differences in Participation Patterns

Emmett (1977) has found that gender as well as social class, occupation, academic attainment, and peer group allegiances exert an influence on recreational involvement. The gender statistics taken from the General Household Survey of 1980 (Office of Population and Survey, 1980) are especially noteworthy because they indicated far less involvement in sporting activities among young females than among young males. These lower rates of participation have resulted in a concerted effort by the Sports Council to provide greater encouragement and opportunity for young women to take part in sport.

The Organization of Youth Sport

Physical education programs in secondary schools provide a range of recreative and competitive opportunities for young people. Interschool competitions are organized at the local or district level, country or provincial level, and at the national level. In addition, there are 42 national school organizations governing 27 different sports.

Youth clubs and organizations provide opportunities away from the school environment. These clubs range from purpose-built centers owned by local authorities to one-night-a-week village clubs using shared premises. The National Association of Youth Clubs (NAYC) is an umbrella oganization serving and representing Associations of Youth Clubs in counties and metropolitan areas of England, Northern Ireland, Scotland, and Wales. This association is comprised of 731,552 members in 6,455 clubs under the guidance of 3,306 full-time youth workers, 12,630 part-time workers, and 28,261 volunteers. The NAYC promotes a wide range of sporting and recreational activities for all age levels which include national competitive events, local events, local sports, introduction sessions, and instructional courses. Other organizations particularly involved with youth include some sporting activities. Furthermore, local leisure and recreation departments provide a wide range of recreational and competitive opportunities for youths based at local facilities in their area.

Funding of Youth Sport

Statutory Provision

Physical education programs are supported as part of the school curriculum by the various education authorities. Some effort is also made through these same authorities to fund a youth service. Facilities for sport have developed steadily throughout the 1970s with a marked growth in the number of swimming pools, outdoor playing pitches, and indoor sports centers. This growth has given a greater range of opportunities to a greater number of people.

Voluntary Provision

Unfortunately, financial support from the voluntary sector of sport is almost impossible to assess accurately. Thousands of sports clubs and organizations (no figures are available to estimate the number of youth members) operate independently of any statutory body and raise their own funds by any available means.

Commercial Involvement

Commercial involvement in sport has shown a marked increase with various companies wishing to be particularly associated with youth sport. Proficiency award schemes, training programs, and championship competitions have been the main focus of their attention.

The Education of Youth Sport Coaches

Sport-Specific and Technique Education

Sport-specific and technique education is largely undertaken by the 123 national governing bodies of sport, each working independently. Many of the national governing bodies have developed their own sport specific coaching education programs that take into account different levels of expertise and provide instruction for coaches ranging from elementary to advanced levels. All of the national governing bodies belong to an umbrella organization called the Central Council of Physical Recreation. This organization has recently initiated a community sports leaders' award (certification) to recruit a large body of young people and adults who are willing to be trained in the basic teaching-coaching principles and in the simple organizational arrangements concerned with their chosen activity. This award (10 hours in length) is for individuals who have not reached a Level 1 Coaching Certification in a national governing body program, but who are involved in youth sport.

Sport Science and Medicine Education

The National Coaching Foundation has recently been established to provide information services programs and technical data from home and overseas for coaches at both the local and national levels. The staff of this organization is working closely with the national governing bodies to develop coaching education materials. Specifically, the foundation has two objectives: (a) to promote at the local and national level, the education, instruction, and training of coaches and other interested persons in performance-related knowledge applied to all kinds of sports; and (b) to promote and disseminate knowledge in pursuit of the first objective.

The Status of Youth Sport Research

Scope and Current Status of Youth Sport Research

Previous research relevant to youth sport can be classified into four categories. These include (a) studies specifically related to the training of young athletes (very few); (b) studies of groups of young people who might be expected to have experiences or problems similar to those of young athletes (e.g., ballet dancers); (c) studies of the effects of training on adult athletes; and (d) studies of (mainly adult) sport injuries. Unfortunately, little research is being done relating specifically to young athletes. However, of those studies being conducted, topics receiving the greatest attention include growth and development, sexual maturation, and psychological equilibrium.

Major Questions Studied

The Sports Council is hoping to commission a study to determine how to eliminate, avoid, minimize, and control any negative effects of training. The basis for concern is the widespread belief that the training of (especially elite) young athletes may have adverse effects in terms of damage to general health, injury, disturbance of maturational processes, psychological damage, interruption to and retardation of educational development, and disruption of social and family life.

Most Pressing Research Questions

Many important issues still need consideration. These include the identification of physiological and psychological capacities of children at different ages; the type of game adaptations which are necessary; the rate of skill development appropriate to children at various ages; and the potential physical and mental damage caused by intensive training and competition.

Major Strengths and Areas Needing Improvement in Youth Sport

It would be impossible to briefly summarize the full position of youth sport in the United Kingdom today. There has always been a strong tradition of youth sport in the past which ensured a good foundation for the future. However, the nature of sport is changing, and the number of areas of concern is growing. Both the strengths and areas needing improvement in United Kingdom youth sport are outlined below.

Strengths

- A major strength is the high standard of physical education in the schools. Specifically, the professional training of sports teachers is of the highest standard, and sport is an integral part of the school curriculum.
- The national governing bodies of Sport provide a clear framework of sport-specific training for coaches in many sports.
- The enormous range of sporting opportunities available to young people is a tremendous asset.
- A growing awareness of the potential of sport as a powerful tool that may be used to the benefit of the community, particularly with the unemployed and with other groups with special needs in the inner city.

Areas Needing Improvement

- The decline in sport participation after leaving school has been a matter of concern since it was highlighted in the Wolfenden Report in 1960. The Sports Council in its document, "The Next Ten Years," states that one of its major tasks is to work through and with the education system to ensure that more former students maintain one or more of the many skills and interests developed through the curriculum.
- A clear pattern of training for coaches in the nonsport-specific areas of study must be established. With a few major exceptions, most sports concentrate almost entirely on technical skills with little or no reference to performance-related knowledge (sport science).
- More low-level sports leaders working at grass roots level in the community must be provided.
- Because of a growing concern of the potential damage too much vigorous participation in sport causes children, more physiological and psychological investigation must be conducted.
- Young athletes involved in high-level competition must be monitored to ensure that training produces the maximum benefits.

References

Emmett, I. (1977). *Report to the Sports Council on the decline in sports participation after leaving school*. Unpublished draft report. London: Sports Council.

Martin, W. & Mason, S. (1981). *The U.K. sports market*. Sudbury, Suffolk: Leisure Consultants.

Office of Population Censuses and Surveys (1980). *General household survey*. London: HMSO.

The Sports Council (1982). *Sport in the community—The next ten years*. London: Sports Council.

Wolfenden Report (1960). *Sport in the community*. The Report of the Wolfenden Committee. London: Central Council of Physical Recreation.

5

Youth Sport in the USA

Rainer Martens
UNIVERSITY OF ILLINOIS AT URBANA-CHAMPAIGN
URBANA, ILLINOIS, USA

This report provides a brief look at the status of youth sport in the United States. The topics considered include (a) the demographics of youth sport participation, (b) the organization of youth sport, (c) coaching education, (d) the status of youth sport research, and (e) conclusions about the strengths and weaknesses of American youth sport programs.

The Scope of Youth Sport Participation

Estimates of the number of young people (ages 6-18) participating in nonschool sports are made in Table 1. These estimates were first made in 1977 (Martens, 1978) by determining the percent of youth participating in a sport for a known population and then projecting that percent to a national population of youth in this age category. Data for the estimates were obtained from a wide variety of sources and should be viewed as rough approximations. All estimates were revised and updated for this report.

Several observations from the data in Table 1 are noteworthy. Participation has increased by over 5 million. However, it is incorrect to conclude that 5 million more children are playing, because these data do not represent children participating, but rather indicate the number of participants in each sport, with many children being multiple-sport participants. About 20 million of the 45 million youth in this age range participate in nonschool youth sport, or 44% of this population. In addition, the National High School Federation estimates that 3.35 million boys and 1.78 million girls, or a total of 5.13 million young people, participate in high school sport. (No estimates of elementary and junior high school participation could be obtained.)

Table 1. Estimate of participation in nonschool sports among children ages 6 to 18 (in millions)

Sport	Boys 1977	Boys 1984	Girls 1977	Girls 1984	Combined 1977	Combined 1984
Baseball	4.20	3.91	0.79	0.62	4.99	4.53
Softball	1.97	2.10	2.41	2.62	4.38	4.72
Swimming	1.71	1.85	1.91	2.08	3.62	3.93
Bowling	2.07	2.07	1.51	1.50	3.58	3.57
Basketball	2.13	2.13	1.22	1.22	3.35	3.35
Football (tackle)	1.56	1.16	0.29	0.10	1.85	1.26
Tennis	0.88	1.35	0.95	1.24	1.83	2.59
Gymnastics	0.59	0.75	1.17	1.50	1.76	2.25
Football (flag)	1.11	1.20	0.36	0.45	1.47	1.65
Track & Field	0.76	1.00	0.54	0.75	1.30	1.75
Soccer	0.72	2.20	0.52	1.70	1.24	3.90
Wrestling	—	0.25	—	0.0	—	0.25
Other	1.24	1.00	0.79	0.80	2.03	1.80
Totals	18.94	20.97	12.46	14.58	30.41	35.55
% by sex	62%	59%	38%	41%		

Gender

The pattern of participation by gender is clearly shown in Table 1. Girls' participation has increased by just over 2 million, and now represents 41% of the participants as compared to 38% in 1977. Softball, dethroning baseball, is now America's number 1 youth sport. Soccer has made the most dramatic increase, moving from 11th to 4th in popularity with an increase in total participants of 2.66 million. Gymnastics and tennis also increased significantly in the number of participants, while American football declined 600,000, and baseball by ½ million.

Age

Estimates also were made of the age at which children begin participating in organized competitive sport. Swimming and gymnastics won honors for introducing children to sport at the ripe old age of 3 years. The mean age for the 12 sports for the "earliest" participation was 5.83 years. The mean of the mean beginning age is 11 years, which is somewhat older than might be expected.

Organization of Youth Sport

One of the few generalizations that can be made about the organization of sport in the United States is that it has not been organized by the federal government. Although sport in recent times is being influenced more by federal legislation (e.g., Title IX, Amateur Sport Act of 1978), sport, more than most elements of American life, has avoided government intervention.

The types of agencies that organize sport in the United States and an example of a specific agency are shown in Table 3. Unlike some other nations, the organization of sport in this country is diverse, without any one agency providing national coordination of all youth sport programs. Sport in America

Table 2. Age children begin participation in sports

Sport	Earliest age	Mean beginning age
Baseball	5	9
Softball	7	10
Swimming	3	11
Bowling	6	14
Basketball	7	12
Football (tackle)	8	12
Tennis	8	14
Gymnastics	3	8
Football (flag)	7	10
Track & Field	5	11
Soccer	6	10
Wrestling	5	11
Average age	5.83	11.0

Table 3. Categories of agencies who organize youth sports

Type of Agency	Example of type
National youth sport organization	PONY Baseball
National youth agency	Boys Clubs of America
National governing body	U.S. Wrestling
National service organization	American Legion Baseball
National religious organization	Catholic Youth Organization
Regional youth sport organization	Soccer Association for Youth
State school activity association	Illinois High School Activity Association
Local school district	Hutchinson, KS Public School
Local service club	Champaign Optimist Club
Municipal recreation department	Champaign Park District
Private sports clubs	Urbana Wrestling Club

is not the prerogative of any level of government or societal institution as can be seen from Table 3. In fact, in some sports such as baseball, there are so many organizations that an organization of baseball organizations exists.

On the other hand, organizers of sport, especially Olympic sport, have recognized the value in having some centralization of sport. Through the creation of the Amateur Sport Act of 1978, a procedure was developed under the United States Olympic Committee to form National Governing Bodies (NGBs) for each Olympic sport. Thus, for at least Olympic and international competition, there is a central governing body for each sport in the United States, but these NGBs only govern a small percent of the total participants in youth sport.

Funding for Youth Sport

The funding for youth sport comes mostly from five sources. These include taxes, individual donations, participation fees, business sponsorships, and service club donations. Sport in the United States is not heavily supported by tax dollars as it is in some other countries.

Education of Youth Sport Coaches

The number of volunteer coaches in the United States is estimated at about 2.5 million, with another 1/2 million professional or paid coaches. Most of the volunteer coaches and many of the professional coaches have no training in sport medicine and science. The vast majority of coaching education in the United States consists of sport-specific training with emphasis on technique and strategy. The only systematic coaching education which has been offered in the United States, which combines sport specific training with sport medicine and science training, has been through universities and colleges. However, this training has been available to only a few.

School coaches must meet minimum certification standards in only 13 states, with these standards varying from 6 to 18 semester hours of coursework in physical education. The other states assume that if a person has a teaching certificate, he or she is qualified to coach.

Because fewer and fewer teachers wish to be coaches in the public schools, it has become necessary to hire nonteacher coaches to meet the need. The qualifications of these individuals to coach tends to be based on their experience playing or coaching the sport, not on their training in sport medicine and science. In general, a belief prevails in the United States that a person is qualified to coach by having played the sport, and the better the person had played, the better coach he or she will be. This belief may be properly labelled a myth.

In the 1970s, interest grew in providing coaching education programs which emphasized sport medicine and science, especially for the 2.5 million volunteers. Several of the national youth sport organizations and the NGBs for Olympic sport began offering limited coaching education clinics. At the same time, and in some cases in cooperation with these sport organizations, several agencies emerged to help educate coaches. The three prominent programs are the Michigan Youth Sport Institute, the National Youth Sport Coaches Association, and the American Coaching Effectiveness Program.

The Michigan program is limited mostly to that state. Its primary activity is a series of workshops conducted by faculty at Michigan State University. The National Youth Sport Coaches Association has been adopted by some municipal recreation departments and United States military youth sport programs. It relies exclusively on video tapes to present very limited information to coaches about technique, strategies, and sport medicine.

The American Coaching Effectiveness Program is more comprehensive than the other programs and has now trained over 25,000 coaches. The Level 1 program has been adopted by 12 NGBs, the YMCA of the USA, the Boys Clubs of America, hundreds of local recreation and youth sport agencies, and several major national sport agencies such as PONY Baseball.

Status of Youth Sport Research

This section needs to be prefaced with the statement that any research in the sport medicine and science field which increases our knowledge of how humans function or behave will be useful for youth sport. Thus, from this perspective, the research being done in sport physiology, sport biomechanics, motor learning and control, motor development, sport psychology, and sociology of sport contributes to youth sport when children are used as subjects.

During the 1970s, a substantial interest developed in studying the phenomenon of youth sport in the United States. For a period of about 5 years (1976-81), conferences abounded, publications rolled off the presses, and academicians pontificated about youth sport in America. While the topic is by no means dead today, the fashionable topic of the late '70s has at least experienced a recession.

Most of this research has been descriptive (e.g., State of Michigan, 1976; Martens & Gould, 1979), seeking answers to such questions as how many people are involved in youth sport; players, parents, and coaches attitudes about a variety of issues; the number and types of injuries; and the number and reasons for children dropping out of sport programs. A major exception to the descriptive research has been the coaching behavior study by Smith, Smoll, and Curtis (1978). They developed a coaching training program, delivered it to a group of coaches, and compared the difference in coaching behaviors between trained and untrained coaches.

Some of the other topics which have been studied include anxiety in sport, motivation, perceptions of competence, aggression, attributions, moral development, self-esteem, and socialization into and through sport. Gould (1982) concluded from his review of the youth sport research that those studies contributing the most (a) asked important practical questions, (b) integrated previous research or theory into the study, and (c) employed a series of studies on the problem. More of this type of research is needed.

Major Strengths and Need for Improvement

The following are the major strengths of youth sport programs in the USA:

- Millions of children are playing and enjoying sport.
- The programs offered are diverse in types of sport, skill levels, and age groups.
- Sport is increasingly available to all children, regardless of sex, race, or economic status.
- Sport is quite safe, with remarkably low-injury rates when compared to unorganized activities and the potential for injury.
- Sport is readily available because Americans donate large sums of money and time to provide children the opportunity to play through many different types of agencies.
- The facilities for many sport programs are good to excellent. It is hard to imagine, however, that many other nations have more pools, gymnasia, ice rinks, and playing fields per capita than the United States.

Although youth sport is amazingly successful in the United States, it is not difficult to find room for improvement. The following are areas which I recommend be given priority:

- Continue improving coaches' education about sport sciences and sport-specific knowledge.
- Educate parents about their role and contribution to their children's participation in youth sport.
- Modify children's sport based on biomechanical, physiological, and developmental research to make that sport appropriate for various developmental levels.
- Reduce injury rates even further.
- Eliminate boxing and contact karate as sports permitted to be played in our society.
- Increase the age children first begin to play competitively in certain sports and emphasize learning fundamental skills early.
- Increase the availability of daily physical education in the elementary schools so that children develop basic movement skills under the leadership of professional instructors.
- Deemphasize the value in our society of being a winner, and emphasize the value of pursuing personal excellence.

References

Gould, D. (1982). Sport psychology in the 1980s: Status, direction, and challenge in youth sports research. *Journal of Sport Psychology, 4*(3), 203-218.

Martens, R., (1978). *Joy and sadness in children's sports*. Champaign, IL: Human Kinetics.

Martens, R., & Gould, D. (1979). Why do adults volunteer to coach children's sports? In G. Roberts & K.M. Newell (Eds.), *Psychology of motor behavior and sport—1978* (pp. 79-89). Champaign, IL: Human Kinetics.

Smith, R. E., Smoll, F. L., & Curtis, B. (1978). Coaching behaviors in Little League baseball. In F. L. Smoll & R. E. Smith (Eds.), *Psychological perspectives in youth sports*. Washington, D.C.: Hemisphere Publishing.

State of Michigan. (1976). *Joint legislative study on youth sports programs: Agency sponsored sports (Phase I report)*. Lansing, MI: State of Michigan.

6

Youth Sport in the Soviet Union

Stephen C. Jefferies
AMERICAN COACHING EFFECTIVENESS PROGRAM
CHAMPAIGN, ILLINOIS, USA

This paper is a brief review of the status of youth sport in the Soviet Union. The following topics are considered: (a) the scope of youth sport participation in the USSR, (b) the organization of youth sport, (c) the education of youth sport coaches, (d) the status of youth sport research, and (e) an assessment of the major strengths and weaknesses of Soviet youth sport.

Scope of Youth Sport Participation in the USSR

Soviet statistics on youth sport participation require elaboration because a clear distinction is made between elite-sport programs and recreational activities. Young athletes participating in elite-sport programs numbered approximately 2 million in 1976. A more recent estimate put the figure between 4 to 6 million (Filin, 1982). Of the 46 million children attending public schools, it was reported that 18 million are involved in some type of sport program (Kirillyuk, 1980, p. 20).

Organized physical activity begins in the kindergartens (ages 3 to 6). Walks to the park and free play in children's playgrounds are typical daily exercise activities. In the public schools, there is a nationally regulated physical education program. This is currently undergoing revision with the goal of catering more effectively to the diverse needs of Soviet school children throughout the 15 republics.

Training in elite-sport programs depends on the sport. The youngest participants (ages 4 to 5) are in women's gymnastics, swimming, and figure skating. The USSR has an age-based training program which regulates the age children may begin training and the number of permissible training hours. For some sports, for example, track and field and wrestling, training is not recommended until children have reached an age where development is compatible with the skills required. In recent years, the apparent decrease in the age of champion athletes, especially in sports like gymnastics and swimming, spurred a movement to begin training earlier. However, many Soviet specialists have since questioned the assumption that the number of years spent in training is proportional or even related to the level of final skill development.

Soviet sport is based on the Olympic program. Official sport policy regulates training in these areas. Soccer is probably the most generally popular sport, but individual republics and regions or cities within these republics have their own favorites. The small town of Vladimir, outside of Moscow, has traditionally produced outstanding male gymnasts (e.g., Nikolai Andrianov). Georgian and Ukrainian soccer players inevitably occupy the majority of the positions on the Soviet national team. The severe Soviet climate also offers ideal conditions for cross-country skiing, ice hockey, and skating.

Gender differences in sport participation almost certainly exist insofar as the Olympic program remains dominated by male sports. Consequently, opportunities for males exceed those for females. However, Soviet women have contributed significantly to the success of the USSR in international sport, a fact Soviets claim illustrates the emancipation of women in the Soviet Union.

Organization of Youth Sport

Since 1968, the Sports Committee of the USSR has been responsible for all Soviet sport development. Located in Moscow, the Sports Committee disseminates information through local sport committees in the republics, regions, districts, and cities. A unique feature of the Soviet sport system is the participation of the Ministry of Education in the organization and regulation of youth sport. Approximately two thirds of all Soviet sport schools are organized by this ministry. The sport school training program was developed by the Sports Committee in cooperation with the sport department of the Ministry of Education

Although the Sports Committee retains overall control of policy, the practical application of its directives is divided between various governmental and public organizations. Each unit has special interest for one section of the community and is totally responsible for funding its programs. Figure 1 illustrates this relationship.

The Pioneer and Komsomol youth organizations take an active part in the development of sport and physical activity, especially through the national award for fitness and physical skill, the GTO (Gotov k trudy i oboroniye [Ready for labor and defense]). Pioneer summer camps attract 10-12 million children annually (Kondratyeva & Taborko, 1979, p. 6). The Komsomol coordinates national youth sport competitions like the Leather Ball (soccer), Golden Puck (ice hockey), Olympic Snowflake (cross-country skiing), and Neptune (swimming). Other national youth sport competitions include a popular interschool,

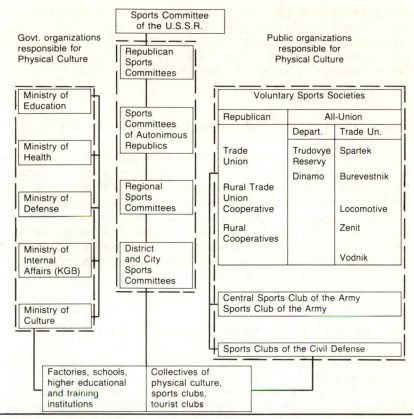

Figure 1. Organizational structure of the Soviet physical culture movement.

interclass contest named the ''Hopeful Starts,'' and an interfamily fun competition called ''Daddy, Mommy, and me.''

Collectives of physical culture based in the public schools, offer extracurricular physical activity for young people. In 1977, for example, it was estimated these totaled 96,000 (Filin, 1977b, p. 9). Within these collectives, sport sections are organized 2 to 3 times per week by the physical education staff. Activities depend on the interests of the staff, facilities, and climate.

The most athletically gifted children are recruited into the sport school system. There are three basic types of sport schools, each catering to a specific segment of the population, with the total number of sport schools estimated at 6,700 (*Sovietsky Sport*, September 1, 1983). The sport schools combine excellent facilities with high quality, carefully supervised training programs. The different types of sport schools provide young athletes with ongoing support from beginning to international skill levels. The Soviets have implemented revisions to the public school program to help young athletes successfully combine educational studies and sport training (See Jefferies, 1984, for more information about Soviet sport school organization). Sport boarding schools (approximately 34 distributed around the country) provide educational and training opportunities for talented children whose families live in rural areas.

The Education of Youth Sport Coaches in the USSR

Volunteers are used extensively in recreation and leisure programs. Short training courses provide them with the essential skills necessary for conducting these programs. The Soviets believe that outstanding talent is most effectively nurtured by professionally trained, full-time coaches, rather than part-time coaches or school teachers. Sport school coaches must complete 4-year training programs in their sport specialization. Entrance to a training institute is dependent on a satisfactory combination of academic ability and sport skill. Although coaches specialize in *one* sport, all Soviet coaches are trained to apply similar methodological and organizational principles.

The Status of Youth Sport Research in the USSR

Following the revolution, the existing Russian sport system was revised to serve the goals of the newly emerging Soviet society. Initially, the paramount need was for physically fit and well-trained military personnel. Sport schools first began in the 1930s. Following the war, an interest in skill development reemerged and the trend toward early sport specialization began. Sport selection was a dominant theme in the 1960s. Interest was directed at the interrelationship between age and the emergence of different physical abilities. The means and methods of long-term training were investigated in the 1970s; this provided information for the development of the current age-based training system.

A new discipline entitled the "Theory and Methods of Youth Sports" began in 1975-76 at the Central State Institute for Physical Culture in Moscow. This was dedicated to the application of the sport sciences to the needs and abilities of younger populations. Preparation in youth sport is a major concern because an estimated 70% of the institute's graduates find work in the sport school system (Filin, 1977a, p. 17). Current research is coordinated by this institute together with the Department of Youth Sports at the All-Union Research Institute for Physical Culture in Moscow. Applied research is emphasized, and projects are regularly conducted in cooperation with coaches and athletes in the various training institutions. For example, the Alekseyev track school in Leningrad has its own Sports Measurement Laboratory.

At the All-Union Research Institute for Physical Culture, attention has recently been directed to the idea of "modeling": that is, identifying desirable physical characteristics of young athletes at different stages of the long-term training process. Plotting the progressions of champion athletes provides objective data for developmental programs. Attention is directed at general principles in an effort to retain the methodological consistency of the system regardless of specialization.

No data specific to the incidence of youth sport injuries is known. A concern widely expressed is the potentially harmful effects of "premature sport specialization." Soviet sport scientists advise "optimal sport specialization": That is, specialized sport techniques should only be taught to children who have the physical and mental qualities necessary to sustain these skills. The development of general physical abilities should precede and form a foundation for the coaching of specific sport skills.

Major Strengths and Weaknesses in Soviet Youth Sport

Strengths

In the USSR, opportunities for participation in elite-youth sport are dependent solely on ability, rather than economic status. Participation is free and facilities are available within easy access of most Soviet homes. The age-based training system is methodologically consistent among all sports throughout the nation and conducted by full-time, professionally trained coaches. There is an effective system of recruitment and selection, and participation in youth sport is actively encouraged. Soviet authorities have accepted responsibility for attempting to find solutions to the "education versus athletics" dilemma athletes in the West must resolve on their own. A natural career pathway exists for youth athletes to continue their interest in sport by becoming coaches. This ensures that the Soviet sport system retains its most talented and experienced athletes.

Weaknesses

Improvements are being sought at the lower levels of participation. Without diminishing the excellent achievements of the national teams, more opportunities must be made available for mass participation. Broadening the base of mass participation improves the general health of the nation and enhances the quality and quantity of athletes capable of performing successfully in Olympic and world competitions. Closer connections between the public schools and sport schools need to be established. The current program of reform in public school physical education is designed to improve the effectiveness of the mass sport movement. The USSR lags significantly behind the West in sport technology. This includes everything from sophisticated computers and other advanced high-tech equipment, to everyday items of sport apparel.

References

Filin, V. P. (1977a). Osnovy yunosheskogo sporta [The foundations of youth sport]. In *Metodicheskiye razrabotki dlya prepodavatelei i studentov institutov fizicheskoi kul'tury* (pp. 3-22). Moscow: Central State Institute for Physical Culture.

Filin, V. P. (1977b). Stanovleniye nauchnykh i metodicheskikh osnov detsko-yunosheskogo sporta [The formation of the scientific and methodological foundations of children's and youth sport]. *Teoriya i praktika fizicheskoi kul'tury*, **11**, 46-51.

Filin, V. P. (1982, March). Personal communication.

Jefferies, S. C. (1984). Sport and education: Theory and practice in the USSR. *Quest*, **36**, 164-176.

Kirillyuk, V. (1981). *Sport: The Soviet Union today and tomorrow*. Moscow: Novosti Press Agency Publishing House.

Kondratyeva, M., & Taborko, V. (1979). *Children and sport in the USSR*. Moscow: Progress Publishers.

PART II

When Should Children Begin Competing?

With the continuing growth and popularity of organized youth sport programs, it is not uncommon for concerned parents and coaches to ask questions regarding the physical and psychological welfare of their children as sport participants. One of the most frequently raised questions is, What age should children begin competing in sport? Although this question appears simplistic on the surface, it is most complex. Not only is physical maturation a primary consideration in the decision to begin competitive involvement, but social, emotional, and cognitive maturity levels also play major roles.

This part of the volume explores the issues of competitive sport readiness from an interdisciplinary perspective. In the opening paper, Robert Malina provides a comprehensive definition of readiness and emphasizes the need to consider physical, social, emotional, and cognitive aspects of competitive maturity. Malina contends that physical and motor components are most frequently considered, while social and emotional aspects are often neglected. For example, such behaviors as proper attitude, social interaction skills, independence, and motivation are critical when one talks about readiness for competition.

Brian Sharkey takes a physiological perspective of the topic and focuses on the question, When should children begin training for competition? Effective guidelines for strength and endurance training in young athletes are primary areas of his discussion.

Then, Michael Passer looks at the psychological ramifications of readiness for organized participation. He focuses on children's capabilities for engaging in social comparison at various ages, arguing that children should not begin competing until they have the appropriate social comparison and cognitive reasoning abilities to understand the competitive process.

From a sociological standpoint, Jay Coakley suggests that a child's understanding of social relationships is critical for the enjoyable and motivational benefit of the sport competition experience. His discussion of the stages of role-taking ability (i.e., the ability to put oneself in the role of others' perspectives) provides insight into the behaviors of children at varying cognitive and social stages of development; in addition, he discusses the importance that these skills have for a meaningful experience of competitive participation. Coakley also provides several implications of the information pertaining to role-taking abilities.

Finally, John Halbert, writing from a full-time coaching perspective, takes the stance that policy statements regarding the age at which children should start competition are likely to be ignored by coaches and parents who, in the past, have been more than willing to start children in competition at very young ages. Instead, Halbert contends that we must direct our efforts toward educating coaches so that maximal positive outcomes are achieved, and children's needs are met through sport experiences. He shares insights regarding some critical questions to address in the preparation of youth sport coaches.

7

Readiness for Competitive Youth Sport

Robert M. Malina
UNIVERSITY OF TEXAS
AUSTIN, TEXAS, USA

Competitive sport for children and youth is an established feature in many areas of the world. It has clear social sanction, not only in the culture of children and youth, but in the broader cultural complex within which the youngsters live. Given the positive social sanction for youth sport, there have been, as one would expect, numerous discussions of the role of competitive sport in childhood and youth. An important component of such discussions is the readiness of a youngster for competitive sport. This paper addresses the concept of readiness in general, and several specific applications to youth sport.

The Readiness Concept

The concept of readiness is used most often in the context of reading and of school; that is, is the child ready to read or is the child ready for school? In other words, is the child able to successfully handle the demands of reading or the demands of the classroom? The same can be asked for competitive sport. Is a given youngster ready for the demands of competitive sport?

Readiness is closely related to the notion of maturation. Although definitions of maturation vary, it is most often viewed in the context of genetic regulation of developmental changes and in combination with learning. Maturation refers to the potential or limits, while learning refers to environmental influences, that is, the nature-nurture interaction. There are other views of readiness, and the reader is referred to the comprehensive overview of Brenner (1957).

The term *maturation* thus implies genotypic control, and the result is a genetic-environment interaction. The term *readiness* fits into this discussion

quite easily. It refers to the match between the child's current level of maturation and the demands presented by a specific situation or situations; for example, is the child sufficiently mature to benefit from specific instruction in a
given task? This question has direct relevance to skills related to sport. When
is a child sufficiently mature or ready to benefit from specific instruction and
practice in motor skills? Are there indicators of such readiness?

The demands of youth sport are rather complex, including physical, motor,
perceptual, social, emotional, and intellectual components. All too often, the
physical (size and biological maturity) and motor (skill) components are emphasized in selecting youngsters for sport. A more comprehensive view of
readiness is essential. A youngster might have the size requisites for a sport,
but may not have sufficient motor control or sufficient emotional competence
to handle stressful situations.

Operational Definition

It is in this context that an operational definition of readiness for competitive
youth sport is offered. Readiness for sport can be defined in terms of the match
between a child's level of growth, maturity, and development on one hand,
and the tasks/demands presented by competitive sport on the other. Further
clarification is in order because the terms *growth*, *maturity*, and *development*
are used variably and at times interchangeably by different professionals involved with children and youth. Growth refers to measurable changes in body
size, for example, height, weight, fatness. Maturation refers to the child's
biological clock that marks progress toward the mature state. It is viewed most
often in terms of skeletal and sexual maturation and the timing of the adolescent growth spurt. Development is a broader concept than growth and maturation. I prefer to view it in the context of the development of competence in
a variety of interrelated domains during childhood and youth, that is, social
competence, intellectual and/or cognitive competence, motor competence, and
so on. Thus, from this perspective, growth and maturation are essentially
biological processes, while development is a broader concept which encompasses the many facets of childhood and youth—the social, emotional, intellectual, and motor domains.

Obviously, growth, maturation, and development are related. For example, there are reasonably well-established relationships between size and motor
performance, or social and emotional correlates of advanced or delayed
biological maturation. Individual variation in growth, maturation, and development contributes directly to the child's self-concept, an important developmental
component that is often overlooked. Individual variation in biological maturation and associated changes in size, physique, body composition, and performance is the backdrop against which youth evaluate and interpret their own
growth and maturation. The adolescent growth spurt and sexual maturation
do not occur in a social vacuum, and sport is an important part of the youngster's
world. Although many children begin participation in competitive sport prior
to adolescence, it is during early adolescence (approximately 9 through 14
years) that youth sport is a dominant force in the youngster's life; thus success
in athletics is a significant form of positive social reinforcement at this time.

Individual Characteristics and Sport Task Demand

The demands of sport are many, and readiness for sport is based on the match between the characteristics of the individual child and the demands of a sport. It is a functional relationship. In the words of Brenner (1957, p. 122), "Readiness is a functional, interrelated unity of subject-object orientation, of individual-task or individual-goal directedness." This concept can be easily applied to sport. The basic ingredients are the individual and his or her unique make-up, the specific tasks of a given sport, and the goal of a sport, which is more often than not, winning. Orientation and direction vary. The issue of readiness for sport is rendered more complex by the fundamental nature of many youth sports. They are team sports which require the coordination and cooperation of several individuals each of whom is unique.

At the level of the individual, success or failure in sport can be viewed as dependent upon the balance between the child's ability and the task demands of a sport. This is schematically illustrated in Figure 1. According to this scheme, which is modified after that of Brenner (1957) for school readiness, readiness occurs when a child's ability, defined as the matrix of growth, maturity, and developmental characteristics (Individual Volume, IV) is commensurate or exceeds the tasks demands of a sport (Task Volume, TV). There is unreadiness when the child's ability is exceeded by the demands of a sport.

The identification and definition of task demands for a specific sport are rather straightforward in a technical sense. On the other hand, many issues come to mind when individual readiness for a sport is considered. For example, what are the criteria of readiness for a given sport? Is there a best time for entrance into competitive sport? Individual variation in growth, maturation, and development—that is, readiness—is great, and obviously, there is no single answer. Just as there are readiness tests for reading and arithmetic, and aptitude tests for music and art, should there be such tests for youth sport?

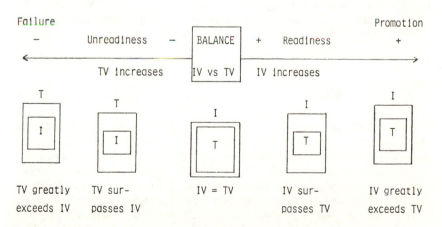

Figure 1. Readiness for sport: a balance between individual volume (IV) and task volume (TV). From "Nature and meaning of readiness for school" by A. Brenner, 1957, *Merrill-Palmer Quarterly*, **3**, p. 135. Copyright 1957 by Wayne State University Press. Adapted by permission.

Given the premium placed upon motor skills in most sports, should tests of perceptual development, motor control, and motor performance be used in youth sport? On the other hand, some sports, such as running, place rather heavy physiological demands on the developing child. Hence, one may inquire about assessing the trainability of the aerobic system of the child. Similar issues of assessment may be addressed in terms of the readiness of the youngster for group participation and cooperation in a competitive situation or social interaction skills with peers and adults. The latter is especially relevant to youth sport. The youngster must be able to interact with the coaches in teaching, practice, and game situations.

Children who appear at a try-out for a sport demonstrate varying degrees of readiness. Most often selections are made on the basis of the motor skill demands of a sport and in some sports on body size, or both. Other demands, such as attitude, social interaction skills, independence, receptivity to coaching, ability to follow instructions, motivation, and so on are generally not considered. Yet, the latter do play a signficant role in success or failure in many sports. There is a need for systematic study of the selection procedures used by coaches at the local level. There is much to be learned from men and women who have many years of experience in working with children in competitive sport. One Little League coach, for example, made his selection criteria quite explicit to the families of boys he selected, and among them, the child's attitude, as he perceived it, was of primary importance. These men and women spend many hours observing the youngsters compete from 6 years of age on, and by the time they are 10 or 12 years of age, they have a good idea as to the unique attributes, that is, the readiness of each child for higher competitive levels.

The preceding has focused on issues related to the readiness of an individual child. On the other hand, the child's perception of his or her own readiness for sport merits equal concern. How does the child experience readiness for sport in contrast to the perceptions of parents and coaches? Such data probably do not exist, although parents and coaches most likely can fill volumes with anecdotal information.

Parent Readiness

Parents are another issue in any discussion of youth sport and readiness for sport. Concern is most often expressed for the child's readiness. However, a legitimate concern is the readiness of parents for their child in sport. How do we assess parental readiness? To use a bit of anecdotal information, coaches were overheard discussing a particular prospect for Little League baseball. The general opinion was rather straightforward: The child is talented; however, if you draft him you must also "draft" his mother! The demands of youth sport on parents are many, not only in time, but also in the emotional involvement in their child's success or failure. Are parents ready to allow their child to participate in sport without constantly interceding on his or her behalf? Is the child motivated to participate, or is it a front for parental motivation? Parental readiness for competitive sport in childhood is ordinarily not considered in the literature, although steps are being taken in many quarters to orient parents to various youth sport programs (Feltz, 1983).

The concern for parental readiness can also be extended to the readiness of coaches to handle, teach, and work with a group of children, each of whom uniquely varies in readiness for sport. Some progress in the coaching area is being made as evidenced, for example, in the first level of the National Coaching Certification Program of Canada which is aimed at local and school coaches working with youngsters 6 to 16 years of age (National Coaching Certification Council, 1978).

Characteristics of Talented Young Athletes

Youngsters who excel in sport are often labeled "talented" or "gifted." It is of interest to inquire whether talented young athletes share characteristics in common with youngsters successful in other competitions, such as music, the arts, and mathematics. Bloom (1982) did a detailed retrospective study of individuals who attained "world class" status at a very early age (i.e., as early as 17 and as late as 35 years) in sport, music, and mathematics. Sport was represented by Olympic swimmers, music by concert pianists, and mathematics by research mathematicians. Successful individuals in these diverse areas of endeavor showed three characteristics in common: (a) willingness to do great amounts of work aimed at high goals; (b) great competitiveness; and (c) ability to learn rapidly. The successful swimmers also demonstrated two additional characteristics: ease in the water and a special "feel" for the water. The physical characteristics of the swimmers were also postulated as important, primarily in providing early competitive advantages and in securing expert coaching:

> Natural physical characteristics that give an individual some initial advantage over his or her age mates are likely to function to motivate the individual to enter and compete in a sport. They also help him or her secure the teaching and training needed to convert an individual with small initial advantages into a world-class athlete. (Bloom, 1982, p. 515)

The native talents of the youngster, although important at early competitive levels, are probably not as significant at later ages when international competition occurs. At such levels, athletes have much in common so that other factors, many quite subtle, are important in obtaining the so-called competitive edge.

An essential ingredient in Bloom's consideration of talent in diverse areas was the recognition of talent. Clearly this is related to the issue of readiness. In the course of analyzing the comments of the gifted individuals, their parents, teachers, and coaches, certain characteristics regularly surfaced as markers: "The attributions of uniqueness or special qualities to the individual...[which]...are used to rationalize or justify some course of action" (Bloom, 1982, p. 519). Individual variation in markers is obviously great. However, the important thing is the recognition and perception of the markers by parents and perhaps teachers and coaches. This is done selectively in keeping with the values and interests of the parents. In Bloom's study, for example, parents of gifted young musicians rarely noted the child's athletic interests or abilities, while the parents of gifted young swimmers rarely noted musical interests or abilities. These findings clearly indicate a significant role for parental values in influencing the notion of readiness of their child for sport. The values will influence the identification and selective emphasis of certain markers.

Summary

Readiness for sport is a function of the child's characteristics, that is, growth, maturation and development, and the demands of the sport. It is not entirely a child-sport issue, however. It also includes readiness of parents to permit or tolerate their child in sport, and of coaches to work with children who bring to the sport situation a variety of unique individual characteristics and backgrounds. Readiness for competitive sport must consider the whole child, including his or her family, and perhaps the community. Nevertheless, the focus of youth sport should be youth. This is an Olympic year and at times this focus is distorted. It is our task as professionals concerned and involved with children in sport to avoid such distortions and maintain the focus on youth in youth sport.

References

Bloom, B.S. (1982). The role of gifts and markers in the development of talent. *Exceptional Children, 48*, 510-522.

Brenner, A. (1957). Nature and meaning of readiness for school. *Merrill-Palmer Quarterly, 3*, 114-135.

Feltz, D. (1983). Orienting parents to your youth sports program. *Spotlight on Youth Sports, 6*(4), 1-2, 5.

National Coaching Certification Council (1978). *Coaching theory: Level one.* Ottawa: Coaching Association of Canada.

8

When Should Children Begin Competing? A Physiological Perspective

Brian J. Sharkey
UNIVERSITY OF MONTANA
MISSOULA, MONTANA, USA

In biological terms, competition for food, attention, and other needs begins at birth. Schools foster competition for grades, awards, offices, and parts in the band or play. But not until play turns to organized sport do we begin to worry about the physical and emotional risks of competition. The trend toward athletic competition at younger ages is a parallel of the effort to move algebra and other subjects into the lower grades. While early exposure to sport or algebra will make better young athletes and mathematicians, what will the early pressure accomplish in the long run?

The question of early competition can be considered on several levels: what actually goes on, what experts say should go on (authoritative opinion), and what research has to say. Parents and children have learned that authoritative opinion is often too conservative or even incorrect. It seldom changes attitudes or behavior. Research, when it is available, does not change behavior until it is overwhelmingly obvious or negative. Positve opinions or research are relatively ineffective when it comes to shifting participation to safe, developmental sports such as soccer or cross-country skiing (from football and ice hockey, for example).

Therefore, this paper deals with the more realistic question, When should children begin training for competition? Strength and endurance are the two major areas of training considered. In each case actual practices are contrasted to authoritative opinion and available research; there is also a discussion of how the positions can be brought closer together in a safer, more productive system of training and competition.

Strength Training

When should children begin strength training? Conventional wisdom and authoritative opinion agree that children should avoid weight lifting until puberty. Most experts agree that prepubescent children can engage in resistance training for endurance using calisthenic-like exercises (push-ups, sit-ups, chin-ups). But because androgen levels are low before puberty, strength training is unproductive and could be dangerous. The American Academy of Pediatrics (AAP) has cautioned that preadolescents should avoid weight training because of high potential for injury—if not practiced correctly or safely (author emphasis).

A 1979 Consumer Product Safety Commission report listed over 35,000 weight-lifting injuries requiring visits to the emergency room, such as sprains, strains, fractures, epiphyseal damage, shoulder, back and knee injuries. Half the injuries were in the 10 to 19-year age group. In spite of the danger, sporting goods stores continue to sell millions of pounds of weights for home use, and the availability of weight machines in schools and health clubs has exploded in recent years. Children will be encouraged to use these weights to improve athletic performance; therefore, effective guidelines are necessary for their use.

It is often said that preadolescents do not significantly improve strength or muscle mass in a strength-training program. This bit of conventional wisdom is about as true as the folklore that says females do not increase muscle mass with strength training. Preadolescents can and do increase strength. Vrijens (1978) found improvements in back and abdomen muscles but no significant improvements in the strength of the limbs. Micheli (1982) trained 9 to 11-year-old children and found a dramatic increase in strength (52% over 12 weeks of training). Most remarkable is the case of the young Bulgarian who started weight lifting at a relatively early age, achieved international prominence at 14 years, and set world records 2 years later. At 16 years of age, pound for pound, he is the strongest lifter in the history of the sport. Thus it appears that children can improve strength, but that does not necessarily argue that they should engage in strength training. That decision depends on the purposes of the program and the sport itself. In many sports, muscular endurance or power are more related to success, and these techniques, which employ less resistance and more repetitions, are considered safer and more acceptable by most experts.

Endurance Training

While the American Academy of Pediatrics (1982) has yet to establish distance-running guidelines for children, it has said that long distance-running events intended primarily for adults are not recommended for children prior to physical maturity. The Academy is convinced that immature youths (less than Tanner Stage 5) should avoid the full marathon distance. While few would argue with this conservative attitude, it is useful to compare it to the opinion that prevented women from competing in longer distance events. In 1984, the year of the first Olympic Marathon for women, those Victorian notions seem rather wistful.

Will the concerns for children follow the same course? Children can and do train for and compete in endurance-running events, including the full marathon. Many more train for competition in age-group swimming, cycling, and cross-country skiing.

Since the myth of the athletic heart was put to rest several decades ago, researchers have attempted to discover the optimal age for endurance training. It is known that training in the teens allows greater development than that which begins after the age of 20. Still unknown, however, is whether prepubescent training yields greater rewards in the development of the oxygen transport system. Some studies show improved endurance with early training; others do not. Endurance training leads to improved running performances, but improvements seem related more to increased leg length (growth) than changes in aerobic power. Conversely, studies on young swimmers show improvements in aerobic power and endurance performance.

Recent evidence suggests that human muscle fibers show remarkable plasticity, that changes in fiber type and metabolic profile are possible, that fast glycolytic fibers can become more oxidative, and that fast fibers can take on slow-twitch characteristics. These findings will create more interest in determining the optimal age for endurance training.

However, of less concern is the optimal age for training and competition than is the possibility that others might exploit young athletes via the use of anabolic steroids, growth hormone, or even pericardium removal (to improve stroke volume and cardiac output). Sports physiologists should do what they can to establish reasonable training goals and teach in coaching education programs to make the youth sport experience more suitable for the participants; but they are less well equipped to monitor the ethics of those who would manipulate and exploit young athletes to serve adult purposes.

Perspective

Aside from the actual cases of physical and emotional trauma that can accompany improper strength or endurance training (Stanish, 1984), the major risk is the eventual loss of interest that occurs when preadolescent athletes train too hard and compete too often in sport. This syndrome may be more common in the American way of sport, which is characterized by the short seasons and inadequate training time allotted in school sport programs. The European or club sport approach allows a longer view of participation that reduces the tendency for overtraining and overcompetition in the early years. Surprisingly, this approach is making a comeback in the United States.

Financial pressures, equal opportunity laws, and greater emphasis on academics are causing changes in school sport programs. Schools and colleges are returning to the club system that characterized American sport at the turn of the century. Some fear this will signal a return to poor coaching and overemphasis, but that is not necessarily the case. While most states now allow nonteachers to coach, many youth sport organizations have coaching certification programs (few school coaches are certified to coach). Organizations like the U.S. Wrestling Federation and the U.S. Ski Coaches Association are training coaches to conduct sensible programs with an emphasis on healthy, long-term participation, rather than short-term results. Most athletes on the U. S. Nordic Ski Team begin participation at an early age. After a few years of club competition, they move up to regional and then national competition. A few who make the national team in their teens have continued international competition into their late 20s or early 30s. This continued interest does not occur when athletes are pushed to the limit at every level.

Summary

While it is true that young athletes in swimming, gymnastics, and wrestling seem to prosper with early training, these athletes often leave competition before they achieve physiological maturity. This early burn-out is common when rigorous training and competition start early, and it suggests the need for an approach which emphasizes skill development and age-related training and competition for preadolescent children, saving the more intense training and competition for later years.

References

American Academy of Pediatrics (1982). Risks in long-distance running for children. *Physician and Sportsmedicine*, **10**, 82-86.

Micheli, L. (1983). (Cited by G. Legwold) Preadolescent show dramatic strength gains. *Physician and Sportsmedicine*, **11**, 25.

Stanish, W. (1984). Overuse injuries in athletes: A perspective. *Medicine and Science in Sports and Exercise*, **16**, 1-7.

Vrijens, J. (1978). Muscle strength development in the pre- and postpubescent age. *Medicine and Sport*, **11**, 152-158.

9

When Should Children Begin Competing? A Psychological Perspective

Michael W. Passer
UNIVERSITY OF WASHINGTON
SEATTLE, WASHINGTON, USA

This paper focuses on psychological evidence pertaining to children's age-readiness for participation in organized competitive sport. The research cited here is based primarily on children from the United States and other industrialized Western countries. Because socialization processes exert considerable influence on the timing and nature of children's competitive behavior (McPherson, 1982; Sherif, 1976), conclusions about psychological age-readiness for competition ultimately must be viewed within a broader cultural framework, with generalizations made cautiously.

Social Comparison and Competition

Numerous investigators have emphasized that competition is a social comparison process and that very young children cannot and do not compete or socially compare with others (Roberts, 1980; Scanlan, 1982; Sherif, 1976). From around 1-1/2 to 2-1/2 years of age, children develop a well-organized autonomous achievement orientation that evolves from a more basic mastery or competence motivation (Veroff, 1969). The child masters new skills via exploration and play and readily evaluates mastery attempt outcomes. Competence is judged based on autonomous standards, and satisfaction is derived from successful mastery attempts. From 3-1/2 to 5-1/2 years of age, children increasingly act to maximize their self-gain at the expense of others when placed in conflict-of-interest situations (see Pepitone, 1980). To adults it often appears that these children are competing, rather than cooperating, because they vie with peers for desired objects or limited rewards. But this is not competition in a social comparison sense. Rather, these children simply act to acquire more of something they value (Pepitone, 1980). In essence, they are still pursuing autonomous achievement goals.

Evaluation of Own Competence

Veroff (1969) contends that not until the age of 5 or 6 do children begin to spontaneously compare their performance with that of other children in order to evaluate their own competence. He also notes that this social comparison orientation strengthens in the early school years. Several studies support Veroff's contentions (see Pepitone, 1980; Veroff, 1969; Weiner & Kun, 1978). Children's interest in competition stems directly from this burgeoning desire for social comparison. Naturalistic observation studies (Rowen, 1973) indicate that around the ages of 6 to 7 children begin to transform all sorts of situations into competitive ones to see who is "the best." Based on gaming research, Toda, Shinotsuka, McClintock, and Stech (1978) propose that competition becomes an independent social motive around the age of 7. This research also indicates that children from various countries will increase their competitive behavior when social comparison information is made available (Toda et al., 1978).

In short, findings from diverse lines of research suggest that the early elementary school years are when most children are able to compete and seek out competitive situations for their social comparison value. Sport competition is particularly important to many children because it is an arena in which they can compare their motor and athletic abilities, which are highly valued attributes among children of elementary and secondary school age (Scanlan, 1982).

Competitive Ability of Preschoolers

Are younger children truly unable to compete in sport? Perhaps the social comparison function of competition has been overemphasized. After all, children who developmentally are not in a social comparison stage surely can participate in sport, have fun, and learn skills; furthermore, they can attempt goals and gain feedback about their abilities that would feed into their autonomous achievement orientation. All this is very true, but the point is that to satisfy these other psychological functions there is absolutely no need to formalize and structure physical activity settings into highly organized competitive games.

Another qualifier stems from the social comparison literature itself. Veroff (1969) notes that even 4-year-olds can learn social comparison standards and are capable of comparing themselves to others if they are asked. Furthermore, these children may intrinsically become socially comparative if their environment (e.g., attending preschool) orients them toward this (Veroff, 1969). Some recent findings suggest that preschool-age boys, but not girls, may in fact make social comparison judgments when placed in athletic contest situations (Pascuzzi, 1981). Thus, it could be argued that 4-year-olds are capable of social comparison when externally prompted, that some of them are intrinsically oriented to compare with others, and that for those children who are not comparison-oriented, involving them in competitive sport will accelerate their capacity for and interest in social comparison and competition. Whether this is a desirable developmental goal can only be answered in relation to one's personal values about childhood.

Cognitive Readiness for Competition

Compelling arguments propose that early elementary school-age children are not psychologically ready to participate in organized youth sport even though they possess social comparison motivation. For example, Roberts (1980) indicates that children's cognitive reasoning abilities are such that they do not develop a mature understanding of the competition process until they are 10 to 12 years old, and, therefore, should be discouraged from organized sport until the age of 13. Weiner and Kun's (1978) attributional analysis of the growth of achievement motivation lends support to Robert's arguments. For example, to accurately assess one's competence based on performance outcomes (e.g., success-failure) in sport requires (a) an awareness that such outcomes are the product of interactive causal factors (e.g. one's or an opponent's physical ability, strategy, and effort in relation to objective task difficulty), and (b) a sensitivity to numerous antecedent cues (e.g., own and opponent's past success history, pattern of current performance) from which the operation of these causes can be inferred. Only in the latter elementary and early secondary school years do these cognitive capabilities become more fully developed (Roberts, 1980; Weiner & Kun, 1978)

These developmental shifts in cognitive reasoning influence not only how children of different ages will assess their competence based on performance outcomes, but also how they will respond emotionally to those outcomes, what their future performance aspirations and success expectancies will be, and how they will approve or disapprove of other children based on those children's outcomes. For example, at age 6 children's expectancies of future success begin to be influenced by their past task outcomes, but it may not be until 10 to 12 years of age that the attributions they make for these outcomes will affect these success expectancies (see Weiner & Kun, 1978). As Weiner and Kun (1978) note, the cognitive development of attribution-expectancy linkages may be essential to the formation of realistic performance expectancies and achievement aspirations.

Resolving the Issues

To summarize, given the necessary motor development, children of virtually any age can be placed in athletic events that are organized and labeled by adults as "competition." But it is not until the early elementary school years that most children will have a fairly well-developed orientation to perceive these contests as competition in the same social comparison sense that adults view them, much less spontaneously seek out competitive sport situations for their social comparison value. Psychological arguments can be given for involving younger children and, alternatively, for delaying their involvement. The issue is further complicated by the considerable differences that exist in the rate of children's psychological development and in the kinds of competitive sport environments to which they are exposed.

Given the preceding considerations, the author's belief is that children younger than 7 or 8 should be discouraged from participating in organized youth sport, and that this is a somewhat liberal recommendation. Certainly the age of initial involvement should be pushed back in specific sports if concerns about physiological capacity, anatomical development, or other physical growth matters exist. In light of Roberts' (1980) and Weiner and Kun's (1978) important attributional analyses, it is essential that among other educational goals, the parents and coaches of preteens competing in youth sport be made aware of the ways in which children's cognitive capacities differ from those of adults. Finally, it should be noted that the arguments raised in this paper should not be construed as evidence for or against involving children in organized youth sport in the first place. That is another matter entirely.

References

McPherson, B. D. (1982). The child in competitive sport: Influence of the social milieu. In R. A. Magill, M. J. Ash, & F. L. Smoll (Eds.), *Children in sport* (pp. 247-278). Champaign, IL: Human Kinetics.

Pascuzzi, D.L. (1981, May). Young children's perception of success and failure [Abstract]. In *Psychology of motor behavior and sport—1981*, p. 97. (Available from Michael Passer, Department of Psychology, University of Washington, Seattle, WA.) D.C. Heath & Company.

Roberts, G. (1980). Children in competition: A theoretical perspective and recommendations for practice. *Motor Skills: Theory Into Practice*, **4**, 37-50.

Rowen, B. (1973). *The children we see: An observational approach to child study*. New York: Holt, Rinehart, & Winston, Inc.

Scanlan, T. K. (1982). Social evaluation: A key developmental element in the competition process. In R. A. Magill, M. J. Ash, & F. L. Smoll (Eds.), *Children in sport* (pp. 138-152). Champaign, IL: Human Kinetics.

Sherif, C. (1976). The social context of competition. In D. Landers (Ed.), *Social problems in athletics* (pp. 18-36). Urbana, IL: University of Illinois Press.

Toda, M., Shinotsuka, H., McClintock, C.G., & Stech, F.J. (1978). Development of competitive behavior as a function of culture, age, and social comparison. *Journal of Personality and Social Psychology*, **36**, 825-839.

Veroff, J. (1969). Social comparison and the development of achievement motivation. In C. P. Smith (Ed.), *Achievement-related motives in children* (pp. 46-101). New York: Russel Sage Foundation.

Weiner, B., & Kun, A. (1978). The development of causal attributions and the growth of achievement and social motivation. Unpublished manuscript. University of California, Los Angeles.

10

When Should Children Begin Competing? A Sociological Perspective

Jay Coakley
UNIVERSITY OF COLORADO
COLORADO SPRINGS, COLORADO, USA

Let me begin by clarifying an important point related to the issue of children in sport. I would argue that it is *never* too early for a child to engage in expressive physical activities. In fact, the more, the better; and the more diversified—both socially and physically, the better. This is true for both boys and girls, but especially for girls, because at this point, they are more likely to receive messages, subtle and otherwise, that sometimes inhibit involvement.

When it comes to competitive physical activities, I have to qualify this position. Competition changes the social setting in which physical activities occur. In particular, it formally alters the relationships between participants; and the interaction skills required to handle those relationships are formed over time through developmental and socialization processes. Fortunately, the competitive component of sport activities can be manipulated to accommodate the interaction skill levels of children at different stages of social development.

This means that I have two answers to the question, "When should children begin competing?" The first answer is that organized sport competition *should not begin before age 8*, because prior to that time, a child's understanding of social relationships is such that competitive sport activities would not be understood in a way that would make them exciting or motivational. This is not to say that these activities would be harmful, although they could interfere with developing physical skills and experiencing the intrinsic satisfaction associated with demonstrating those skills.

The second answer is that competition is acceptable after 8 years old as long as (a) competitive reward structures and relationships are controlled to make them compatible with the interaction skills of participants; and (b) adults establish their performance expectations for participants on the basis of realistic developmental criteria. These answers are based on what we know about the nature of sport competition and about the role-taking abilities of children.

Contrient Interdependence in Competitive Sport

Without going into a detailed discussion on the *nature of competition*, let me simply say that all formal competitive activities are based on reward structures in which there is some degree of contrient interdependence between opponents. In other words, everyone cannot win; competitive goals are mutually exclusive. However, it is possible to control both the degree and the subjective importance of contrient interdependence in sport activities. In fact, when children are playing in situations not supervised by adults, they are masters at inventing these forms of control. "Do-overs," "interference" calls, elaborate handicap systems, and rules serving as catalysts for action and high scores are all attempts to mediate competitive relationships and soften the impact of competitive outcomes. Organized sport programs for children under 12 years old would do quite well to incorporate variations of these forms of control into their own games.

The degree of contrient interdependence in competitive sport also varies with the nature of the tasks performed in the activity. In coactive sports (e.g., swimming, track) task performance involves little or no direct interaction with opponents, although success is determined by a comparison of individual accomplishments. In counteractive sports (e.g., wrestling, basketball), task performance involves direct interaction with opponents; and success requires overt domination of those opponents.

Role Taking Abilities

In order to fully understand the nature of the challenge involved in either of these forms of competition, individuals must be able to put themselves into the roles of other participants. The inability to engage in this type of role taking interferes with competition becoming a source of excitement and motivation. In other words, the ability to compete and the subjective perception of the competitive experience is grounded in a participant's role-taking abilities. This is obvious in sports involving conditions of counteraction such as football, basketball, hockey, soccer, and softball. But it also applies to sports involving conditions of coaction such as swimming, distance running, or long jumping, in which competition itself would be an irrelevant basis of experience if one is not able to conceptualize the competitive relationship from an opponent's perspective or from what might be called a third party perspective apart from self or opponent. This is not to say that the activity would necessarily be boring or harmful if a child was not able to engage in a relatively sophisticated level of role taking, but only that motivation and satisfaction would be based on something other than the process of social comparison that occurs in competition. Therefore, imposing a competitive reward structure on the sport activities of children who do not possess these social-cognitive skills is at best senseless and futile.

Role taking abilities depend on a combination of cognitive development and social experience. Without being able to put oneself into the role of another and understand that other person's point of view in a particular situation, it is impossible to comprehend competition and compete with an opponent on a meaningful level. Without this ability, there is no basis for creating the reciprocity necessary for any form of contrient interdependence to exist.

Stages

Research by Selman (1971, 1976) suggests that the role-taking abilities of children become increasingly sophisticated as the children move through a series of developmental stages. During the ages of 4 to 6 (Stage zero), children are in an egocentric stage; they are able to differentiate themselves from others and the rest of the social environment, but they are not yet able to take the point of view of another person. (To illustrate this, try to explain to a 5-year-old that her uncle is her grandmother's son). Then from the ages of 6 to 8 (Stage 1), children start to be able to understand the point of view held by another person, but they perceive their own point of view as the correct one. During these two periods, interdependence may exist in social relationships, but it only occurs incidentally. Social behavior is characterized by little reciprocity; it is based on an internal conception of what should be rather than on the emergent dynamics of interpersonal relationships. (Watching a group of 3- to 7-year-olds "playing house" will confirm this point about reciprocity).

It is not until the 8- to 10-year-old period (Stage 2) that children begin to develop the role-taking abilities that enable them to understand and to accept another person's point of view. Then between the ages of 10 to 12 (Stage 3), they begin to develop the ability to distinguish more than a single other point of view and are able to assess differences between these perspectives in a reasonably objective manner. This enables them to take what could be called a third party perspective—one that is not simply limited to their own view or the view of a single other person.

Finally, after age 12 (Stage 4), the ability to engage in formal reasoning operations combined with increasingly diversified social experiences adds another dimension to the role-taking process. During early adolescence, it becomes possible to put oneself simultaneously into the roles of a number of others and form a "group perspective" on the social environment and their relationship to it. Such a perspective is essentially grounded in past experience, but it is not associated with any single experience. Instead, it is based on a weighted synthesis of the points of view of many others. It has no immediate interpersonal referents, and it is independent of any specific relationships between self and others.

Implications

What, then, are the implications of these stages for our question on competition? First, the existence of these stages suggests that before children reach 12 years of age, there is good reason to formally and systematically control competitive reward structures and competitive relationships. For children under 8 years old, the emphasis in organized programs should be almost exclusively on individual physical skill development. Competition is generally irrelevant to the experiences of participants before this age. For children between the ages of 8 and 12, an emphasis on individual skill development should be *gradually* balanced with an emphasis on rules, structured relationships, and both offensive and defensive strategies. However, until children reach 12 years of age, it is unrealistic to have competitive reward structures and competitive relationships as the primary focus in a program. Such a focus presumes the existence of social skills not acquired at least until early adolescence.

Second, it means that performance expectations held by adults should be modified so that parents and coaches do not strive to have their children and teams act like miniature versions of adults. They must realize that only a few children under age 10 will be able to conceptually grasp the idea of a team being composed of an interrelated set of positions that shift in response to one another, in response to the placement of opponents, and in response to the placement of the ball or other objects of attention. In fact, most 10-to 12-year-olds still have problems grasping this idea.

Conclusion

Thus, 9-year-old soccer players are destined to forever play "beehive soccer" in spite of the advice and planning of coaches. Immediately following the opening kick, there will be forty 9-year-old legs within 10 yards of the soccer ball, and they will follow that ball like a swarm of bees following its queen. Meanwhile, there are sideline pleas to "stay in position" and "get back to where you belong." The only way to avoid beehive soccer and its equivalents in other team sports is to carefully and tediously condition players under age 10 (and sometimes under age 12) to respond in certain ways to on-the-field contingencies. Such a tactic may win a few games, but it destroys much of the action that children look for in their sport experiences. It is better to accept some chaos and teach children basic skills than to tediously establish strategic, behavioral response patterns in a group of children who are cognitively unable to grasp the notion of team strategy, and who are socially unable to handle the role-taking demands occasioned by competitive relationships.

After children reach 13 years of age, it is possible to lift many of the controls that are appropriate in the programs for preteen children. During adolescence, the self-conceptions of young people gradually take on the complexity that permits them to integrate their sport experiences into this generalized group perspective that outlines their individual relationships with the rest of the social world. Before that time, self-concepts are more unidimensional in nature, and explicit care must be taken to make sure that sport experiences serve to enhance self-esteem and provide young people with the opportunities to develop physical and social skills. Such results are unlikely if competitive reward structures and competitive relationships are not controlled to key into the role-taking abilities of participants.

References

Selman, R. L. (1971). Taking another's perspective: Role-taking development in early childhood. *Child Development*, **42**, 1721-1734.

Selman, R. L. (1976). Social-cognitive understanding: A guide to educational and clinical practice. In T. Lickona (Ed.), *Moral development and behavior* (pp. 299-316). New York: Holt, Rinehart & Winston.

11

When Should Children Begin Competing? A Coach's Perspective

John A. Halbert
SOUTH AUSTRALIAN COLLEGE OF ADVANCED EDUCATION
UNDERDALE, SOUTH AUSTRALIA, AUSTRALIA

Sport as an educational experience for children has been a topic of debate for many years. Yet despite the increase in the fervor of this controversy in the last decade, we have seen tremendous growth in organized programs of sport for children (Martens, 1978). There is certainly no evidence that this tendency will be reversed or that it has reached its peak of involvement.

Recently, much attention has been directed to the establishment of adequate guidelines for children's sport (Canadian Council on Children, 1979; Martens & Seefeldt, 1979). In Australia, a group consisting of representatives from the Confederation of Australian Sport, the Australian Council of Health, Physical Education and Recreation, and the Australian Sports Medicine Federation (1983) has completed a policy statement entitled "Children in Sport". A problem associated with such documents is that they are not always prepared by people who are in close contact with those administering and involved in children's sport. The Australian document contains this statement: "It is recommended that no structured competition be provided for children under the age of ten years" (p. 3). This statement will not be acceptable to the vast majority of organizers and parents in the children's sporting community. Robertson (1983) reported that almost 60% of the children involved in competitive sport in primary or elementary schools were under 10 years of age, and that 80% of coaches stated that they felt that children should become involved in sport before the age of 10 years.

Surely, it is the responsibility of each particular sporting association to determine when children are ready to commence competition in that sport. Obviously, the age of readiness will vary considerably from one sport to another and according to the developmental level of each individual child. I find it hard to believe, as would many administrators in different sports, that some so-called authorities in little contact with children's sport are adequately informed to make such a blanket recommendation for all sports! The danger of such a recommendation is that it will lead to the rejection of the document and disregard for many good points made in the policy statement such as those concerning modifications of major games, the integration of skill and fitness in the training programs, and the flexibility in agreements made between coaches involved in children's sport at a local level. The hope of the joint committee "that national sporting bodies will give careful consideration to encouraging member associations and clubs to adopt the recommendations it contains" (p. 1) is unlikely to be realized. While we must not abdicate our responsibility to improve the quality of experiences for children involved in sport, we practice ostrich-like behavior if we believe that we can dictate such involvement.

Critical Issues for Consideration

What, then, is the reaction of a coach to the question, "When should children begin to compete?" Such a question is likely to evoke the same general answers wherever it is raised. We might say that children should begin when their attitude is correct or when they have expressed an interest to do so. The question of readiness would be raised: Have they the size and physical development to cope? Are their skills sufficiently developed? Does the game expect more of them than their physical, mental, psychological, or social development can accommodate? Many conferences have not, and are not likely to come up with any more definitive answers than the general statements already outlined. Thus, the best question may not be, "When should children begin competing?" but rather, "What are the critical issues to consider with regard to readiness for competition?" I contend that we should accept youth sport competition as a phenomenon of our time and our society, and *seek to educate coaches and parents to make it the positive experience that so many believe that it can be*. That is the stance which will be adopted for the remainder of this paper.

What are ways in which we can maximize the positive outcomes and minimize the negative ones in competitive sport? As Alley (1974) once said, "Athletics in education should be thought of as a two-edged sword, capable of cutting in opposite directions. The direction of the sword cut depends on those who swing it, not on the sword itself" (p. 104). In the case of youth sport, it is the coaches and parents who swing the sword; thus, it is our responsibility to provide as much help as possible to our volunteer coaches, who in so many cases are also the parents of some of the children involved.

The Dropout Factor

Perhaps a major resource when it comes to discussing motives for sport involvement is the children themselves. Orlick (1974) interviewed children as to reasons why they dropped out of involvement in ice hockey; he then identified factors relating either to the competitive emphasis or problems associated with conflicts of interest. By far, the greater percentage of dropouts was due to the competitive emphasis either within the program itself or the emphasis related to the coaches' behavior. More recently, Robertson (1984) surveyed children who were involved in competitive sport in primary or elementary schools in South Australia and asked them about the "turn-offs" in their sport. Thirty percent offered no criticism, 40% referred to the similar program emphasis identified by Orlick, while the remaining percentage was spread over adult problems, injuries, and a range of miscellaneous comments. The reasons, which do not differ greatly throughout the world revolve around certain undesirable aspects of adult behavior as a result of differing perspectives of what children want in their sport. While children feel that the most important things about their sport are opportunities to play, to play as well as they are able, and to have fun, and that the least important is to beat their opponent, adults are seen to place too much emphasis on the importance of winning. Surely the children's sporting environment should reflect their priorities and not those of adults.

Educating Coaches

Smoll and Smith (1980) suggested that the relationship between the coach and player is a primary determinant of the ways in which children are ultimately affected by their participation. Coaches become the ones who are the vital links in establishing a psychologically healthy environment for the children in their sport. It is their education which is the crucial step toward helping to solve many of the problems associated with children's sport. Yet surveys conducted in Canada, the United States (Illinois), and South Australia have all indicated that less than 50% of coaches, and more in the order of only 30%, have received *any* formal training for the task (Halbert, 1979; Martens & Gould, 1979; Valeriote, 1979). It seems incredible that in this important aspect of a child's development, we should entrust the task so blithely to unqualified adults.

Robertson's (1983) survey indicated that few would be willing to undertake the lengthy courses of training proposed by the various accreditation courses offered in many countries. However, most would consider attending workshops of a 2- to 3-hour duration. At least, such workshops would fill the void between those who have no training and the desirability of these coaches doing accredited courses. Certainly, many of the coaches working with children recognize their inadequate training and want some education, albeit in a very limited form.

Without exploring in detail the content of such clinics or workshops, there are some aspects which need to be highlighted, and some techniques of presentation which could assist the educative process. First, priority in such courses must move away from information on the skills and strategies of the particular sport to focus on children and their development, desires, and expectations. Coaches of children need to know more about children. For example, How do children grow and develop? What motivates them? What are the best communication patterns to use with children?

Second, in the planning of any such workshops or clinics, the void between what coaches say and what they do must be recognized. When coaches of competitive children's sport are questioned, they almost invariably give the "expected'' answers about the objectives and practices which guide their coaching. Yet a closer examination of what they actually do reveals frequent violations of those principles even though most have motives which are commendable. Smoll and Smith (1980) indicated that most coaches have incorrect perceptions of how they behave in coaching and are amazed when shown their behavior categories by trained observers. Obviously, it is not possible for those coaches who work with children to have access to trained observers able to provide such feedback. However, they should be encouraged to set up means of providing such feedback, either from their players and their parents or by using simple self-monitoring or evaluating techniques. Clinics should provide coaches with suggestions of how this evaluation could be undertaken.

Summary

Consideration of the question, "When should children begin to compete?" is a difficult undertaking. In such a situation, it would seem best to direct our attention to the ways in which we can educate the various groups involved in competitive children's sport so that some of the recognized problems can be eliminated or at least alleviated. The coaches are the prime group in need of such education. To condemn the operation of children's sport or attempt to direct those involved with definite statements which have little concrete evidence to support them would be a negative approach. This would alienate the community of voluntary enthusiasts to the ultimate detriment of the children who play. The following statement (Nettleton, 1975) would seem an excellent summary of the stance taken in this paper:

> Contemporary criticism of the negative aspects of sport as an educational influence will have performed a useful function if it causes us to focus upon the removal of various abuses of sport, but I would argue strongly that if the criticism causes us to make attempts to ignore experiences offered by sport altogether, the experiences of many children will be the poorer (p. 5).

References

Alley, L. E. (1974, October). Athletics in education: The double-aged sword. *Phi Delta Kappan*, pp. 102-113.

Canadian Council on Children and Youth. (1979). *Fair play codes for children in sport*. Canada: National Task Force on Children's Play.

Confederation of Australian Sport, The Australian Council of Health, Physical Education and Recreation, & The Australian Sports Medicine Federation. (1983). *Children in sport*. Adelaide: ACHPER Publications.

Graham, R. H., & Carron, A. V. (1983). Impact of coaching certification on coaching attitudes. *Canadian Journal of Applied Sports Sciences*, **8**,(3), 180-188.

Halbert, J. A. (1979). *Sport coaches questionnaire*. Unpublished manuscript, South Australian College of Advanced Education.

Martens, R. (1978). *Joy and sadness in children's sports*. Champaign, IL: Human Kinetics.

Martens, R., & Gould, D. (1979). Why do adults volunteer to coach children's sports? In G.C. Roberts & K.M. Newell (Eds.), *Psychology of motor behavior and sports—1978* (pp. 78-89). Champaign, IL: Human Kinetics.

Martens, R., & Seefeldt, V. (1979). *Guidelines for children's sports*. Washington, DC: American Alliance for Health, Physical Education, Recreation, and Dance.

Nettleton, B. (1975). *Teaching sport*. Adelaide: ACHPER Publications.

Orlick, T. (1974, November/December). The athletic dropout—a high price for inefficiency. *Canadian Association of Health, Physical Education and Recreation Journal*, **41**(2), 11-13.

Robertson, I. (1983, October). *Values, attributes and educational needs of primary school sports coaches*. Report to the Professional Development Centre, Central Western Region, Education Department of South Australia.

Robertson, I. (1984). Sport in the lives of South Australian children. *Sports Coach*, **7**(4), 3-6.

Smoll, F. L. & Smith, R. E. (1980). Techniques for improving self-awareness of youth sports coaches. *Journal of Physical Education and Recreation*, **51**, 46-49.

Valeriote, T. (1979). Coaching certification: Certification top priority. *Coaching Review*, **1**, 11-13.

PART III

The Pursuit of Competence
Motivation in Youth Sport

In Part III youth sport is approached from a theoretical perspective by first reviewing an "early" theory of motivation. This competence or effectance motivation theory (White, 1959), recently revived and modified by Susan Harter and her colleagues, focuses on the developmental and socialization factors influencing children's achievement, motivation, and self-esteem in competence domains such as classrooms, sport environments, and peer interactions. Clearly shown in the chapters of this section is that Harter's competence motivation theory offers an especially pertinent model for guiding sport psychologists who wish to study psychosocial development through sport from a developmental perspective.

In the opening paper, Weiss provides a discussion of the theoretical model underlying an understanding of competence motivation. Central to the model are key components and constructs such as socialization history, perceived competence, perceived control, and motivational orientation. This approach is especially significant because of the emphasis placed on the role that cognitive developmental factors play in a child's psychosocial growth.

Following this introduction to competence motivation theory, the two remaining papers empirically test the tenets of competence motivation theory in the sport domain. First, Horn and Hasbrook pursue the question of how children and youth evaluate their physical performance and form judgments about their self-worth. A questionnaire, designed to identify particular sources of information which children use to evaluate their physical competence, was administered to 273 children ranging from 8 to 14 years of age. As predicted, results revealed that certain information sources underlying children's judgments of competence differed across age groups. The authors state that these findings indicate that sensitivity to certain information sources may be influenced by maturational changes in children's cognitive capabilities, as well as factors such as prior performance success and trait measures such as locus of control and anxiety. Horn and Hasbrook conclude by suggesting that researchers and practitioners alike should recognize that qualitative, and not only quantitative, differences in cognitive processes exist for children and youth, and that this information should be used for better understanding children's achievement behavior in sport.

In the second empirical paper, the research team of Weiss, Bredemeier, and Shewchuk explore interrelationships among perceived competence, perceived control, motivational orientation, and physical achievement in youth sports. Using information from both competence motivation theory and prior research, they formulated and analyzed a causal model hypothesized to describe the directional influences of these constructs. Their results supported a self-consistency model in which children's perceptions of their physical competence causally influenced achievement both directly and indirectly through motivational orientation. Further, perceived unknown control, that is, the degree to which a child understood the causes of successful or unsuccessful outcomes, was a catalyst for motivational orientation. The authors also suggest implications for these findings and encourage the use of more causal modeling analyses in youth sport psychological research.

12

A Theoretical Overview of Competence Motivation

Maureen R. Weiss

UNIVERSITY OF OREGON
EUGENE, OREGON, USA

The study of motivation in sport has received considerable attention in the sport psychology literature. Researchers have examined motivational topics such as why people participate or discontinue involvement in sport, attributions given for success and failure outcomes, how extrinsic rewards affect intrinsic motivation, and the arousal-performance relationship.

One of the more recent approaches to studying motivation employs a developmental interpretation of White's (1959) mastery or competence model (Harter, 1978; 1981a). The notion of competence or effectance motivation is that a child is impelled to deal effectively with the environment and does so by engaging in mastery attempts. If an attempt is successful (i.e., if it results in competent performance), feelings of inherent pleasure or efficacy are experienced. This, in turn, maintains or increases competence motivation in the individual. Mastery, curiosity, challenge, and play were all viewed by White as behaviors in which the child's urge toward competence was satisfied by feelings of intrinsic pleasure.

White's (1959) conceptualization of competence motivation was especially attractive because it incorporated behavioral aspects especially relevant for the developing child. However, a major problem with White's presentation of the competence motivation construct was that it was not operationalized and thus not open to empirical test. Over the last 6 years, Susan Harter and her colleagues (Harter, 1978, 1981a, 1981b, 1982; Harter & Connell, 1981) have attempted to remedy this problem and have achieved a great deal of success in doing so.

Harter's Model of Competence Motivation Theory

Harter's (1978, 1981a) refinement and extension of White's competence motivation theory paved the way for empirical testing primarily by operationally defining model components and formulating self-report scales to assess constructs integral to the model. Specifically, competence motivation was not viewed by Harter as a global or unitary construct, but rather as a multidimensional motive. In addition, this multidimensional motive is hypothesized to be responsive to the influence of four psychological constructs not mentioned by White. First, although White focused primarily on the antecedents and consequences of successful experiences, Harter included the role that failure experiences play in subsequent perceptions of self. Second, Harter clarified the definition of success per se, and has found that successful experiences which offer an optimal challenge (the degree of task difficulty is moderate or carefully matched to the learner's developmental capabilities) result in the greatest amount of intrinsic pleasure. Third, Harter emphasized the need to consider influences from significant others, and especially their role in maintaining or attenuating intrinsic motivation and perceptions of self through reinforcement and modeling patterns. Additionally, Harter noted the importance of reinforcement history on the development of a self-reward system and the internalization of mastery goals.

The components of Harter's model that have received the most attention in empirical research are the relative strength of intrinsic versus extrinsic motivational orientations and perceptions of competence and control. In addition, Harter delineated mastery attempts in three specific competence domains: cognitive (school performance), social (peer relationships), and physical (athletic prowess). Individuals are capable of having degrees of motivational orientation, perceived competence, and perceived control which differ in each of these three domains. Of particular interest to Harter has been the developmental change and individual difference factors associated with her reformulated model. This focus seems especially promising for sport psychologists interested in a developmental perspective as prior studies on motivation using experimental paradigms have typically neglected developmental considerations (Halliwell, 1978; Weiss & Bredemeier, 1982).

The relationships among intrinsic/extrinsic motivational orientation, perceived competence, perceived control, and one's actual achievement is of special interest to sport psychologists. The study of these interrelationships would simplify the various ways motivation has been viewed in the social psychological study of youth in sport. Motivational orientation is defined by Harter as the motivational stance which the child adopts toward a specific achievement domain (e.g., intrinsic orientation regarding sport participation) and provides a measure of the underlying reasons for engaging in particular achievement-related behaviors. Perceived competence provides a domain-specific measure of self-esteem, and perceived control is a domain-specific measure of children's perceptions of who or what is responsible for one's success or failure in a particular achievement area.

Harter (1981a) has found that these three constructs, along with actual achievement interrelate in the following way: Children who are oriented toward intrinsic mastery[1] are those who perceive themselves as competent and identify themselves as primarily responsible for their success and failure. Also, these children are actually competent, as reflected in achievement scores. The converse is true of children oriented toward extrinsic mastery.

An understanding of these interrelationships offers a great deal of insight into the experiences of children and adolescents. Moreover, Harter's model is congruent with Deci's (1975) conceptualization of intrinsic motivation as behavior motivated by the need to feel competent and self-determining in dealing with one's environment, and which has served as a popular research paradigm in sport psychology (Thomas & Tennant, 1978; Vallerand & Reid, 1984). The advantage of using Harter's model is that the causal relationships among these factors can be determined empirically with sensitivity to developmental and individual differences. The causal relationships found, in turn, carry implications for sport psychologists and practitioners who wish to employ intervention strategies for enhancing intrinsic motivation.

Empirical Testing of Competence Motivation Theory

Despite the intuitive appeal of competence motivation theory, few studies have actually been conducted to test its predictions in the sport domain (Feltz & Petlichkoff, 1983; Horn, in press; Roberts, Kleiber, & Duda, 1981). Roberts et al. (1981) conducted one of the first studies in sport based on Harter's competence motivation theory. These investigators hypothesized that a relationship would be found between perceived physical competence and children's future expectancies of success in sport, persistence in such activities, and attributions of ability for success. Results revealed that children with higher levels of self-regard were more likely to be sport participants than were those with low perceived competence. Furthermore, there was some indication that children high in perceived physical competence attributed success to ability, persisted at tasks longer, and had more positive expectations of future success than did individuals scoring low on this measure.

In another study, Horn (in press) investigated the influence of coaching behaviors on athletes' psychosocial growth, specifically, their perceptions of competence and control. Coaches of five junior high interscholastic softball teams were observed over several practices and games, and their behaviors were coded using the Coaching Behavior Assessment System, commonly known as CBAS (Smoll, Smith, Curtis, & Hunt, 1978). Athletes' perceptions of competence and control were assessed during pre- and postseason and analyzed as a function of the player's skill level and a number of spontaneous and reactive behaviors displayed by the coach. Results revealed that attained skill level accounted for the majority of the variance in psychosocial growth

---

[1]*Intrinsic mastery* was defined as preference for challenging rather than easy tasks, incentive to work to satisfy one's own interest rather than for pleasing teachers and getting good grades, and preference to figure out problems on one's own in contrast to depending on the teacher for help and guidance.

of the players, but certain coaching behaviors contributed significantly to perceived physical competence above and beyond that of skill level. Specifically, the coaches' use of reinforcement, nonreinforcement, and punishment were the most influential contributors to an explanation of psychosocial growth. In this study, then, Horn examined the influence of socializing agents' reinforcement patterns on players' perceptions of self-regard.

Feltz and Petlichkoff (1983) were interested in understanding why children participate or discontinue sport involvement and investigated this question from the standpoint of competence motivation theory. They obtained measures of perceived physical competence from a number of school-sponsored competitors and former competitors in a variety of team and individual sports. Results showed that participants demonstrated higher levels of perceived physical competence than dropouts. Additionally, a significant gender effect was also found, with males having higher scores than females. If patterns of motivated behavior can be delineated by measures of self-perceptions, then instructional strategies to enhance participants' needs and to foster continued interest in sport participation can perhaps be devised and implemented.

Unfortunately, no studies to date have examined the relationships between other constructs germane to the physical domain of the competence model, that is, to motivational orientation, perceptions of competence, perceptions of control, and actual achievement. A major limiting factor has been the paucity and global nature of measures available for assessing these constructs. Self-concept and perceptions of control have traditionally been assessed with global measures of such constructs, reporting low to moderate correlations between these measures and actual achievement. Harter and Connell (1981) claimed that it is not surprising that global self-evaluative measures have shown low correlations with specific measures of achievement; thus, they and other colleagues constructed psychometrically sound, specific self-evaluative instruments for perceived competence, perceived control, and motivational orientation. This battery of tests was found valid and reliable across large and diverse samples, and is especially geared to the developmental capabilities of children from the third through ninth grades. A short description of two of these scales—perceived competence and perceived control—is outlined below.

Perceived Competence Scale for Children

Perceived competence is assessed with the Perceived Competence Scale for Children (Harter, 1982). The scale consists of 28 items, 7 in each of three specific domains (cognitive, social, physical) and 7 that tap a child's general sense of self-worth. The questionnaire format is one that first asks the child to choose between one of two statements. For example, the child is asked to choose between "Some kids do very well at all kinds of sports, BUT Others don't feel that they are very good when it comes to sports." After the child chooses one of these statements, he or she is then asked to decide whether the statement is "sort of" or "really" true for him or her. Each item is thus scored on a 4 point scale where a score of 4 indicates the highest degree of perceived competence, and 1 indicates the lowest degree of perceived competence.

Multidimentional Measure of Children's Perceptions of Control

The construct of perceived control is assessed through administration of the Multidimensional Measure of Children's Perceptions of Control (Connell, 1980). Similar to the Perceived Competence Scale, cognitive, social, and physical domains are tapped. Three independent sources of control are measured. Two of the sources, *internal* control, and *external* control in the form of powerful others, have been employed on previous scales (Nowicki & Strickland, 1973). The third source of control, *unknown*, emerged in the construction phases of the scale, in which children indicated that they simply did not know who or what was responsible for their successes and failures.

The items on this questionnaire are presented in the form of a statement such as, "When I try to catch a ball and I miss it, it's usually because I didn't try hard enough." Children are then asked to indicate whether it is "very true," "sort of true," "not very true," or "not at all true." These responses are scored 4, 3, 2, 1, respectively. This particular example denotes internal control. A sample external or powerful others control item would be, "When I lose an outdoor game, it is usually because the kid I played against was much better at the game to begin with."

Summary

Thus, with valid and reliable measures derived from a developmental theory of motivation well suited for the study of psychosocial growth through sport, researchers are now able to explore how the constructs of motivational orientation, perceived competence, perceived control, and actual achievement interrelate and explain phenomena in the physical domain. With further research to test the components of competence motivation theory in the physical domain, and with refinements to the interrelationships among relevant constructs, the value of such results should provide physical educators with some general guidelines for enhancing intrinsic motivation in sport.

References

Connell, J. (1980). *A multidimensional measure of children's perceptions of control*. Denver, CO: University of Denver.

Deci, E. L. (1975). *Intrinsic motivation*. New York: Plenum Press.

Feltz, D. L., & Petlichkoff, L. (1983). Perceived competence among interscholastic sport participants and dropouts. *Canadian Journal of Applied Sport Sciences*, **8**, 231-35.

Halliwell, W. R. (1978). A reaction to Deci's paper on intrinsic motivation. In D. M. Landers & R. W. Christina (Eds.), *Psychology of motor behavior and sport—1977* (pp. 397-402). Champaign, IL: Human Kinetics.

Harter, S. (1978). Effectance motivation reconsidered: Toward a developmental model. *Human Development*, **21**, 34-64.

Harter, S. (1981a). A model of intrinsic mastery motivation in children: Individual differences and developmental change. In W. C. Collins (Ed.), *Minnesota Symposium on Child Psychology (Vol. 14).* (pp. 215-254). New Jersey: Erlbaum.

Harter, S. (1981b). A new self-report scale of intrinsic versus extrinsic orientation and the classroom: Motivational and informational components. *Developmental Psychology*, **17**, 300-312.

Harter, S. (1982). The perceived competence scale for children. *Child Development*, **53**, 87-97.

Harter, S., & Connell, J. P. (1984). A model of children's achievement and related self-perceptions of competence, control, and motivational orientation. In J. Nicholls (Ed.), *Advances in motivation and achievement, Vol. 3.* (pp. 219-250). Greenwich, CT: JAI Press.

Horn, T. S. (in press). Coaching behaviors and their relationship to athletes' self-perceptions. *Journal of Educational Psychology*.

Nowicki, S., & Strickland, B. (1973). A locus of control scale for children. *Journal of Consulting and Clinical Psychology*, **40**, 148-154.

Roberts, G. C., Kleiber, D. A., & Duda, J. L. (1981). An analysis of motivation in children's sport: The role of perceived competence in participation. *Journal of Sport Psychology*, **3**, 206-216.

Smoll, F. L., Smith, R. E., Curtis, B., & Hunt, E. (1978) Toward a mediational model of coach-player relationships. *Research Quarterly*, **49**, 528-541.

Thomas, J. R., & Tennant, L. K. (1978). Effects of rewards on changes in children's motivation for an athletic task. In F. L. Smoll & R. E. Smith (Eds.), *Psychological perspectives in youth sports* (pp. 123-144). Washington: Hemisphere Publishing.

Vallerand, R. J., & Reid, G. (1984). On the causal effects of perceived competence on intrinsic motivation: A test cognitive evaluation theory. *Journal of Sport Psychology*, **6**, 94-102.

Weiss, M. R., & Bredemeier, B. J. (1983). Developmental sport psychology: A theoretical approach for studying children in sport. *Journal of Sport Psychology*, **5**, 216-230.

White, R. (1959). Motivation reconsidered: The concept of competence. *Psychological Review*, **66**, 297-323.

13

Informational Components Influencing Children's Perceptions of Their Physical Competence

Thelma Sternberg Horn and Cynthia Hasbrook
UNIVERSITY OF WISCONSIN-MILWAUKEE
MILWAUKEE, WISCONSIN, USA

Harter's (1978) theory of competence motivation asserts that the judgments which children form about their capabilities in a particular achievement domain will affect their motivation as well as their performance in that context. Application of this theory to the youth sport setting would lead to the conclusion that it is very important for young athletes to develop and to maintain a positive view of themselves and their competencies. However, very little information is available regarding the *processes* by which children form such positive self-perceptions. That is, we do not know how children evaluate their physical performance or what information they use to make judgments about their self-worth.

In the athletic environment, as well as in any achievement context, there are many *potential* sources of information that can be used for self-assessment (Minton, 1979; Scanlan, 1982). Available sources include (a) the evaluative feedback provided by significant adults and/or peers, (b) the performance of comparison others, (c) internal cues or stimuli (e.g., degree of effort exerted or enjoyment of the activity), and (d) actual performance outcome.

Although all of these information sources may be available in a particular achievement arena, theory and research from the psychological literature suggest that the susceptibility of children to particular information sources is age-dependent (Ruble, Boggiano, Feldman, & Loebl, 1980; Veroff, 1969). In early childhood, for example, children tend to base their competence judgments on autonomous performance standards (successful completion of a task) in combination with the feedback of significant adults (Boggiano & Ruble, 1979; Ruble, Parsons, & Ross, 1976; Stipek, 1981). However, with the acquisition of higher levels of cognitive functioning (i.e., decentration), which generally occurs around the ages of 5 or 6, children begin to use peer performance in judging their own competence (Cook & Stingle, 1974; Ruble et al., 1980).

The saliency of social comparison information appears to increase over the elementary school years and to reach highest intensity in late childhood and early adolescence (Cook & Stingle, 1974). Although considerably less information is available concerning competence judgments in older children, it has been speculated that the maturational changes in cognitive or intellectual functioning that occur during the adolescent years may be associated with changes in the self-assessment process. That is, children in late adolescence may show an expansion in their competence judgments by moving away from primary dependence on peer comparison toward the integrated use of many systems of information and toward the establishment of self-determined or internal standards of performance (Harter, 1978; Veroff, 1969).

In addition to age-related differences in the self-evaluation process, previous research in the cognitive achievement domain has also revealed gender differences in the saliency of particular information sources. Specifically, girls tend to exhibit less orientation toward peer comparison than do boys throughout the elementary school years (Ruble et al., 1976; Veroff, 1969). In contrast, girls may be considerably more dependent on adult feedback in evaluating their competence than are their male peers (Dweck & Bush, 1976; Lenney, 1977).

This paper reports a study designed to investigate these developmental and gender issues in the physical activity context. Specifically, the researchers' intent was to determine what sources of information are used by boys and girls at each of three age levels (e.g., middle childhood to early adolescence) in forming perceptions of their physical competence.

Method

Subjects

A total of 273 children ranging from 8 to 14 years of age served as the subjects for this study. All of the children were members of an age-group soccer league that drew its players from a large metropolitan city and several surrounding rural communities. For purposes related to this study, statistical analyses of children's responses were conducted by using three specific age categories: Group 1: 8- and 9-year-olds; Group 2: 10- and 11-year-olds; and Group 3: 12- to 14-year-olds. There were 42 boys and 32 girls in Group 1, 30 boys and 64 girls in Group 2, and 35 boys and 70 girls in Group 3.

Assessment of Information Sources

To identify the particular sources of information on which children depend in evaluating their competence, a paper-and-pencil instrument, an adaptation of Minton's (1979) Competence Information Scale, was developed. Minton's inventory was formulated on the basis of extensive interviews with children to ascertain the dimensions of information underlying their judgments of their own competence. These interview responses were then used to develop a scale which incorporated the identified information sources for each of the achievement domains (i.e., cognitive, physical, and social). For the present study, the information sources identified for the physical achievement domain were used to develop a sport-specific competence information scale. To complete this scale, children were first asked to make a judgment regarding their sport competence and then to indicate (via a Likert-type rating) how important each of 12 information sources was in helping them know that the chosen competence statement was true for them. The 12 information sources included the following: coaches' feedback, teammates' feedback, teammates' performance, opponents' performance, personal attraction toward the sport, degree of perceived effort exerted in practice, parents' feedback, spectators' feedback, self-rating of game performance, team won-loss record, degree of skill improvement, and ease in learning new skills. For psychometric purposes, four test items were written to assess each of the 12 information sources.[1] Thus, the complete Sport Competence Information Scale contained 48 items. This scale was administered to all consenting athletes on each team during a specially organized 30-minute team session.

Results

Because it was anticipated that the 12 different information sources assessed in this study would actually be representative of more general latent constructs, an exploratory factor analysis was employed. Initial factors were extracted using a minimum eigenvalue of 1.0, and varimax rotation of the extracted factors yielded a six-factor solution.[2]

Examination of these six factors (see Table 1) indicated that the information sources available in the athletic environment were indeed separated into conceptually distinct categories. Factor 1 loaded heavily on items reflecting social comparison (i.e., using the performance of teammates and opponent players to judge own ability). Factors 2 and 4 were both labeled social evaluation because each primarily loaded highly on items suggesting the use of feedback from significant others. However, the two factors differed from each other in the particular significant others to which each referred. Coaches, peers, and spectators loaded highly on Factor 2, while parents and spectators

---

[1]Assessment of the internal consistency of this instrument was tested by using Cronbach's alpha to determine whether the four items comprising each of the 12 sources were answered consistently by the respondents. Obtained alpha coefficients for all 12 sources ranged from .71 to .88 as assessed for each age group.

[2]Due to the broad range of chronological ages (e.g., 8 to 14) which characterized the children in this study, additional factor analyses for each age and gender group were conducted to determine if the underlying factor structure would differ across any of these levels. Because each of these separate analyses yielded factor patterns virtually identical to those for the combined sample, all subsequent analyses were conducted using only the combined sample factor results.

dominated Factor 4. This separation of significant others into two different categories probably reflects a tendency by children to make a conceptual distinction between the feedback received from their coaches and teammates versus that received from their parents.

Factor 3 reflected more internal sources of information and indicated that young athletes may be using such cues as (a) the amount of effort they exert in practices, (b) the degree of improvement in their skill performance, and (c) the ease with which they acquire new skills to judge their ability. Factor

Table 1. Factor analysis results: Sources of competence information

Information Sources	Item no.	Factor Weights					
		1	2	3	4	5	6
Coaches' Feedback	1	.08	.57	.19	.19	-.01	.11
Coaches' Feedback	2	.36	.55	.18	.13	.14	-.01
Coaches' Feedback	3	.21	.53	.15	.26	.11	-.05
Coaches' Feedback	4	.09	.71	.22	.13	.18	.06
Peers' Feedback	1	.31	.50	.04	.11	-.06	.02
Peers' Feedback	2	.26	.55	.11	.28	-.01	.12
Peers' Feedback	3	.25	.44	.09	.22	.10	-.01
Peers' Feedback	4	.31	.63	.08	.20	.10	.12
Perceived Effort	1	.07	-.03	.52	-.10	-.01	-.02
Perceived Effort	2	.04	.15	.62	.10	-.02	.23
Perceived Effort	3	.13	-.04	.67	.11	.07	.03
Perceived Effort	4	-.01	.15	.60	-.03	.04	.04
Teammate Comparison	1	.52	.16	.14	-.08	.01	-.11
Teammate Comparison	2	.52	.22	.18	-.04	.07	-.12
Teammate Comparison	3	.63	.13	.10	.03	.09	.09
Teammate Comparison	4	.56	.39	.09	.06	.02	.09
Parents' Feedback	1	.02	.25	.01	.71	.24	.17
Parents' Feedback	2	.08	.18	.09	.70	.24	.22
Parents' Feedback	3	.12	.14	.09	.69	.21	.13
Parents' Feedback	4	.02	.31	.05	.69	.24	.14
Game Performance	1	.35	.15	.06	.19	-.16	.10
Game Performance	2	.45	.17	.42	.05	.01	.02
Game Performance	3	.41	-.01	.20	.11	.04	.11
Game Performance	4	.39	.16	.41	-.07	.06	.11
Ease in Learning	1	.34	.11	.38	.07	.13	.05
Ease in Learning	2	.40	.04	.50	.22	.09	-.04
Ease in Learning	3	.33	.02	.54	.15	.06	.09
Ease in Learning	4	.32	.17	.58	.10	.08	.01
Team Record	1	.04	.11	-.01	.14	.80	.18
Team Record	2	.07	.05	.08	.18	.80	.11
Team Record	3	-.03	.06	.03	.22	.77	.04
Team Record	4	.14	.10	.12	.32	.57	.02
Skill Improvement	1	.01	.22	.47	-.01	-.01	.12
Skill Improvement	2	.11	.04	.42	.21	-.07	.39
Skill Improvement	3	.09	.06	.54	.05	.06	.18
Skill Improvement	4	-.01	.21	.44	.04	.06	.30

(Cont.)

Table 1. (Cont.)

Opponent Comparison	1	.55	.19	.02	.22	.02	.04
Opponent Comparison	2	.38	.29	.22	.15	.03	.23
Opponent Comparison	3	.66	.08	.09	.18	.08	.06
Opponent Comparison	4	.52	.29	.07	.12	.07	.13
Attraction to Sport	1	-.04	.15	-.01	.15	.16	.62
Attraction to Sport	2	.15	.02	.26	.20	.08	.69
Attraction to Sport	3	.06	.01	.10	.22	.20	.45
Attraction to Sport	4	-.05	.12	.28	.15	.11	.52
Spectators' Feedback	1	.24	.35	.01	.52	.19	.16
Spectators' Feedback	2	.32	.40	.09	.46	.09	.15
Spectators' Feedback	3	.34	.42	.04	.49	.11	.02
Spectators' Feedback	4	.32	.56	-.01	.26	.14	.08
Eigenvalue		12.5	3.6	2.8	1.8	1.6	1.1
Percent of Variance		49.9	14.2	11.4	7.1	6.2	4.5

Note. A minimum loading of .40 was used as a criterion value in the interpretation of individual factors.

5 suggested the use of game outcome (i.e., team won-loss record), while Factor 6 indicated a reliance on affect (i.e., degree of liking for the sport) as a basis for competence judgments.

Developmental and Gender Differences

According to psychological theory, the saliency of the particular sources of information available in the sport achievement setting should be age- and/or gender-dependent. Specifically, given the age range of the children in this study, the use of social evaluation (primarily provided by adults) was expected to decline with increasing age while the use of social/peer comparison should correspondingly increase. Additionally, females at all three age levels were expected to exhibit less dependence on social/peer comparison but greater dependence on the social evaluation provided by significant adults. In order to test for such group differences, factor scores were calculated for each subject using the obtained factor pattern weights.

A 3 × 2 (Age Level × Gender) multivariate analysis of variance (MANOVA) was then conducted using the six factor scores as the criterion or dependent variables. Because the statistical design was nonorthogonal in nature, the main and interaction effects were tested in stepwise order beginning with the age by gender interaction. Application of the Wilk's lambda multivariate F-test showed the single interaction term to be nonsignificant, F (12,524) = 1.05, $p < .41$. Similarly, the main effect for gender also did not reach significance, F (6,262) = 1.82, $p < .10$. As hypothesized, however, the main effect for age level was significant at the .0001 level, F (12, 524) = 4.28.

Univariate and discriminant function analyses were employed as follow-up procedures for the obtained significant multivariate finding. These results (see Table 2) indicated that three criterion variables (the factors for Social Com-

Table 2. Univariate and multivariate ANOVA results

Effect	Multivariate F Value	Univariate F Value		Standardized Discriminant Coefficient
Age Level	4.28*	Factor 1:	2.98*	.362
		Factor 2:	.07	-.019
		Factor 3:	.42	.055
		Factor 4:	9.20**	-.601
		Factor 5:	13.18**	-.726
		Factor 6:	1.03	-.079
Gender	1.82			
Gender by Age Level	1.05			

*$p < .05$.
**$p < .001$.

parison, Social Evaluation, and Game Outcome) accounted for the greatest amount of age-group differentiation. Posthoc Scheffe testing revealed that the athletes in the oldest age group, the 12- to 14-year-olds, rated the social com parison information sources significantly higher in importance than did either of the other two groups (M Group 1 = -.101; M Group 2 = -.103; M Group 3 = .164). In contrast, both of the younger groups rated evaluative feedback from parents and spectators as a more important source of information than did the oldest age group (M Group 1 = .274; M Group 2 = .089; M Group 3 = -.273). Finally, the younger groups also indicated a greater reliance on game outcome (winning/losing) as a source of competence judgments than did the oldest group (M Group 1 = .347; M Group 2 = .089; M Group 3 = -.324).

Discussion

The results of these multivariate and univariate analyses indicate that the dimensions of information underlying children's competence perceptions do differ across age. Furthermore, these obtained differences are quite consistent with predictions based on the literature from developmental psychology. As expected, the dependence on adult feedback (particularly from parents) declined with age while the use of peer comparison increased. Interestingly, younger children in this study exhibited a tendency to rely more heavily on game outcome as an important information source. It is quite likely that team win-loss record represents a very concrete and easily interpretable source of information for younger children who tend to process information in concrete rather than abstract ways.

No support was found in this study for the predicted gender differences. These results are in direct contrast to the significant differences reported by Roberts and Duda (1984) who found that collegiate females involved in a recreational racquetball class used different criteria to evaluate their sport ability than did their male peers. The differential findings from these two studies are quite likely due in part to differences in the selected sample (e.g., collegiate versus school-aged females, recreational sport participants versus competitive athletes, etc.). In addition, the two studies also differed with regard to the conceptualization and measurement of perceived ability. The present study utilized perceived competence as a measure of the individual's *general* belief concerning his or her personal sport ability. In contrast, Roberts and Duda measured perceived ability as the individual's assessment of his or her competence as demonstrated in a *particular* instance (i.e., in one game situation). At this point, then, we might tentatively conclude that gender differences in regard to personal competence judgments, while evident in certain contexts, may not be consistently found across all ages or in all sport situations. Therefore, further research is needed to clarify issues related to gender differences in self-perceptions of physical ability.

The significant differences found in this study between age groups suggest that sensitivity to particular information sources might well be affected by maturational changes in children's cognitive and intellectual capabilities. However, it is also important to note that choice of information sources is obviously not solely dependent on children's age. The considerable variation evident in this study between children within each age group suggests that the particular criteria used to evaluate personal competence may also be a function of other identifiable factors. Such factors might include the degree of sport experience and the level of past performance success an athlete has had. Additionally, certain psychological characteristics, such as level of perceived competence, locus of control, and/or trait anxiety might affect the criteria on which an athlete depends for self-assessment of physical ability. Support for this hypothesis can be found in previously reported research in the sport psychology domain. That is, children with certain psychological characteristics (i.e., low self-esteem, low perceived competence, and high competitive trait anxiety) have been found to be more sensitive to adult evaluation than are children with contrasting psychological characteristics (Horn, 1982; Passer, 1983; Smith, Smoll, & Curtis, 1979). This research, in combination with the results from the present study, clearly suggests that children may not only differ from each other in their quantitative scores on the perceived competence scale but also in the qualitative criteria they use to evaluate that competence. Therefore, the recognition by researchers and practitioners that such qualitative differences in cognitive processes do exist should contribute to a clearer understanding of children's achievement behavior in sport contexts.

References

Boggiano, A. K., & Ruble, D. N. (1979). Competence and the overjustification effect: A developmental study. *Journal of Personality and Social Psychology*, **37**, 1462-1468.

Cook, H., & Stingle, S. (1974). Cooperative behavior in children. *Psychological Bulletin*, **81**, 918-933.

Dweck, C. S., & Bush, E. S. (1976). Sex differences in learned helplessness: I. Differential debilitation with peer and adult evaluators. *Developmental Psychology*, **12**, 147-156.

Harter, S. (1978). Effectance motivation reconsidered: Toward a developmental model. *Human Development*, **21**, 34-64.

Horn, T. S. (1982). *The influence of coaching behaviors on young athletes' perceptions of competence and control.* Unpublished doctoral dissertation, Michigan State University, East Lansing.

Lenney, E. (1977). Women's self-confidence in achievement situations. *Psychological Bulletin, 84,* 1-13.

Minton, B. (1979, April). *Dimensions of information underlying children's judgments of their competence.* Paper presented at the meeting of Society for Research in Child Development, San Fransisco, CA.

Passer, M. W. (1983). Fear of failure, fear of evaluation, perceived competence, and self-esteem in competitive trait-anxious children. *Journal of Sport Psychology, 5,* 172-188.

Roberts, G. C., & Duda, J. L. (1984). Motivation in sport: The mediating role of perceived ability. *Journal of Sport Psychology, 6,* 312-324.

Ruble, D., Boggiano, A., Feldman, N., & Loebl, J. (1980). Developmental analysis of the role of social comparison in self-evaluation. *Developmental Psychology, 16,* 105-115.

Ruble, D., Parsons, J., & Ross, J. (1976). Self-evaluative responses of children in an achievement setting. *Child Development, 47,* 990-997.

Scanlan, T. K. (1982). Social evaluation: A key developmental element in the competition process. In R. A. Magill, M. J. Ash, & F. L. Smoll (Eds.), *Children in Sport* (pp. 138-152). Champaign, IL: Human Kinetics.

Smith, R. E., Smoll, F. L., & Curtis, B. (1979). Coach effectiveness training: A cognitive-behavioral approach to enhancing relationship skills in youth sport coaches. *Journal of Sport Psychology, 1,* 59-75.

Stipek, D. (1981). Children's perceptions of their own and their classmates' ability. *Journal of Educational Psychology, 73,* 404-410.

Veroff, J. (1969). Social comparison and the development of achievement motivation. In C. P. Smith (Ed.), *Achievement-related motives in children* (pp. 46-101). New York: Russell Sage Foundation.

14

The Dynamics of Perceived Competence, Perceived Control, and Motivational Orientation in Youth Sport

Maureen R. Weiss
UNIVERSITY OF OREGON
EUGENE, OREGON, USA

Brenda Jo Bredemeier
UNIVERSITY OF CALIFORNIA
BERKELEY, CALIFORNIA, USA

Richard M. Shewchuk
TEXAS RESEARCH INSTITUTE OF MENTAL SCIENCES
HOUSTON, TEXAS, USA

Susan Harter's (1978, 1981c) competence motivation theory appears to be especially useful in the study of children's psychosocial growth because of its sensitivity to developmental change and individual differences within developmental level (Harter, 1981b; Harter & Connell, 1981). Recently, Roberts (1984) has emphasized the need for sport psychology researchers to consider how cognitive developmental variability among children influences their perceptions and interpretations of their sport experiences. In fact, the components of Harter's model, including the role of significant others in the development of competence motivation, the functions of reward, the notion of optimal challenge, and the constructs of motivational orientation, perceived competence, and perceived control, have all been given extensive attention in the sport psychological literature on youth sport.

Harter's (1978) original model of competence motivation was designed to identify relationships among motivational orientation, perceived competence, perceived control, and actual achievement. Specifically, Harter hypothesized that the child who is intrinsically motivated within a given mastery domain (cognitive, social, physical) would also perceive him or herself to be relatively competent in that domain, and would take personal responsibility for his or her successes and failures. These positive feelings of competence and perceptions of personal control over outcomes, in turn, would be associated with higher levels of actual achievement. Lower levels of achievement would be expected from a child whose motivational orientation was more extrinsic, whose perceptions of competence were relatively low, and whose perceptions of control were attributed to powerful others.

Within the educational literature, the topics of perceptions of self and motivational orientation have received considerable attention in empirical research. For example, there has been an ongoing debate over the causal relationship between self-esteem and achievement (Wylie, 1979). It is not clear whether successful achievement in various task settings result in positive self-regard, or if one's high self-esteem increases the likelihood for successful accomplishment. Because both of these interrelated constructs represent desirable outcomes of sport participation, the ability to determine the direction of causality would provide important insight as to instructional strategies and communication styles needed to maximize positive sport experiences.

Causal Predominance in the Achievement-Self-Esteem Relationship

Two different theoretical positions identify the hypothesized directional influence of self-esteem and achievement. Researchers adopting a behavioristic view (see Carlsyn & Kenny, 1977; Purkey, 1970) posit that achievement behavior is the primary factor influencing self-esteem development. That is, achievement causes the child to emerge from the performance situation with self-views consistent with that level of performance. These theorists further contend that motivation for achievement is obtained from social approval given for desirable performance in particular tasks.

In contrast, self-consistency or self-enhancement theorists (Lecky, 1945) argue that self-esteem is causally predominant over achievement. Children who see themselves as competent and worthy are predicted to act in ways consistent with the way they view themselves and will thus experience successful task performances, while children with low self-regard will not. Foremost in the philosophy of self-consistency theory is that augmented performance will result from an enriched self-esteem and enhanced motivation for learning.

Although the causal predominance of the achievement-self-esteem relationship is an important topic, studies attempting to unravel the answers have typically employed correlational techniques using global measures of self-esteem and achievement. It is not surprising that these global measures have yielded only low to moderate correlations between these two variables. In addition, researchers who have suggested that increases in one variable (e.g., achievement) *cause* increases in the other (e.g., self-esteem), have disregarded the fact that inferences of causality stemming from correlational studies are unwarranted.

In one of the few studies to investigate the causal predominance question in the sport setting, Shewchuk (1983) used causal-modeling techniques to test the self-consistency theory that self-esteem precedes physical achievement. It was hypothesized that the evaluative self-perceptions of preadolescent boys and girls would exert a causal influence on their performances in a variety of sport skills and on their peer-relevant appraisals of those tasks. Shewchuk found that the model's representation of the data was accurate, although there were differences for the boys and girls. Specifically, while self-esteem was the strongest causal influence on girl's achievement, anxiety was the most powerful mediator in the relationship between self-esteem and motor performance for boys.

Despite increasing interest in the constructs of motivational orientation, perceived competence, perceived control, and achievement in youth sport, their interrelationships remain virtually unexamined. In the cognitive domain, Harter and Connell (1981) have investigated the causal influences of these four variables by comparing models from four theoretical approaches. Using structural modeling techniques, they found that the best-fitting model was one in which unknown perceived control, a variable depicting the level to which one understands why one succeeds or fails, was a critical variable in the sequence of events describing the causal relationships among the variables. Specifically, unknown control was found to be a significant causal determinant of achievement, which impacted on perceptions of competence, and which in turn were found to be causal of motivational orientation. The authors suggested that attempts to improve the child's understanding of why he or she succeeds or fails would improve academic endeavors. Furthermore, enhanced achievement should have a direct and positive impact on the child's perceived competence and motivation to learn and be challenged in academic achievement settings.

The purpose of the study reported in this paper was to investigate the causal relationships among motivational orientation, perceived competence, perceived control, and achievement in the physical domain. Based on Harter's (1978, 1981a) competence motivation model and on the recent youth sport research on the relationship between self-esteem and physical competence (Roberts, Kleiber, & Duda, 1981; Shewchuk, 1983), the authors adopted a self-consistency stance to develop a causal model to test the interrelationships among these variables. Additionally, results from the Harter and Connell (1981) study were used to further enhance the model with regard to the causal influence of perceived control on achievement and motivation.

The general model tested in this study is depicted in Figure 1. It was hypothesized that perceived control causally determines levels of physical achievement and motivational orientation. Further, perceived competence was predicted to causally influence achievement directly and indirectly via motivation. Finally, perceptions of control and perceptions of competence were correlated in this particular model.

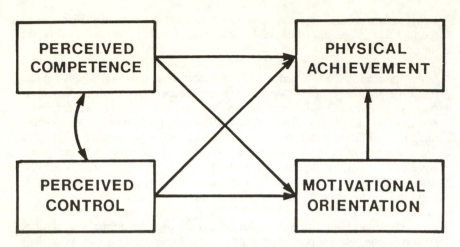

Figure 1. General causal model of perceived competence and control tested in this study.

Method

Sample

Children (N = 155) participating in a 7-week summer sport program at the University of Oregon were subjects in this study. Children's ages ranged from 8 to 12 years (M = 10.2 years, SD = 1.4 years) and included third through sixth graders. Of these, 86 were boys and 69 were girls. Permission for children's participation was granted by parents prior to the start of the program.

The sport program in which these children were enrolled emphasized the educational goals of physical and interpersonal skill development. Because it was not structured to promote intense competition among individuals or teams, it resembled a physical education environment and thus may not reflect the "typical" youth sport situation.

Measures

Figure 2 presents an operationally defined analog to the causal model pictured in Figure 1. Specifically, the *measures* used to assess each of the constructs of perceived competence, physical achievement, perceived control, and motivational orientation are set in the same causal diagram as that in Figure 1. A description of these measures are provided below.[1]

Perceived Competence

Perceived physical competence (PC) was assessed with Harter's (1982) Perceived Competence Scale for Children using only the seven items pertaining to sports and outdoor games. The format for the questionnaire can be seen in Chapter 12, "A Theoretical Overview of Competence Motivation" (this volume).

---

[1]The paper and pencil measures used in this study are available upon request from the first author.

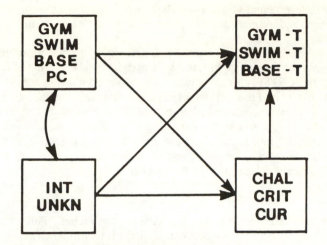

Figure 2. The causal model operationally defined.

Because the perceived physical competence questions tapped a child's overall sense of physical self-worth, an attempt was made to solicit sport-specific measures of perceived competence. This was done by having the child rate his or her ability in comparison to same-gender group members in gymnastics (GYM), swimming (SWIM), baseball (for boys), or softball (for girls) (BASE). Children rated themselves on one 5-point Likert scale for each activity.

Physical Achievement
The child's actual physical competence was assessed by teacher's ratings of their abilities in each of the specific sports of gymnastics (GYM-T), swimming (SWIM-T), and baseball/softball (BASE-T). Teachers of these respective activities completed the short form of the Teacher's Rating of Child's Actual Competence also developed by Harter (1979). This questionnaire includes three items identical to the self-descriptive items completed by the children on the Perceived Competence Scale for Children, and it also included an overall assessment item of the child's physical competence in the sport.

Perceived Control
Measures of the child's perceived internal, powerful others, and unknown sources of control were assessed with Connell's (1980) Multidimensional Measure of Children's Perceptions of Control scale. This scale consists of 12 items depicting perceived physical control, 4 items for each of the three subscales (internal, powerful others, unknown). Two scores were utilized in the actual statistical procedures: unknown control (UNKN), and relative internality (INT), which was calculated by subtracting the powerful others score from the internal control score (Harter & Connell, 1981).

Motivational Orientation
In an earlier study, we (Weiss, Bredemeier, & Shewchuk, 1985) reported the development of a Motivational Orientation in Sport scale. For the present investigation, we chose to employ measures of three of the scales—Challenge,

Curiosity/Interest, and Criteria—as these were significantly correlated with one another and represented the most reliable scales in terms of internal consistency.

The Challenge (CHAL) subscale was defined as a child's preference for challenge versus preference for easy work assigned and consisted of five items. The Criteria (CRIT) subscale is composed of seven items designed to determine whether a child has an internal sense of whether he or she has succeeded or done poorly on a task, or whether the child is dependent on external sources of evaluation such as teacher feedback or grades. Finally, the Curiosity (CUR) subscale includes four items which distinguish a work incentive motivated by one's own interest and curiosity, and an incentive derived from a desire to please significant others such as the teacher.

Procedure

Children were administered the Perceived Competence, Perceived Sport-Specific Competence, Perceived Control, and Motivational Orientation scales in two sessions that occurred a week apart during the sport program. Children worked independently but were helped with reading or understanding items when necessary. Instructions for administering the questionnaires were in accordance with those outlined in the manuals authored by Harter (1979, 1980) and Connell (Connell, 1980).

Model Estimation

We derived the model of the causal relations among perceived competence, perceived control, physical achievement, and motivational orientation (see Figure 1) based on earlier formulations by Harter (1978), Harter and Connell (1981), and Shewchuk (1983). Correlations were obtained for each of the pertinent variables used in the study and which have been described above. These data were then analyzed using a technique called structural equation modeling, or what is commonly known as LISREL.

LISREL is a technique that analyzes structural relationships using the method of maximum likelihood statistics. For the causal structure specified for the variables depicted in Figure 2, LISREL estimates the parameters of the linear structural equations and evaluates the overall goodness-of-fit of the model using a chi-square statistic. Unlike most test statistics which are used to reject a null hypothesis, the smaller the chi-square relative to its degrees of freedom, the better the fit of the data to the underlying covariance structure of the hypothesized model.

Although causal modeling or LISREL is relatively new to sport psychological research, it is especially well suited for examining the relationships among a set of variables which are guided by a particular theory (such as competence motivation). As with other multivariate procedures, there are basically three critical steps in conducting a causal analysis of the data generated for the variables of interest (Finn, 1974): (a) Specify the model to be tested in the study (which must be guided by theory and/or previous empirical research establishing the causal relationships among variables); (b) estimate the parameters of the model (using the software LISREL V developed by Joreskog and Sorbum [1981]; and (c) test the fit of the data to the specified model, (i.e., the model is subjected to empirical verification) also using the LISREL V program. Use of structural equation modeling is especially attractive if one embraces Landers' (1983) position regarding the need for theory testing in sport psychological research.

For the model pictured in Figure 2, we can specify a linear structural equation for each dependent or endogenous variable. According to the model, these variables are explained by independent or exogenous variables residing within the causal structure and other endogenous variables. The structural equations are represented by the general formula:

$$Y = \beta y + \gamma x + \zeta$$

As the terms imply, exogenous variables are determined by factors residing outside the specified causal structure, while endogenous variables are causally influenced by factors within the hypothesized model. In the equation above, y represents a vector of observed endogenous variables measured without error. There were six endogenous variables: gymnastics achievement, swimming achievement, baseball/softball achievement, challenge, criteria and curiosity. Beta (β) is a matrix of causal coefficients relating the endogenous variables.

The next term in the equation reveals x, a vector of observed exogenous variables measured without error. There were six exogenous variables: perceived physical competence, perceived gymnastics competence, perceived swimming competence, perceived baseball/softball competence, relative internality, and perceived unknown control. Gamma (γ) is a matrix of coefficients reflecting the influence of these exogenous variables on endogenous variables. Finally, zeta (ζ) represents a vector of errors in equations, also referred to as residuals or disturbance terms.

Results

The final structural equation model, contained in Figure 3, demonstrated excellent compatibility or fitting of the data to the hypothesized causal structure. All indices of goodness-of-fit supported the tenability of our model for explaining the causal relationships among the measured variables, $\chi^2 = 16.87$, $p = .822$; goodness-of-fit index $= .940$, and adjusted goodness-of-fit $= .891$. Thus, we can confidently state that this model is a likely candidate for describing the assumed causal structure of the processes hypothesized to generate the data.

In order to understand this somewhat complex model, we must examine the causal influences (straight arrows) which are signified by the coefficients, γ and β. One should also note the curved lines which designate intercorrelations, for example, among the exogenous variables, and among the residuals or ζ. Psi (ψ) indicates a covariance matrix of the residuals or errors in the structural equations. In the model pictured in Figure 2, all the causal and correlational influences contributed to the excellent fitting of the data to the model. However, to discern which of the causal influences were significant and meaningful, we must examine the standardized coefficients and their associated T values.

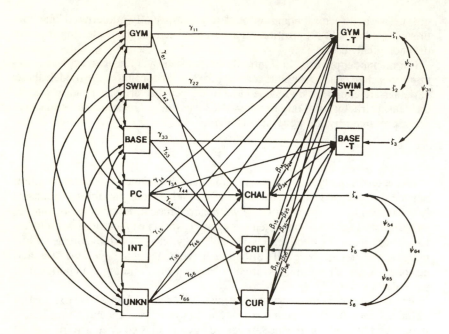

Figure 3. Final structural equation model.

Table 1 contains the standardized LISREL estimates and the *T* values of the parameters pertinent to the structural equation model. *T* values are obtained by dividing the parameter estimate by its standard error and have an underlying *z*-distribution. Therefore, a *T* value greater than 1.96 indicates that the coefficients are statistically significant at the .05 level and should be considered meaningful.

Because we obtained the standardized estimates of the coefficients, their relative magnitudes can be directly compared within a particular sample. Inspection of Table 1 reveals that several of the gamma coefficients (causal influences from independent to dependent variables) were significant. Gymnastics achievement was causally influenced by perceived gymnastics competence and perceived physical competence, and negatively influenced by unknown control and relative internality. Swimming achievement was significantly influenced only by perceived swimming competence, just as baseball/softball achievement was causally determined only by perceived physical competence. The motivational subscale of challenge was significantly influenced by perceived swimming competence and perceived physical competence, and was negatively influenced by unknown control. The gamma coefficient from perceived physical competence to criteria was significant, as were the causal coefficients (negative influence) from unknown control to both criteria and curiosity.

In summary, it is clear that achievement in sport areas such as gymnastics, swimming, and baseball/softball could be causally attributed to sport-specific and overall perceptions of physical competence. Perceived control did not emerge as a major causal influence of achievement, although the coefficients from both unknown control and relative internality to gymnastics achievement were significant. The unknown perceived control variable had a negative causal influence on the motivational orientation subscales of challenge, criteria, and curiosity; that is, children who did not know who or what was responsible for their success or failure in sport had lower motivational scores than children who could identify the sources of control. The gamma coefficients which were most important to the model (had the highest coefficient values) were γ^{11} (GYM to GYM-T), γ^{22} (SWIM to SWIM-T), γ^{24} (PC to BASE-T), and γ^{54} (PC to CHALLENGE).

The percentage of variance explained for the achievement variables was good considering the limited number of causal variables included in the model. For example, the squared multiple correlations (R^2) for gymnastics achievement was 35.4%; for swimming achievement, 27.1%; and for baseball/softball achievement, 33.5%. The percentage of variance explained for the motiva-

Table 1. Standardized LISREL estimates and T values for the structural equation model

Parameter	Standardized Coefficient	T Value
γ_{11}	.476	6.26
γ_{14}	.190	2.71
γ_{15}	− .229	− 3.47
γ_{16}	− .189	− 2.71
γ_{22}	.435	7.48
γ_{33}	.019	.24
γ_{34}	.499	5.74
γ_{42}	.191	2.79
γ_{44}	.314	4.58
γ_{46}	− .258	− 3.44
γ_{53}	− .163	− 1.82
γ_{54}	.280	3.12
γ_{56}	− .263	− 3.37
γ_{61}	.112	1.57
γ_{66}	− .275	− 3.44
β_{14}	.208	2.61
β_{15}	− .082	− 1.10
β_{16}	− .225	− 2.86
β_{24}	.220	2.70
β_{25}	.085	1.10
β_{26}	− .083	− 1.02
β_{34}	.174	2.15
β_{35}	− .075	− .99
β_{36}	− .155	− 1.97
ψ_{21}	.200	3.41
ψ_{31}	.130	2.43
ψ_{54}	.175	2.46
ψ_{64}	.349	4.51
ψ_{65}	.254	3.28

tional variables was somewhat lower: challenge (19.7%), criteria (13.5%), and curiosity (8.5%).

The beta coefficients (causal influences of dependent variables on other dependent variables) also revealed a number of significant effects of motivation on achievement variables in the model. Inspection of Table 1 reveals that gymnastics achievement was causally influenced by challenge and negatively influenced by curiosity. Swimming achievement was also causally determined by challenge, while baseball/softball achievement was positively influenced by challenge and negatively influenced by curiosity. The most important beta coefficients appeared to be β^{14} (challenge to gymnastics achievement); β^{24} (challenge to swimming achievement); and β^{16} (negative influence of curiosity to gymnastics achievement).

In all, then, achievement measures were causally influenced by perceived competence and motivational orientation subscales. Additionally, perceived unknown control exerted a consistent and negative causal influence on motivational orientation, while perceived competence positively influenced the challenge and criteria subscales of motivation. Thus, physical achievement was directly and indirectly influenced by perceived competence as well as indirectly influenced by perceived control through motivational orientation.

As stated earlier, psi (ψ) is a covariance matrix of the residuals (errors) in the structural equations. An examination of the T values for the coefficients indicated that not only were the errors of "unspecified causes" significant, but also their correlations were significant. Thus, although the model tested in the present analysis fit the data very well and provides some evidence of "causality" among the variables specified in the model, there may be other competing models which may fit the data equally well. While we are not working within what we might call a "closed system" of functional relationships, we are, however, operating within the confines of a theory or what is presently known. Thus, we are confident, in spite of the rather large residual paths (ζ's), that the present model has captured the essential mechanisms of those processes responsible for generating the covariances among the observed variables.

Discussion

The results of this study offer support for the view that individuals act in ways that are consistent with their perceptions of self. That is, the causal coefficients estimated by LISREL showed that perceptions of one's competence in physical activity (e.g., in swimming) impacts on actual competence directly and indirectly through motivational orientation. Enhancement of one's perceived physical competence was also found to be significantly associated with two motivational measures: challenge and criteria. This suggests that higher levels of perceived competence directly enhance the child's preference to perform hard, challenging work as opposed to easier work assigned by the teacher. Higher levels of perceived competence also encourage the child to develop an internal sense of whether he or she has succeeded or done poorly criteria) as opposed to depending on external sources of evaluation such as teacher feedback.

The results of this study also reflect the significant impact of the unknown control construct on achievement and motivation. Significant negative causal coefficients were found when examining the influence of unknown control on gymnastics achievement, challenge, criteria, and curiosity. The importance that the unknown control variable plays in this network of psychosocial variables is consistent with findings by Harter and Connell (1981). They found that the extent to which a child feels that he or she knows or does not know the causes of successful or unsuccessful outcomes was most directly related to academic achievement. In the present study, it was the child who received a low unknown control score (indicating an understanding of what was responsible for his or her success and failure) that experienced high levels of gymnastics achievement and expressed high degrees of motivation on the challenge, criteria, and curiosity subscales. These findings imply that by improving the child's understanding of why he or she succeeds or fails, his or her level of intrinsic motivation and physical achievement level will improve.

According to the beta coefficients found in the present structural equation model, high scores on the challenge subscale of motivational orientation was found to significantly influence gymnastics, swimming, and baseball/softball achievement. This suggests that children who show an intrinsic orientation for their preference for challenging tasks will most likely show the highest gains in improvement of skills.

Interestingly, the curiosity scale was found to negatively influence gymnastics and baseball/softball achievement. A closer look at the definition of this subscale may add some insight to this finding. The curiosity/interest subscale is characterized by Harter as a measure of the incentive to work to satisfy one's own interest and curiosity versus working to please the teacher and obtain good grades. For example, the following is a sample item from this subscale:

Some kids practice their skills because the teacher tells them to BUT Other kids practice their skills to find out about a lot of things they've been wanting to know.

It is plausible that within the structure of youth sport, children who work to please the physical education teacher or coach actually fare better in terms of skill development than those who work to satisfy one's interest. The regimentation often seen in the organization of youth leagues may reward individuals with a more extrinsic orientation when it comes to curiosity/interest than those with a more intrinsic interest. In an earlier study (Weiss, Bredemeier, & Shewchuk, 1985), it was found that with increasing age, children went from an intrinsic orientation in independent mastery (the degree to which a child prefers to figure out skills on his or her own), to an extrinsic orientation (a dependence on the teacher for help and guidance, particularly when it comes to figuring out skills and strategies). The mastery subscale was not examined in the present study, but it is possible that the same kind of rationale might hold for the curiosity/interest subscale.

The results of this study also support those of Shewchuk (1983) and suggest that it is perceptions of competence and control that are the primary causal factors of achievement and motivational orientation. Carlsyn and Kenny (1977) use the term "causally predominant" so as not to preclude reciprocal causation. The residuals found in this study indicated the existence of some as yet "unaccounted for" variables in the model and suggested that other competing models may fit the data as well as our model. It is apparent, however, that the model proposed to represent the causal mechanisms underlying the variables is an excellent one and was formulated based on a theoretical framework describing the relationship between self-esteem and achievement, as well as prior empirical research.

We feel that this study was an important step in determining the causal relationships among the constructs of perceived competence, perceived control, motivational orientation, and actual achievement in the physical domain. It is apparent, however, that further studies must be conducted to replicate and extend the findings of these empirical investigations. Additionally, other components of Harter's model need to be tested to determine their relevance to an understanding of competence motivation in the physical domain. For example, the role of affect, most notably intrinsic pleasure and anxiety, is an integral part of Harter's (1978) model. Similarly, a line of research that has received considerable attention in sport psychology is that of competitive anxiety and its effects on performance and motivation. Thus, investigators could focus on the correlates of anxiety in sport using Harter's theoretical framework to discover the interplay of anxiety with the constructs of perceived competence, perceived control, motivation, and physical achievement.

Another important component of Harter's competence model is the role of significant other's evaluations on perceptions of competence and control. It is hypothesized that positive reinforcement and approval for independent mastery attempts will lead to augmented self-views while the lack of such reinforcement and approval will attenuate psychosocial growth. Recently, Horn (in press) examined the influence of coaching behaviors on junior high school softball players' subsequent perceptions of competence and control. Results suggested that certain coaching behaviors (reinforcement, nonreinforcement, punishment) added significant variance above and beyond the athlete's attained skill level over the season. Additional research is needed to delineate those communication strategies that are most likely to have a beneficial impact on children's sport experiences.

Causal-Modeling Techniques

Finally, the use of causal-modeling techniques is especially suited for examining a variety of sport psychological issues, such as the tenets of competence motivation theory (Shewchuk, 1983). Such procedures include cross-lagged panel correlations, path analysis, and analysis of covariance structures. Causal modeling enables researchers to test the relationships among a set of variables which are guided by a particular theory. A set of mathematical equations is generated which permit one to predict the effects of changes in the values of one variable on other variables in the model. Finally, the parameters of the model are estimated from the equations and the model is subjected to empirical verification. Causal-modeling procedures can provide social science researchers with a means for exploring important questions regarding causal relationships among variables that previously have not been amenable to traditional correlational or experimental approaches (Shewchuk, 1983). It is hoped that researchers will use causal-modeling techniques more frequently in the future so that important directional interrelationships can be uncovered. Certainly, with regard to competence motivation theory, the time is ripe for employing this technique.

References

Carlsyn, R. J., & Kenny, D. A. (1977). Self-concept of ability and perceived evaluation of others: Cause or effect of academic achievement? *Journal of Educational Psychology*, **69**, 136-145.

Connell, J. P. (1980). *A multidimensional measure of children's perceptions of control*. Unpublished master's thesis, University of Denver.

Finn, J. D. (1974). *A general model for multivariate analysis*. New York: Holt, Rinehart, & Winston.

Harter, S. (1978). Effectance motivation reconsidered: Toward a developmental model. *Human Development*, **21**, 34-64.

Harter, S. (1979). *Perceived competence scale for children (Form 0)*. Unpublished manuscript, University of Denver, Denver, CO.

Harter, S. (1980). *Intrinsic/extrinsic motivational orientation in the classroom*. Unpublished manuscript, University of Denver, Denver, CO.

Harter, S. (1981a). A model of intrinsic mastery motivation in children: Individual differences and developmental change. In W. C. Collins (Ed.), *Minnesota Symposium on Child Psychology (Vol. 14)* (pp. 215-254). New Jersey: Erlbaum.

Harter, S. (1981b). A new self-report scale of intrinsic versus extrinsic orientation and the classroom: Motivational and informational components. *Developmental Psychology*, **17**, 300-312.

Harter, S. (1982). The perceived competence scale for children. *Child Development*, **53**, 87-97.

Harter, S., & Connell, J. P. (1981). A model of children's achievement and related self-perceptions of competence, control, and motivational orientation. In J. Nicholls (Ed.), *Advances in Motivation and Achievement, Vol 3* (pp. 219-250). Greenwich, CT: JAI Press.

Horn, T. S. (in press). Coaching behaviors and their relationship to athletes' self-perceptions. *Journal of Educational Psychology*.

Joreskog, K. G., & Sorbum, D. (1981). *LISREL V: Analyzing of linear structural relationships by the method of maximum likelihood*. Chicago: International Educational Services.

Landers, D. M. (1983). Whatever happened to theory testing? *Journal of Sport Psychology*, **5**, 135-151.

Lecky, P. (1945). *Self-consistency: A theory of personality*. Long Island, NY: Island Press.

Purkey, W. W. (1970). *Self-concept and school achievement*. Englewood Cliffs, NJ: Prentice-Hall.

Roberts, G.C. (1984). Toward a new theory of motivation in sport: The role of perceived ability. In J.M. Silva and R.S. Weinberg (Eds.), *Psychological foundations of sport* (pp. 214-228). Champaign, IL: Human Kinetics.

Roberts, G. C., Kleiber, D. A., & Duda, J. L. (1981). An analysis of motivation in children's sport: The role of perceived competence in participation. *Journal of Sport Psychology*, **3**, 206-216.

Shewchuk, R. M. (1983). *Self-concept and physical performance of preadolescent children: A causal analysis*. Unpublished doctoral dissertation, University of Oregon.

Weiss, M. R., Bredemeier, B. J., & Shewchuk, R. M. (1985). An intrinsic/extrinsic motivation scale for the youth sport setting: A confirmatory factor analysis. *Journal of Sport Psychology, 7* (1), 75-91.

Wylie, R. C. (1979). *The self-concept: Theory and research on selected topics (Vol. 2).* Lincoln, NE: University of Nebraska Press.

PART IV

Perceptions of Stress in Young Athletes

Understanding the stress and anxiety young athletes experience has long been a concern for those involved in youth sport. In fact, a recent survey[1] of youth sport leaders revealed that understanding the competitive stress placed on young athletes and helping young athletes cope with competitive stress are two of the most important issues requiring study in children's sport. Not surprising, then, is the considerable attention that the examination of competitive stress in young athletes has received in recent years.

Although researchers have studied stress in young athletes for some time, the integration of this research and provision of a conceptual framework to guide and interpret it was lacking. This part seeks to accomplish this goal. It includes four interrelated papers written by authors who have been extensively involved in conducting research on young athletes.

In the first paper, Ron Smith, a clinical psychologist, provides a theoretical framework for understanding the stress process. Specifically, his model of athletic stress examines the relationship between the athletic situation, the young athlete's cognitive appraisal of various aspects of the situation, actual physiological responses, and behavioral attempts to cope with the situation. The model not only provides a conceptual framework for guiding youth sport stress research, but also serves as a framework for designing intervention programs used for reducing stress.

Next, Tara Scanlan discusses individual and situational factors that are associated with both pre- and postcompetitive stress that young athletes experience. These factors have been identified from a landmark series of studies

[1]Gould, D. (1982). Sport psychology in the 1980s: Status, direction, and challenge in youth sports research. *Journal of Sport Psychology, 4,* 203–218.

conducted by Scanlan and her associates. Following Scanlan, Glyn Roberts extends existing conceptualizations of the stress process by examining how the achievement goals children hold in competitive sport and their developmental capacity to process information affect their perceptions of stress. His innovative approach identifies unexplored relationships between achievement goals and stress and should serve as a guide for future research.

Frank Smoll, in the final paper in this section, uses the model developed by Smith and discusses intervention strategies which can be used to help minimize sources of stress placed on young athletes. In particular, Smoll identifies behavioral, physiological, and cognitive coping strategies, as well as intervention procedures to reduce situational sources of stress. These include modification of the sport, implementation of various coaching strategies, and development of parental education programs.

15

A Component Analysis of Athletic Stress

Ronald E. Smith
UNIVERSITY OF WASHINGTON
SEATTLE, WASHINGTON, USA

At all competitive levels, athletes are subjected to both physical and psychological demands. When these demands tax the physiological, behavioral, and psychological resources of the competitor, athletic stress is said to exist. While stress is endemic to the athletic setting, it is well recognized that extreme levels of stress can have adverse consequences on performance, enjoyment of the activity, and the physical and psychological welfare of the athlete (Passer, 1984; Smith, 1984; Smith & Smoll, 1982). Given the critical role that stress can play in athletics, it is not surprising that athletic stress has been the focus of much empirical attention in recent years. Research has been directed at an exploration of the nature of stress, its antecedents, and its consequences. Recent attention has also been directed to the development of methods for reducing psychological stress at both the situational level (Smoll & Smith, 1984) and through intervention programs directed at athletes (Smith, 1984).

Whether attention is focused on the dynamics of stress or on the methods designed to alleviate it, the presence of a conceptual model can facilitate progress at both the theoretical and applied levels. The focus of the present discussion is on a conceptual model of stress that can serve to guide research while also having implications for the development of intervention programs. Later in this volume, Smoll explores some of the implications of this type of a model for designing stress reduction-intervention programs for young athletes. This paper's discussion focuses primarily on the components of the model and the relationship among these components.

The term *stress* is typically used in two different but related ways. The first refers to situations that tax the physical and/or psychological capabilities of the individual. The focus here is on the balance between the demands of the situation and on the personal and social resources the person has to cope with

107

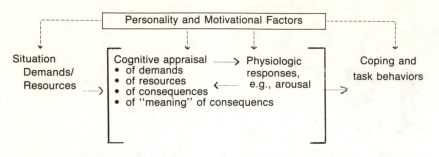

Figure 1. A conceptual model of stress showing hypothesized relationships among situational, cognitive, physiological, and behavioral components. Motivational and personality variables are assumed to affect and interact with each of the components.

these demands. Situations are likely to be labeled as stressful when their demands test or exceed the resources of a person. The second use of the term *stress* refers to a person's cognitive, emotional, and behavioral responses to situational demands. Clearly, these two uses of the word are not synonomous because people may vary considerably in how "stressful" they find the same situation to be.

Figure 1 contains a conceptual model of stress that takes both the situation and the individual's reactions into account. The model encompasses relationships among the situation, the athlete's congitive appraisal of various aspects of the situation, physiological arousal responses, and behavioral attempts to cope with the situation. Each of these components is, in turn, influenced by personality and motivational variables.

The Situational Component

The first component of the model, the situation, involves interaction between environmental demands and personal or environmental resources. Whenever a young athlete encounters a demand, resources are mobilized to meet it. When demands and resources are relatively balanced, stress is minimal. When demands slightly exceed resources, the situation is likely to be viewed as challenging. But when a significant imbalance occurs because of increased demands or decreases in the resources for meeting them, then the situation is likely to be regarded as stressful. Athletic demands can be *external*, as when a young athlete is faced with a strong opponent in an important contest, or when the athlete is interacting with an abusive or highly demanding coach or a critical group of teammates.

Other situational demands have an *internal* locus of causation, resulting from personality or motivational factors. Internal demands include desired goals, personal standards of performance relating to values or commitments, or unconscious motives and conflicts. Motivational and personality variables influence which of the complex of environmental demands will be most salient or demanding. Needs for competence, mastery, affiliation, or power each can cause the athlete to focus on and respond to particular aspects of the athletic environment. Similarly, different types of resources (e.g., physical skills, social skills, or social support within the environment) may differ in their relative importance to individual athletes in particular situations. In any analysis of situational stress, it is therefore important to take into account the specific demands, resources, and imbalances that are of concern to the individual athlete.

Typically, we think of stress as occurring in situations where demands greatly exceed resources, producing a condition of "overload." However, psychological stress can also result when resources greatly exceed demands. Feelings of boredom, stagnation, and "staleness" are common responses to this state of affairs, and a condition of "underload" may also take a toll on the performance, commitment, and enjoyment a young athlete experiences.

The Cognitive Component

Athletes generally view their emotions as being triggered directly by situational demands. However, in most instances, situations exert their effects on emotions through the intervening influence of thought. Through their own thought processes, people create the psychological reality to which they respond. Thus, the second component of the stress model, cognitive appraisal, plays a central role in understanding stress because the intensity of emotional responses is a function of what people tell themselves about situations, their meaning, and about their ability to cope with the demands of the situation. As part of the active process of perception, people appraise the demands of the situation and the nature and adequacy of the resources they have to cope with them. Such appraisal may or may not be accurate. For example, a young athlete low in self-confidence may perceive a greater discrepancy between demand and resources than is actually the case. Conversely, a self-assured athlete may perceive a smaller discrepancy then actually exists. It follows, however, that it is the perception of balance and imbalance rather than the actual state of affairs that in the end determines how stressed a young athlete will become. Here again, individual difference variables such as self-efficacy and competitive trait anxiety can play a vital role (Passer, 1984).

In addition to mentally evaluating demands and resources, people appraise the possible consequences of failure to meet the demands. If a perceived imbalance between demands and resources threatens harm or the loss of desired goals, the situation is likely to be perceived as stressful or threatening (Lazarus, 1966). Here again, the appraisal process may or may not be accurate. Thus, an athlete who exaggerates or "catastrophizes" about the consequences of failing to successfully deal with the demands may experience needless stress. Distortions may occur regarding the valence of the consequences as well as their likelihood of occurrence. For example, one highly stressed athlete believed that any mistake on her part would certainly lead to demotion to the second team despite assurances from her coach to the contrary. A distortion was clearly occurring at the level of subjective probability of occurrence of a dreaded consequence.

The final aspect of the appraisal prospect is the personal meaning attributed to the consequences. These meanings derive from the athlete's personal beliefs, self-concept, and conditions of self-worth. Ellis (1962) has described in detail the central role of irrational assumptions and beliefs in psychological distress. It is clear that an athlete who believes that his or her basic self-worth is defined by his or her athletic success will attribute different meaning to athletic outcomes than will an athlete whose self-worth is more securely and realistically anchored. For the former, winning can become literally a life-or-death situation, whereas the athlete who can divorce self-worth from success will attribute a less urgent personal meaning to success and failure. Many young athletes appear to be victimized by irrational beliefs concerning the meaning and importance of success and approval of others, and such beliefs predispose them to inappropriate or excessive stress reactions. Modification of such beliefs is an important component of several cognitive-behavioral approaches to teaching athletes stress-management skills (Smith, 1980, 1984).

The Physiological Component

The third component of the model, physiological responses, are reciprocally related to appraisal processes. Despite the recent debate on whether cognition is a necessary condition for emotional arousal (Lazarus, 1984; Zajonc, 1984), it is assumed that whether and to what extent athletes respond with emotional arousal is largely dependent on cognitive mediational responses. When appraisal indicates the existence of threat or danger, physiological arousal occurs as part of the mobilization of resources to deal with the situation. Arousal, in turn, provides feedback concerning the intensity of the emotion being experienced. Arousal feedback contributes to the ongoing process of appraisal and reappraisal. Thus, a young athlete who becomes aware of an increasing level of arousal may appraise the situation as more threatening than one who experiences low arousal in the same situation. This appraisal may, in turn, generate even more emotional arousal. Conversely, a young athlete who experiences low arousal in a potentially stressful situation is likely to appraise the situation as less threatening or as one with which he or she can cope successfully (Smith, 1980).

The Behavioral Component

The fourth and final component of the model consists of the output behaviors that occur in response to the situation. These include task-oriented, social, and coping behaviors that are affected by the demands of the situation, cognitive appraisal processes, and the nature and intensity of emotional responses that may occur. The adequacy or success of these coping behaviors affect the balance between demands and resources as well as the ongoing appraisal process. Thus, a young athlete who experiences herself as being "in the flow" is likely to have a positive affective experience, whereas one who perceives her responses as being inadequate to the demands is more likely to experience negative affect. It is thus seen that all of the components of the model relate in an interactive fashion to one another, so that changes in one component can affect all of the rest.

The implications of the present conceptual model for reducing athletic stress have been explored in greater detail elsewhere (Smith & Smoll, 1982; Smoll, this volume). Intervention can be directed at any of the model's components. Thus, measures may be instituted which decrease situational demands or increase personal and environmental resources (for example, by increasing athletic or social skills). Intervention attempts may also be directed at distortions in the cognitive appraisal process or at helping athletes acquire greater control over physiological arousal response through training in self-control relaxation techniques. It is to be hoped that the conceptual model advanced here will be found to have implications not only for intervention, but also for the development of measuring instruments designed to assess individual differences in the various components of the model. Progress in sport psychology, particularly in studying competitive stress in youth athletes, will most readily be advanced by interrelated advances at the theoretical, empirical, and intervention levels.

References

Ellis, A. (1962). *Reason and emotion in psychotherapy*. New York: Lyle Stuart.

Lazarus, R. S. (1966). *Psychological stress and the coping process*. New York: McGraw-Hill.

Lazarus, R.S. (1984). On the primacy of cognition. *American Psychologist*, **39**, 124-129.

Passer, M. W. (1984). Competitive trait anxiety in children and adolescents: Mediating cognitions, developmental antecedents, and consequences. In J. M. Silva & R. S. Weinberg (Eds.), *Psychological foundations of sport and exercise* (pp. 130-144). Champaign, IL: Human Kinetics.

Smith, R. E. (1980). A cognitive—affective approach to stress management training for athletes. In C. H. Nadeau, W. R. Halliwell, K. M. Newell, & G. C. Roberts (Eds.), *Psychology of motor behavior and sport—1979* (pp. 54-72). Champaign, IL: Human Kinetics.

Smith, R. E. (1984). Theoretical and treatment approaches to anxiety reduction. In J. M. Silva & R. S. Weinberg, (Eds.), *Psychological foundations of sport and exercise*. Champaign, IL: Human Kinetics.

Smith, R. E., & Smoll, F. L. (1982). Psychological stress: A conceptual model and some intervention strategies in youth sports. In R. A. Magill, M. J. Ash, & F. L. Smoll (Eds.), *Children in Sport* (2nd ed.) (pp. 178-195). Champaign, IL: Human Kinetics.

Smoll, F.L. (1986). Stress reduction strategies in youth sports. In M. Weiss & D. Gould (Eds.), *Sport for children and youths* (pp. 127-136). Champaign, IL: Human Kinetics.

Smoll, F.L., & Smith, R.E. (in press). Conducting a sport orientation meeting for parents: A guide for coaches. *Coaching Review*.

Zajonc, R. B. (1984). On the primacy of affect. *American Psychologist*, **39**, 117-123.

16

Competitive Stress in Children

Tara K. Scanlan
UNIVERSITY OF CALIFORNIA—LOS ANGELES
LOS ANGELES, CALIFORNIA, USA

Sport is a public affair. In contrast to achievement in the classroom where passing or failing a math test can be an unobserved private experience, a hit or a strike is witnessed by teammates, opponents, coaches, parents, and spectators. Clearly visible to all is not just the final product of the movement act (e.g., the hit or the strike), but the entire movement process involved in its execution (e.g., a powerful, coordinated swing or a slow, awkward one). In short, all of the people present have a considerable amount of information on which to base their judgments about the young participant's sport ability. By their cheers, groans, and boos, by their looks of approval, disapproval, and disappointment, and by their direct comments, these people convey their judgments to the competitor. These appraisals, combined with the ability information derived from direct social comparisons with teammates and opponents, make the potential for social evaluation in sport high (Scanlan, 1982, 1984).

Social Evaluation

Formally defined, *social evaluation* is the information about one's ability that is received from other people. The developmental literature indicates that social evaluation received from significant adults and peers plays an important role in shaping children's perceptions of their own ability (Scanlan, 1982). Further, emerging evidence in the sport psychology literature suggests that children, and even older competitors, are sensitive to the social evaluation potential in their sports (Griffin, 1972; Hanson, 1967; Johnson, 1949; Simon & Martens, 1979). The underlying theme to these studies appears to be that increases in the social evaluation potential are associated with increases in the amount of competitive stress experienced by the participants (see Scanlan, 1984, for an elaboration).

In sum, competitive sport is where a child's athletic ability is publicly tested, scrutinized, and evaluated. With social evaluation lying at the heart of the competitive experience, sport is an important achievement arena to many participants. Evidence even exists which reveals that children typically consider success in sport to be more important than success in the classroom (Duda, 1981). Accordingly, competitive sport is a stressful endeavor to some children in some circumstances. Reviewed next is a line of research which identifies individual difference and situational factors associated with the stress experienced by children engaged in competitive youth sport.

Predictors of Competitive Stress

Overview and Methodology

Summarized below are the major results of several studies (Scanlan, 1975, 1977; Scanlan & Lewthwaite, 1984; Scanlan & Passer, 1978, 1979) focused on understanding the generic and stable sources of competitive stress in children. The following methodological strategy has been used to achieve this objective. First, a similar research protocol was employed in all of the studies to facilitate the comparison of the results. Competitive stress, the dependent variable, was measured just prior to (precompetition stress) and immediately following (postcompetition stress) a competitive event. The psychological inventories used to measure stress were either the Spielberger State Anxiety Inventory for Children (Spielberger, 1973) or the children's version of the Competitive State Anxiety Inventory (Martens, Burton, Rivkin, & Simon, 1980). State anxiety is the way in which an acute, transitory stress response is operationally defined and measured. Most individual difference factors thought to be predictive of stress were assessed several weeks (competitive trait anxiety, self-esteem) or hours (characteristic prematch thoughts and worries, perceptions of adults) before the contest. Team and personal performance expectancies were measured just before the event and assessments regarding the amount of fun experienced during the competition were made immediately after the contest.

Second, the initial study (Scanlan, 1975, 1977) tested 10- to 12-year-old boys in the controlled setting of the laboratory where the internal validity of the results could best be achieved and causality more clearly established. Third, testing was then conducted in the natural team-sport setting (Scanlan & Passer, 1978) with 11-to 12-year-old male soccer players to assess the ecological validity of the laboratory results (i.e., whether the results would generalize to a real-life setting) and to determine other factors associated with stress. Fourth, a second field study (Scanlan & Passer, 1979) was conducted with female soccer players, participating in the same soccer organization, from the same geographic region, and in the same age division as the previously studied boys. By testing in this manner, not only could the sources of competitive stress in females be examined, but it could also be determined whether the results found with boys generalized to girls as well.

Finally, a third field study (Scanlan & Lewthwaite, 1984) was conducted with 9- to 14-year-old male wrestlers. This study first examined whether the findings generated in the team sport context generalized to the individual sport setting. Then these results and several new potential predictors of stress were analyzed together to examine the relative strength and importance of the various predictors. By using this approach it could be determined, for example, whether a new variable would preempt a previously identified factor as a significant predictor of stress.

The results of these studies are highlighted in the next section with the variables being separated into predictors of precompetition and postcompetition stress. The directions of the relationships are indicated, necessary terms are defined, and the particular studies in which the various results were tested and demonstrated are cited to help the reader evaluate the findings. In a few instances, some brief interpretations are provided which can be pursued in greater depth in the referenced articles.

Precompetition Stress

To date, all of the factors found to be associated with precompetition stress reflect individual difference variables.

Competitive Trait Anxiety

High competitive trait anxious girls and boys experience greater precompetition stress than low competitive trait anxious children. Competitive trait anxiety is a relatively stable personality disposition reflecting the tendency to perceive competitive sport situations as threatening (Martens, 1977). (Finding replicated across all studies.)

Self-esteem

Low self-esteem girls and boys experience greater precompetition stress than high self-esteem children. Self-esteem depicts a child's overall opinion of him or herself and indicates how worthy, capable, and successful the child feels (Coopersmith, 1967; Scanlan & Passer, 1978, 1979.) (Note that self-esteem was found to be significantly correlated with but not predictive of stress in Scanlan & Lewthwaite, 1984).

Team performance expectancies

Girls and boys with lower expectancies for their team to be victorious experience greater precompetition stress than children with higher team expectancies (Scanlan & Passer, 1978, 1979).

Personal performance expectancies

Boys with lower expectancies to personally play well in a soccer game or to win a wrestling match experience greater precompetition stress than boys with higher personal performance expectancies (Scanlan & Passer, 1978; Scanlan & Lewthwaite, 1984). This result was not found for female soccer players (Scanlan & Passer, 1979) and did not account for much of the stress variance for male soccer players. Overall, the results indicate that team expectancies are more important predictors of stress in team sports than personal performance expectancies. However, in individual sports, personal performance expectancies are strong predictors of precompetition stress.

Worries about failure

Boys who worry more frequently about failure before they compete experience greater precompetition stress than boys who are less preoccupied with performing poorly and making mistakes (Scanlan & Lewthwaite, 1984).

Worries about adult expectations and social evaluation

Boys who worry more frequently about the performance expectations and evaluations of their parents and coach tend to experience greater precompetition stress than boys who worry less frequently. The following items reflected this factor: "I worry about letting my mom (dad, coach) down" and "I worry about what my mom (dad, coach) will say if I don't wrestle well." (Scanlan & Lewthwaite, 1984. Note that this factor was found to be significantly correlated with but not predictive of stress.)

Parental pressure to participate

Boys who feel greater pressure from their parents to participate in a sport experience greater precompetition stress than boys who perceive less parental pressure. Items reflecting this factor were "I wrestle because I feel that I have to wrestle to please my mom/dad." (Scanlan & Lewthwaite, 1984. Note that this factor also was significantly correlated with [$r=.56$] the previously presented factor pertaining to adult expectations and social evaluation).

Postcompetition Stress

The two major predictors of postcompetition stress include (a) the situational factor of victory versus defeat, and its various gradations, and (b) the individual difference variable involving the amount of fun children perceive having during the event.

Victory versus defeat

Girls and boys who lose a competitive contest experience greater postcompetition stress than children who win. Relatedly, children who lose experience a significant increase in pre- to postcompetition stress, while children who win manifest a significant decrease. (Result replicated across all studies.)

1. Boys who lose a contest by a very close margin experience greater postcompetition stress than boys who lose by greater margins (Scanlan & Passer, 1978).
2. Girls who tie a contest experience greater postcompetition stress than those who win, and manifest less stress than those who lose (Scanlan & Passer, 1979).
3. Boys who win 50% of a series of consecutive contests experience greater postcompetition stress than boys who win 80%, and manifest less stress than those who win only 20% of the contests. (Scanlan, 1977).

Fun

Girls and boys who perceive that they had less fun during the event experience greater postcompetition stress than children who had more fun. What is important about this finding is that the inverse relationship between fun and stress is independent of victory or defeat. Hence, it is not simply the case that winners have more fun than losers. (Scanlan & Lewthwaite, 1984; Scanlan & Passer, 1978, 1979).

Summary

The findings to date have demonstrated that competitive trait anxiety, performance expectancies pertinent to the particular sport context, victory versus defeat and its varying degrees, and the amount of fun experienced while competing are strong and consistent predictors of competitive stress for both genders across diverse sport contexts. Self-esteem also was found to be a significant, although relatively weak predictor of stress for boys and girls in the soccer studies and was significantly correlated with but not predictive of stress in wrestling (see Scanlan & Lewthwaite, 1984, for a detailed discussion of this result).

Finally, the latest study in this series (Scanlan & Lewthwaite, 1984) has identified several new factors associated with stress that focus on children's characteristic prematch thoughts and worries, as well as their perceptions of the significant adults in their lives. The influence that adults have on children's experience of competitive stress is one of the most exploratory aspects of this work. Understanding the adult's role in the stress process, as well as the part played by peers, is critical to achieving a complete picture of the sources of competitive stress.

References

Coopersmith, S. (1967). *The antecedents of self-esteem*. San Francisco: Freeman.

Duda, J. L. (1981). *A cross-cultural analysis of achievement motivation in sport and the classroom*. Unpublished doctoral dissertation, University of Illinois, Urbana-Champaign.

Griffin, M. R. (1972, Spring). An analysis of state and trait anxiety experienced in sports competition at different age levels. *Foil*, pp. 58-64.

Hanson, D.L. (1967). Cardiac response to participation in Little League baseball competition as determined by telemetry. *Research Quarterly, 38*, 384-388.

Johnson, W. R. (1949). A study of emotion revealed in two types of athletic sports contests. *Research Quarterly, 20*, 72-79.

Martens, R. (1977). *Sport Competition Anxiety Test*. Champaign, IL: Human Kinetics.

Martens, R., Burton, D., Rivkin, F., & Simon, J. (1980). Reliability and validity of the Competitive State Anxiety Inventory (CSAI). In C. H. Nadeau, W. R. Halliwell, K. M. Newell, & G. C. Roberts (Eds.), *Psychology of Motor Behavior and Sport—1979* (91-99). Champaign, IL: Human Kinetics.

Scanlan, T. K. (1975). *The effect of competition trait anxiety and success-failure on the perception of threat in a competitive situation*. Unpublished doctoral dissertation, University of Illinois, Urbana-Champaign.

Scanlan, T. K. (1977). The effects of success-failure on the perception of threat in a competitive situation. *Research Quarterly, 48*, 144-153.

Scanlan, T.K. (1982). Social evaluation: A key developmental element in the competition process. In R.A. Magill, M.J. Ash, & F.L. Smoll (Eds.), *Children in sport* (pp. 138-152). Champaign, IL: Human Kinetics.

Scanlan, T. K. (1984). Competitive stress and the child athlete. In J. M. Silva & R. S. Weinberg (Eds.), *Psychological foundations of sport* (pp. 118-129). Champaign, IL: Human Kinetics.

Scanlan, T. K., & Lewthwaite, R. (1984). Social psychological aspects of the competitive sport experience for male youth sport participants: I. Predictors of competitive stress. *Journal of Sport Psychology*, **6**, 208-226.

Scanlan, T. K., & Passer, M. W. (1978). Factors related to competitive stress among male youth sports participants. *Medicine and Science in Sports*, **10**, 103-108.

Scanlan, T. K., & Passer, M. W. (1979). Sources of competitive stress in young female athletes. *Journal of Sport Psychology*, **1**, 151-159.

Simon, J. A., & Martens, R. (1979). Children's anxiety in sport and nonsport evaluative activities. *Journal of Sport Psychology*, **1**, 160-169.

17

The Perception of Stress: A Potential Source and its Development

Glyn C. Roberts
UNIVERSITY OF ILLINOIS AT URBANA-CHAMPAIGN
URBANA, ILLINOIS, USA

Despite heightened interest and research into the perception of stress on the part of children, one aspect has long been ignored—the information processing capability of the child. The finding that the child perceives stress is well documented (e.g., Hanson, 1967; Lowe & McGrath, 1971; Simon & Martens, 1979). Researchers have given us great insight into the variables which need to be considered (e.g., Smith, this volume) and much data on the association of variables to the perception of stress (e.g., Scanlan, this volume). But *why* does the child perceive stress and does the perception of stress manifest itself differently over the age span? The concern here is with understanding the motivation of children to enter sport programs and how this affects their perception of the competition sport experience and, in turn, their perception of stress.

To understand the perceptions of the child-athlete, we need to make a few assumptions. First, as Scanlan (this volume) expands upon, the competitive sport experience is a highly public and evaluative social comparison environment. Second, participation in sport is very important to children (Duda, 1981). Third, children are intentional, goal-directed individuals who operate in a rational manner.

To fully understand the perception of stress on the part of children, the goals of action must be identified and the function and meaning of behavior must be taken into account. We cannot understand the behaviors or perceptions of children unless we understand their goals for action and the *subjective* meaning of achievement within that context for the child. Thus, we need to understand the achievement goal of the child to fully account for his or her perception of stress and subsequent behavior.

In sport, the first step to understanding the achievement goal of the child is to examine the perceptions of success and failure for the child. It is argued here that perceptions of success and failure are best understood if they are considered to be psychological states based upon the child's interpretation of the outcome of the experience (see Maehr & Nicholls, 1980). If the outcome perceived to reflect desirable qualities about the self, such as competency, courage, virtue, loyalty, then the experience is perceived to be a success and little stress is experienced. If, on the other hand, the outcome is seen as reflecting undesirable qualities about the self, then the experience is perceived to be a failure and stress may be perceived. The perception of stress is exacerbated if the athlete perceives that a desirable personal quality, based upon the goal of action was not demonstrated.

The expectation that one is able, or not able, to demonstrate a desirable personal characteristic clearly affects one's perception of precompetitive stress. If the child expects to achieve the goal, he or she will exhibit little stress. If the goal is likely not to be achieved, then heightened precompetitive stress is experienced. Similarly, if the desirable personal characteristic is demonstrated in competition, then postcompetitive stress is low. If the characteristic is not demonstrated, then postcompetitive stress is heightened. Clearly, to understand the pertinent personal characteristics which affect perception of stress, we need to understand the goal of the child-athlete.

Achievement Goals of Athletes

It is hypothesized that at least three forms of achievement goals exist which affect the perception of stress on the part of the athlete (Maehr & Nicholls, 1980; Roberts, 1984a). These achievement goals are (a) to demonstrate sport competence; (b) to demonstrate sport mastery; and (c) to seek social approval. Let us discuss each in turn with particular emphasis given to how these goals may interact with the sport experience to produce stress.

Sport Competence

The first achievement goal which is predicted to affect the perception of stress is one we term *sport competence* (Roberts, 1984a). This goal is to maximize the subjective probability of attributing high competence to oneself (a desirable personal characteristic), and to minimize attributing low competence to oneself (an undesirable personal characteristic), in competitive sport environments. The primary concern of the athlete is with his or her own ability and how it compares to the ability of others. The focus of attention of the athlete is on social comparison processes where the athlete constantly evaluates his or her own and opponents' competence in order to assess whether ability has been demonstrated. Children generally try hard in order to demonstrate that competence; if, however, they perceive they are unable to exhibit ability, then not trying hard becomes feasible.

One way children perceive they can demonstrate competence is to beat other children in competitive contests. Thus, winning and losing outcomes become important criteria for the child who is motivated by the achievement goal of sport competence. Winning means ability has been demonstrated, and postcompetitive stress is low; losing means insufficient ability has been demonstrated and postcompetitive stress is high. Expectancy of winning means ability is likely to be demonstrated, thus perception of precompetitive stress is reduced; expectancy of losing means insufficient ability is likely to be demonstrated, thus perception of precompetitive stress is exacerbated. However, assessments associated with the achievement goal of sport competence are very complex and are discussed in detail elsewhere (Roberts, 1984b). But it does suggest that future investigations will need to test these predictions by simultaneously examining perception, or experience, of stress and the achievement goal of the young athlete.

Sport Mastery

Some athletes are not concerned with sport competence and with demonstrating higher ability than others. These athletes are still ability-oriented, but a different conceptualization of ability is adopted by these athletes. Rather than being concerned with social comparison processes and assessing their relative ability to others, these athletes focus upon performance within the activity, for the goal of this behavior is to perform as well as possible regardless of the outcome. This type of achievement-goal is termed *sport mastery* (Roberts, 1984a). The athlete directs his or her attention toward achieving mastery, improving, or perfecting a sport skill or task rather than demonstrating higher capacity than that of others. In this sense, high ability is demonstrated when the person exceeds previous levels of performance. These athletes become so engrossed in the activity that they even lose all concept of the passage of time and are often described as being task or intrinsically motivated.

The most interesting aspect of sport mastery oriented children is that they do not perceive much stress in the competitive sport experience (Ewing, 1981; Ewing, Roberts, & Pemberton, 1983). These children are engrossed in the activity itself and merely participating meets this goal, so they do not perceive stress whatever the outcome. These children only perceive stress if the coach or a significant other criticizes their effort or commitment.

Social Approval

The third form of achievement behavior is termed social approval (Roberts, 1984a). These athletes attempt to elicit social approval from significant others, usually parents and/or coaches. In this case, the goal of the athlete is to have significant others attribute a desirable characteristic to him or her rather than focus upon sport competence or sport mastery. Typically, but not always, athletes recognize that social approval is dependent upon the demonstration of effort. To the athlete, trying hard to gain social approval is the goal. This goal is met when the coach signifies approval, but stress is experienced when the coach or significant others fail to signify social approval. How this goal operates in competitive sport will be addressed in more detail later.

The basic premise of the arguments above is that holding one of the achievement goals identified affects one's perception of stress. For example, for the athlete motivated by the sport competence goal, winning and losing becomes a primary criterion for the perception of stress, but not so much for the athlete motivated by the sport mastery goal. Thus, knowledge of the achievement goal has the potential to explain the individual differences typically observed in the perception of stress.

Are there multiple goals? That is an important question which immediately presents itself. Three studies have investigated this issue in the competitive sport environment (Duda, 1981; Ewing, 1981; Ewing, Roberts, & Pemberton, 1983). Utilizing factor analytic procedures, each of these studies has isolated the achievement goals of sport competence, sport mastery, and social approval. The three achievement goals advocated above have been isolated and demonstrated to exist. However, it must be recognized that other achievement goals not only exist (for example, Ewing (1981) found that an intrinsic orientation goal different to task orientation emerged in some situations), but are likely to interact with the competitive sport experience to affect the perception of stress. Again, the important point is that the three goals above always emerge in factor analyses, with one or two other goals emerging on occasion. This is a complex phenomenon, but for the sake of brevity and parsimony, we shall limit discussion to the three goals identified above.

Given that the achievement goals exist in the forms hypothesized, the second important question raised is, How are these goals developed by children?

The Development of Achievement Goals

Children may go through several stages in the development of achievement goals (Maehr & Nicholls, 1980) which affect their perception of stress. Recently, some colleagues and I (Ewing, Roberts, & Pemberton, 1983) investigated the development of achievement goals of children. Utilizing baseball and softball leagues, we gave a questionnaire to children between 9 and 14 years of age. Using factor analytic procedures, we found that achievement goals do not develop at the same rate. For the younger children under 12 years old, we found forms of sport mastery and social approval goals. In this age range, children used statements that strongly reflected effort, an important component of social approval and sport mastery, but always in combination with other statements. Children were unable to differentiate between the relative contributions of effort and ability in determining success and failure outcomes.

Children 12 years or older were able to differentiate between effort and ability, and the achievement goals consistent with our hypotheses emerged. These older children utilized statements consistent with the achievement goals in a reliable manner. Evidently, children are 12 years or older before they are able to process information such that they understand the relative contributions of effort and ability to success and failure outcomes and understand the behavioral implications of holding a particular achievement goal.

This evidence is consistent with other evidence from academic achievement setting which shows that children go through four stages in their understanding of the concepts of effort and ability (Nicholls, 1978). Briefly, Nicholls found that young children, 5 and 6 years old, were unable to differentiate between outcome, ability or effort. In the second stage, 7- to 9-year-old children were similar to the youngest children in the Ewing et al. (1983) study; they recognized that effort contributed to outcome. However, these children believed effort to be the sole cause of outcomes; thus, they believed equal effort led to equal outcomes. In the third stage, children, 9 to 11 years old, began to differentiate between effort and ability, but only when equal effort did not lead to equal outcomes. Then at the fourth stage, children, 12 years or older, began to recognize the relative contributions of ability and effort and recognize that ability is capacity and relatively stable. This evidence from Nicholls is important because the achievement goals identified here depend heavily upon children understanding the relative contributions of effort and ability, and their covariation, to success and failure in competitive sport. Other evidence reveals that effort and ability are the most frequently used elements in attributing success and failure in competitive sport (Bukowski & Moore, 1980; Roberts & Pascuzzi, 1978).

As is evident, children go through several stages in the development of achievement goals with their behavioral ramifications. The next section deals with the implications of the development of achievement goals on the perception of stress.

Implications of the Development of Achievement Goals

The evidence suggests the achievement goals develop at different rates, and age 12 seems to be an important watershed in the development of these goals (Nicholls, 1978; Roberts, 1984b; Ewing et al., 1983). Children younger than 12 years appear to be more concerned with effort behaviors and in pleasing others. Older children, on the other hand, are able to discern not only their effort and its effect upon the comments of significant others, but are able to discern their own competence, too. There is evidence which reveals that the correlation of children's perceived competence and their actual competence gets much higher in a positive direction as children get older (Roberts, 1978). Thus, young children are focusing almost solely upon a limited set of criteria by which they assess success and failure, while older children focus upon a broader set of criteria. Those criteria affect their perception of stress.

The younger players are typically sport mastery and/or social approval oriented. These children are unable to assess their own competence accurately; they focus upon effort, and they believe effort is ability. These children are particularly sensitive to the comments and criticisms of others, especially the coach. When these children participate, they quickly recognize that trying hard is an effective means of obtaining favorable comments and, consequently, trying hard becomes an important criterion for them. When adults, or peers, criticize or praise them for their effort, they are crushed or elated, respectively. For these children, the comments of significant others become the major source of the perception of stress. This is where adults need to be sensitive to the criteria the child is using for success and failure. To the adult, the criticism may be a mild rebuke with the intention of improving a skill. To the child, he or she has failed to please; this is interpreted as a failure experience, and stress is experienced.

Several of my colleagues have pointed out that young children do focus upon the winning and losing outcome and want to win as much as older children. The argument is that if children focus upon outcomes and behave accordingly, they must understand the implications of winning and losing in sport contests. Although that is true, what differs is why children want to win. Young children are information processers and operate in a rational manner; they learn very quickly that winning pleases significant others. One way to please a coach (the only way for some coaches) is to win the game. Older children also want to win and please the coach, but older children also have one other criterion which is important to them—the demonstration of competence. Older children recognize the competence information inherent in outcomes.

Older children are more capable to differentiate between effort and ability and are able to accurately assess their own ability to perform within the activity (Ewing, Roberts, & Pemberton, 1983; Nicholls, 1978). Older children process the information much like adults and are able to deduce their own competence. It is only when children are able to differentiate the causes of outcomes that they are able to judge their own capacity at the task. Older children begin to recognize, probably for the first time, their actual competence. This can be a very exciting or a traumatic discovery.

Children's motivation in sport and their perception of stress should be closely related to their perceived attainment. Those children who perceive themselves as able because they or their team is successful perceive little stress and enjoy the experience; those children who perceive themselves as unable because they or their team is unsuccessful perceive heightened stress and do not enjoy the experience. This should be particularly true of those children who are sport competence goal oriented: Demonstrating ability is their prime motive for participating. Those children who are receiving low competence information in a valued activity probably perceive stress and must ponder their continued involvement. There is evidence to show that dropouts from the competitive sport experience are sport competence goal oriented.

Ewing (1981) looked at youth participants, nonparticipants, and dropouts from competitive sport programs. She found that the individuals who dropped out were most likely to be sport competence oriented, and the survivors were more likely to be social approval oriented. Ewing argued that social approval individuals can meet their goal by sitting on the bench and being a loyal team member. This is not so for the sport competence oriented children: They wish to be playing and demonstrating competence, not just sitting on the bench.

This is discussed in detail elsewhere (Roberts, 1984b), but it is a reasonable hypothesis to state that the development of achievement goals is related to the dropout phenomenon in competitive sports. As we have seen, at age 12 the achievement goals develop in the manner hypothesized, especially the goal of sport competence. It is also at age 12 that we begin to note a significant dropout rate from competitive sport. Between 12 and 17 years old, 80% of all children drop out of competitive sport (Seefeldt, Blievernicht, Bruce, & Gilliam, 1978). For those children perceiving low ability in a highly valued activity, the perception is distressing, and dropping out is one avenue for them to avoid continuing an embarassing and stressful experience. For those who perceive favorable ability assessments, the motivation to continue is enhanced, and perception of stress is low.

The sad aspect of this phenomenon in competitive sport is the extent to which coaches and parents emphasize outcome as the criterion of success and failure. The more the outcome is emphasized, the more likely it is that the child will adopt the same criterion: thus, the goal of sport competence becomes the major goal for that child. If the goal of sport competence is encouraged, then the perception of ability held by the child becomes the major mediating variable of stress and continued involvement of the child.

Conclusion

In this paper, I have tried to illustrate that the perception of stress of children is largely dependent upon the achievement goal of the child: The criteria by which that child perceives are relevant to assessing success or failure of satisfying the achievement goal. My concern has been that we often forget the child is an information-processing organism who operates in a rational manner. However, the criteria important to children may be different than the criteria important to adults. For example, it should be obvious that the criteria of success and failure of a coach motivated by the goal of sport competence is likely to be different than the criteria of success and failure of young children motivated by the goal of social approval.

The above brings us to the question of what we can do to alleviate the perception of stress. This issue is discussed in detail elsewhere (Roberts, 1984b) when the achievement goals are taken into account. That is also the topic addressed by Smoll (this volume), who takes a somewhat broader perspective than the one advocated here. In closing, let me remind you of an obvious caveat—children are not miniature adults! They have their own set of criteria which affect their motivation to participate and their perception of stress.

References

Bukowski, W. M., & Moore, D. (1980). Winners' and losers' attributions for success and failure in series of athletic events. *Journal of Sport Psychology*, **2**, 195-210.

Duda, J. L. (1981). *A Cross-cultural analysis of achievement motivation in sport and the classroom*. Unpublished doctoral dissertation, University of Illinois, Urbana-Champaign.

Ewing, M. E. (1981). *Achievement orientations and sport behavior of males and females*. Doctoral dissertation, University of Illinois, Urbana-Champaign.

Ewing, M. E., Roberts, G. C., & Pemberton, C. L. (1983, May). *A developmental look at children's goals for participating in sport*. Paper presented at the meeting of the North American Society for Psychology of Sport and Physical Activity, Lansing, Michigan.

Hanson, D. L. (1967). Cardiac responses to participation in Little League baseball competition as determined by telemetry. *Research Quarterly*, **38**, 384-388.

Lowe, R., & McGrath, J. E. (1971). *Stress, arousal, and performance: Some findings calling for a new theory* (Report No. AF 1161-67). Washington, DC: Air Force Office of Strategic Research.

Maehr, M. L., & Nicholls, J. G. (1980). Culture and achievement motivation: A second look. In N. Warren (Ed.), *Studies in cross-cultural psychology*. New York: Academic Press.

Nicholls, J. G. (1978). The development of the concepts of effort and ability, perception of own attainment, and the understanding that difficult tasks require more ability. *Child Development*, **49**, 800-814.

Roberts, G. C. (1978). *Causal attributions and perception of competence of children in Australian soccer leagues*. Unpublished manuscript, University of Illinois, Urbana-Champaign.

Roberts, G. C. (1984a). Toward a new theory of motivation in sport: The role of perceived ability. In J. M. Silva & R. S. Weinberg (Eds.), *Psychological foundations of sport and exercise*. Champaign, IL: Human Kinetics.

Roberts, G. C. (1984b). Children's achievement motivation in sport. In J. G. Nicholls (Ed.), *The development of achievement motivation*. Greenwich, CT: JAI Press.

Roberts, G. C., & Pascuzzi, D. L. (1979). Causal attributions in sport: Some theoretical implications. *Journal of Sport Psychology*, **1**, 203-211.

Scanlan, T. K. (1986). Competitive stress in children. In M. Weiss & D. Gould (Eds.), *Sport for children and youths* (pp. 113-118). Champaign, IL: Human Kinetics.

Seefeldt, V., Blievernicht, D., Bruce, R., & Gilliam, T. (1978). *Joint legislative study on youth sport programs, phase II: Agency sponsored sports*. Lansing: State of Michigan.

Simon, J. A., & Martens, R. (1979). Children's anxiety in sport and nonsport evaluative activities. *Journal of Sport Psychology*, **1**, 160-169.

Smith, R. (1986). A component analysis of athletic stress. In M. Weiss & D. Gould (Eds.), *Sport for children and youths (pp. 107-111)*. Champaign, IL: Human Kinetics.

Smoll, F. L. (1986). Stress reduction strategies in youth sports. In M. Weiss & D. Gould (Eds.), *Sport for children and youths* (pp. 127-136). Champaign, IL: Human Kinetics.

18

Stress Reduction Strategies in Youth Sport

Frank L. Smoll
UNIVERSITY OF WASHINGTON
SEATTLE, WASHINGTON, USA

Among the important issues to which sport psychologists have directed their attention is the question of how stressful youth sport is for children. In this volume, Smith, Scanlan, and Roberts have already alluded to the fact that youth sport is stressful. In previous research with young athletes, physiological arousal measures were used (Hanson, 1967; Lowe & McGrath, 1971) raising questions relative to whether arousal reflects an aversive emotional reaction, simple excitement, or something else. Self-report state anxiety measures also have been used (Scanlan & Passer, 1978, 1979). Unfortunately, there are no criteria to determine whether such anxiety scores indicate that the youngsters were *too* stressed (Martens, 1978).

A landmark study by Simon and Martens (1979) assessed how stressful sport is compared with other evaluative activities in which children participate. A self-report state anxiety inventory was administered to 9- to 14-year-old boys just before they competed in one of seven nonschool sports and four other activities: physical education softball class, academic tests, band group, and solo music competitions. None of the sports was found to elicit as much anxiety as band solos. Moreover, wrestling was the only sport that was more anxiety-arousing than school classroom tests. Of the various sports studied, individual sports evoked more anxiety than team sports, which is consistent with an earlier study by Griffin (1972). But, like Scanlan and Passer, Simon and Martens reported that some young athletes experienced relatively high levels of precompetitive stress.

Although there is no simple answer to the question of whether youth sport is too stressful, research results suggest that for most children, sport participation is not exceedingly stressful, especially in comparison with other activites involving performance evaluation. In other words, the amount of stress in youth sport does not appear to be as widespread or as intense as critics have claimed (Martens, 1978; Passer, 1982a, 1982b; R. E. Smith & Smoll, 1982). But it is also evident that the sport setting can produce high levels of stress for a minority of youngsters. Such children undoubtedly find competition to be threatening, and as emphasized by R. E. Smith (this volume), the anxiety which they experience can have deleterious psychological, behavioral, and health-related effects. In view of the negative consequences, development of intervention strategies to minimize sources of undue stress is warranted, along with development of training programs designed to help young athletes acquire more effective coping skills.

The conceptual model of stress formulated by R. E. Smith (this volume) has clear implications for stress reduction in youth sport. In this chapter, consideration will be given to how intervention might be directed at any of the four elements of the model: behavioral, physiological, cognitive, and situational.

Behavioral Component

At the behavioral level, it is intuitively obvious, as well as theoretically sound (Roberts, this volume), that increasing the young athlete's physical prowess can make athletic demands easier to cope with. Training to improve sport skills, thus, should be one way to reduce competitive stress. The rationale for this approach is based on the assumption that youngsters' anxiety reactions are derived in part from deficits in ability. Specifically, feelings of insecurity and heightened anxiety might arise because of perceived lack of skill to cope with a situation. Support for this assumption is provided by recent research indicating that all-star athletes had significantly lower competitive trait anxiety scores than playing substitutes (T. Smith, 1983). Also, Gould, Horn, and Spreeman (1983) reported that low competitive trait anxious (CTA) wrestlers compared to high CTA wrestlers rated themselves higher in ability. Other investigators conversely have reported that self-perceived and actual ability of high CTA children is just as great as that of low CTA youngsters (Magill & Ash, 1979; Passer, 1983; Passer & Scanlan, 1980). Thus, research is equivocal as to whether high CTA youngsters experience competitive stress because of lack of athletic skill. Consequently, the validity of the assumption that underlies the potential efficacy of the proposed intervention strategy is subject to question and merits future empirical attention.

Physiological Arousal and Cognitive Appraisal Components

Reduction of stress at these levels is the focus of intervention programs that seek to teach specific physiological and cognitive coping skills. Training programs in stress management behaviors have promising applications with child athletes for several reasons (R. E. Smith & Smoll, 1982). First, it is highly desirable to acquire adaptive coping responses prior to the turbulent years of adolescence. Second, unlike many adults, children have not generally developed maladaptive coping strategies that are deeply ingrained and therefore difficult to change. Third, the athletic arena requires child athletes to cope with stress-evoking situations on a regular and fairly predictable basis, thereby providing many opportunities to practice and strengthen coping skills in situations that are unlikely to exceed the children's adaptive ability. Finally, developing a range of highly generalizable coping skills should enhance children's ability to handle stress not only in athletics, but also in other aspects of their lives.

The Stress Management Training (SMT) program developed by R. E. Smith (1980) consists of a number of clinical treatment techniques combined into an educational program for self-control of emotion. Originally developed for use in individual and group psychotherapy with clinical populations, the program components have been adapted and combined to form a training package which has been applied to a variety of nonclinical populations, including preadolescent, college, and professional athletes in individual and team sports. In essence, SMT provides for the learning of an *integrated coping response* having physiological-somatic and cognitive components and for the rehearsal of these stress-reducing skills under conditions of high affective arousal. For the purpose of presenting a descriptive overview of the program, SMT can be divided into three major phases: (a) pretraining assessment and conceptualization phase, (b) skill acquisition phase, and (c) skill rehearsal phase.

Pretraining Assessment and Conceptualization

When SMT is administered to individual child athletes, several sessions of the initial phase may be devoted to assessing the nature of their stress responses, the circumstances under which stress occurs, and its effects on performance and other behaviors. Then the children are introduced to a simplified version of the conceptual model of stress to help them understand their problematic stress responses, and they are provided with a rationale for the training program. During the conceptualization phase and throughout training, it is stressed that SMT is not psychotherapy, but an educational program. A second point emphasized is that SMT is a program in *self-control*, and coping abilities that result from the program are a function of how much effort the individual devotes to their acquisition.

Skill Acquisition

The goal of the skill acquisition phase is the development of an integrated coping response having relaxation and cognitive elements. This phase involves (a) the learning of voluntary muscle relaxation skills, and (b) an analysis of thought processes and the replacement of stress-eliciting ideas and self-statements with specific cognitions designed to reduce stress.

Progressive muscle relaxation (Jacobson, 1938) and deep breathing are taught as methods of lowering physiological arousal. The children are taught to breathe slowly and deeply and to emit the mental command "Relax" while they exhale and voluntarily relax their muscles. The command is thus repeatedly paired with the relaxation that occurs with exhalation, so that with time, the mental command becomes an eliciting cue for inducing relaxation, as well as an important component of the integrated coping response that will be learned.

Training in cognitive-coping skills is carried out concurrently with relaxation training. By using two related procedures (cognitive restructuring and self-instructional training), the child is assisted in altering irrational beliefs that cause the competitive situation to be appraised as threatening; and training is provided in replacing self-preoccupational thoughts with task-oriented internal statements. In cognitive restructuring, dysfunctional stress-producing ideas (e.g., "It would be awful if I failed or if someone disapproved of me.") are rationally analyzed, challenged, and replaced with self-statements that are both rationally sound and likely to reduce or prevent a stress response (e.g., "All I can do is give 100%. No one can do more.") In self-instructional training, the focus is on helping children develop and use specific task-relevant self-commands that can be employed in relevant situations (e.g., "Don't get shook up. Just think about what you have to do.")

Eventually, the physiological and cognitive coping responses are combined into an integrated coping response which ties both into the breathing cycle. As children inhale, they emit an antistress self-statement. At the peak of inhalation, they mentally say the word "So," and as they slowly exhale, they instruct themselves to "Relax" and deepen muscular relaxation. Thus, both classes of coping responses are integrated into the breathing cycle.

Skill Rehearsal

The skill rehearsal phase of SMT enables practice of the stress-coping skills under conditions that approximate "real life" situations. In SMT, a variant of a psychotherapeutic procedure known as *induced affect* is used. Children are asked to imagine as vividly as possible stressful athletic situations. They are then asked to focus on the feeling that the imagined situation elicits, and the trainer suggests that as the feeling is focused upon, it becomes increasingly stronger. When a heightened state of arousal is produced, the child is asked to "turn it off" with the relaxation-coping skill. In a later rehearsal, antistress self-statements alone are used. Finally, the integrated coping response is used. After the skill rehearsal phase is completed, the SMT program ends with training in Benson's (1976) meditation procedure, which is presented as a general relaxation and stress-reduction technique that can be used in situations which do not require the athlete to perform.

It should be noted that the goal of SMT is *not* to completely eliminate emotional arousal. Rather, the goal of the training is to give children greater control over emotional responses, so they can reduce or prevent high and aversive levels of arousal that interfere with performance and enjoyment.

Situational Component

Intervention via coping skills programs, such as SMT, have encouraging implications for the reduction of stress in youth sport. However, this kind of direct professional involvement is not always the most practical or economically justifiable approach to solving stress-related problems. Some economical and appropriate measures can be utilized at the situational level to dramatically alter its capacity to generate stress. Reduction of situational sources of stress will be considered relative to (a) changes in certain features of the sport itself, (b) the role of coaches in creating a psychologically healthy athletic environment, and (c) the role of parents in combating competitive stress.

Modification of the Sport

One way to reduce potential sources of stress is to decrease performance demands on young athletes, thereby increasing their chances of experiencing success and enjoyment. This might be accomplished, for example, by lowering the height of the basketball goal or decreasing the distance between the free throw line and the basket. Similarly, changes in playing rules might aptly accommodate youngsters of differing age/ability levels.

The organization and administration of a sport program can be the focus of environmental change aimed at reducing the demands of the competitive situation. Some youth leagues incorporate various homogeneous grouping procedures to organize themselves so that children compete against others of their own ability and size (see Martens & Seefeldt, 1979). Matching children in this way might serve to combat stress associated with inequity of competition and risk of injury. Another kind of organizational modification involves implementing policies to minimize situational demands that many youngsters find stressful. For example, to eliminate the stress-related emphasis on winning, some programs do not keep game scores, league standings, or individual performance statistics (Passer, 1982b).

Coaching Roles and Relationships

It is generally recognized that coaches occupy a position of centrality in the youth sport setting. The manner in which coaches structure the athletic situation, the goal priorities they establish, and the ways in which they relate to athletes are primary determinants of the outcomes of sport participation (Martens, 1978; Seefeldt & Gould, 1980; R. E. Smith, Smoll, Hunt, Curtis, & Coppel, 1979; Smoll, Smith, Curtis, & Hunt, 1978). With specific reference to stress, Scanlan (this volume) and Roberts (this volume) identified coaches among the significant others who have a profound influence on shaping perceptions of achievement demands, capabilities, and consequences of stress. Moreover, Passer's (1984) analysis of the etiology of competitive trait anxiety substantiates that interactions with coaches can be a major source of stress for athletes. Therefore, measures designed to assist coaches in creating a less stressful and more enjoyable athletic atmosphere ultimately should have a significant positive impact on youth sport programs.

Educational programs have been developed to provide coaches with training that assists them in relating more effectively to young athletes. Coach Effectiveness Training (CET) (R. E. Smith, Smoll, & Curtis, 1978) and the American Coaching Effectiveness Program (Martens, 1981) illustrate this approach. Research conducted with CET indicated that coaches who apply specific behaviors (e.g., reinforcement for good performance, encouragement rather than punishment in response to player mistakes) can have beneficial effects on their players' psychological characteristics, such as sport-related attitudes and self-esteem (R. E. Smith et al., 1978). It follows that athletes' stress might be minimized to the extent that coaches establish a supportive psychological climate. Several aspects of CET, which potentially serve to reduce stress, are elaborated in the following discussion.

As previously noted, Scanlan and Passer's (1978, 1979) research confirmed that success-failure outcomes exert a strong influence on postcompetition stress. Winning decreases stress, and losing increases stress. Unfortunately, some coaches adopt a "winning is everything" philosophy, and they may lose sight of other important objectives and values of their program. To place winning in a *healthy* perspective, a four-part philosophy is taught in CET (Smoll & Smith, 1981):

1. *Winning isn't everything, nor is it the only thing.* Young athletes cannot possibly learn from winning and losing if they think the only objective is to beat their opponents. Although winning is an important goal, it is *not* the most important objective.

2. *Failure is not the same thing as losing.* It is important that athletes do not view losing as a sign of failure or as a threat of their personal value.

3. *Success is not synonymous with winning.* Thus, neither success nor failure need depend on the outcome of a contest or a won-lost record. Winning and losing pertain to the outcome of a contest, whereas success and failure do not.

4. *Children should be taught that success is found in striving for victory (i.e., success is related to effort).* Youngsters should be taught that they are never "losers" if they give maximum effort. A major source of athletic stress is fear of failure; knowing that making a mistake or losing a game while giving maximum effort is acceptable to the coach should remove an important source of pressure from the child.

Thus, (point 1) although seeking a victorious outcome is encouraged, this philosophy attempts to reduce the criticality of winning relative to other prized participation motives (e.g., skill and fitness development, affiliation with teammates and friends). In this regard, *fun* is highlighted as a paramount objective. The work of Scanlan and Passer (1978, 1979) suggested that fun is an important intrapersonal factor, the experience of which may help to reduce stress after a defeat. Furthermore, (points 2 & 3) this particular orientation toward winning promotes separation/detachment of the child's feelings of self-worth from the game outcome, and as Gallwey and Kriegel (1977, p.85) affirmed, "the key to overcoming fear of failure is breaking one's attachment to results."

Finally, and perhaps most importantly, (point 4) young athletes are encouraged to attribute their failures to an unstable, controllable factor (i.e., lack of effort) instead of lack of ability. Dweck's (1975) attributional retraining program involved nothing more complicated than explicitly attributing failure to a lack of effort and encouraging subjects to "try harder." Children who received direct instruction in how to interpret the causes of their failures in this way showed improved performance (math problem-solving task) and were better able to cope with failure. Within the realm of sport, one might expect this approach to lessen the negative effects of failure and thereby reduce stress for athletes.

The core of CET consists of a series of behavioral guidelines derived from an empirical data base on coach-athlete relationships (R. E. Smith, Smoll, & Curtis, 1978). The key distinction made within the guidelines is that of positive versus negative approaches to influencing behavior (Smoll & Smith, 1982). The positive approach uses reinforcement and encouragement to strengthen desirable behaviors and to motivate athletes to perform these behaviors. The negative approach uses various forms of punishment to eliminate undesirable behaviors. The guidelines recommend the liberal use of reinforcement for effort as well as performance, the giving of encouragement after mistakes, and the giving of technical instruction in an encouraging and supportive fashion. When technical instruction is given after a mistake, the guidelines recommend, first, complimenting the athlete for something done correctly, then giving the corrective instruction, focusing on the positive things that will happen in the future if the instruction is followed, rather than the negative consequences of the mistake. The use of punitive behaviors is discouraged. Reinforcement is also recommended as a means of establishing and strengthening encouragement and support among teammates as well as compliance with team rules. The ultimate goal of the guidelines is to increase the desire of young athletes to learn and to give maximum effort while reducing their fear of failure.

An important part of the positive approach involves utilization of a cooperative leadership style in which athletes are given a share of the responsibility for determining their own governance. For example, several guidelines are directed at developing a "team rule concept," keeping the lines of coach-athlete interaction open, and fostering two-way communication. This is consistent with the orientation advanced in DeCharms' (1972) personal causation training program in which teachers are taught to treat students as origins as opposed to pawns. Origins are people who perceive themselves as the causes of their behavior and make internal attributions for successes and failures. Pawns, on the other hand, believe that they are impelled to behave by external causes and therefore attribute success and failure to external factors. The CET relationship style of coaching might assist young athletes in perceiving themselves as originators of their behavior. This concomitantly would involve their adopting attributions characteristic of high-need achievers, enabling them to better cope with failure.

CET also includes instructions for coaches on how to organize and conduct a sport orientation meeting with parents (Smoll & Smith, in press). Some purposes of the meeting are to inform parents about their responsibilities for contributing to the success of the sport program and to guide them toward working cooperatively and productively with the coach. Establishing coach-parent rapport in this way might serve to eliminate conflicts that constitute another potential source of environmental stress for young athletes.

Parent Roles and Responsibilities

The literature on sport socialization confirms that parents are instrumental in determining children's sport involvement (see Lewko & Greendorfer, 1982; McPherson, 1982). Furthermore, parental influences constitute an important source of stress for young athletes (see Passer, 1984; Scanlan, this volume). Because of the all too obvious negative impact of overzealous and unknowing adults, some youth leagues have banned parents from attending games in order to reduce the stress placed on children and officials (Martens, 1978). This is an unfortunate example of situational change. More desirable and constructive efforts are reflected in an increasing number of publications concerning parent responsibilities toward their children's sport participation (e.g., Ferrell, Glashagel, & Johnson, 1978; Martens, 1980; Thomas, 1977, Vandeweghe, 1979). With specific reference to stress, *Kidsports* (N.J. Smith, R.E. Smith, & Smoll, 1983) attempts to guide and educate parents about the nature and consequences of athletic stress for children. This volume provides information on how parents might prevent fear of failure as well as teaching them relaxation skills.

In spite of recent literary contributions, there has been no attempt to systematically develop and assess the effects of an educational program for parents to help them facilitate their children's personal growth through athletics. It would appear that many of the same principles and guidelines contained in CET should be included in a program for parents. For example, the conception of success or "winning" as giving maximum effort is as relevant to parents as it is to coaches. Indeed, it may be more important for parents to grasp its implications because they can apply it to many areas of the child's life in addition to athletics. Likewise, the basic principles contained in the positive approach to social influence apply equally to parents. By encouraging youngsters to do as well as they are currently able, by reinforcing effort as well as outcome, and by avoiding use of criticism and punishment when the child fails, parents might foster the development of positive motivation to achieve and prevent the development of fear of failure.

Concluding Comments

Some degree of stress is inherent in sport situations. It is as much a part of sport as is striving for victory. But frequently, unnecessary stress is produced by coaches, parents, and by the unrealistic beliefs and attitudes of athletes themselves. These needless stresses detract from the potential of organized sport to provide children with enjoyment and personal growth. This chapter has explored several potentially valuable strategies for the reduction of stress in youth sport. Although some clinical results have substantiated the positive effects of SMT with child athletes (R. E. Smith, 1980), research concerning the efficacy of other approaches is virtually nonexistent. In addition to developing and applying intervention strategies on sound theoretical bases, sport psychologists must devote considerable future attention to assessing the short- and long-term effects of such efforts.

References

Benson, H. (1976). *The relaxation response*. New York: Avon.

DeCharms, R. (1972). Personal causation training in the schools. *Journal of Applied Social Psychology*, **2**, 95-113.

Dweck, C. S. (1975). The role of expectations and attributions in the alleviation of learned helplessness. *Journal of Personality and Social Psychology*, **31**, 674-685.

Ferrell, J., Glashagel, J., & Johnson, M. (1978). *A family approach to youth sports*. La Grange, IL: Youth Sports Press.

Gallwey, W. T., & Kriegel, R. (1977, November). Fear of skiing. *Psychology Today*, pp. 78-85.

Gould, D., Horn, T., & Spreeman, J. (1983). Competitive anxiety in junior elite wrestlers. *Journal of Sport Psychology*, **5**, 58-71.

Griffin, M. R. (1972, spring). An analysis of state and trait anxiety experienced in sports competition at different levels. *Foil*, pp. 58-64.

Hanson, D. L. (1967). Cardiac response to participation in Little League baseball competition as determined by telemetry. *Research Quarterly*, **38**, 384-388.

Jacobson, E. (1938). *Progressive relaxation*. Chicago: University of Chicago Press.

Lewko, J. H., & Greendorfer, S. L. (1982). Family influence and sex differences in children's socialization into sport: A review. In R. A. Magill, M. J. Ash, & F. L. Smoll (Eds.), *Children in sport* (2nd ed.) (pp. 279-293). Champaign, IL: Human Kinetics.

Lowe, R., & McGrath, J. E. (1971). *Stress, arousal, and performance: Some findings calling for a new theory* (Report No. AF 1161-67). Washington, DC: Air Force Office of Strategic Research.

Magill, R. A., & Ash, M. J. (1979). Academic, psycho-social, and motor characteristics of participants and nonparticipants in children's sport. *Research Quarterly*, **50**, 230-240.

Martens, R. (1978). *Joy and sadness in children's sports*. Champaign, IL: Human Kinetics.

Martens, R. (1980). *Parent guide to kids wrestling*. Champaign, IL: Human Kinetics.

Martens, R. (1981, July-August). American coaching effectiveness program. *Sportsline*, pp. 2-3.

Martens, R., & Seefeldt, V. (1979). *Guidelines for children's sports*. Washington, DC: American Alliance for Health, Physical Education, Recreation and Dance.

McPherson, B. D. (1982). The child in competitive sport: Influence of the social milieu. In R. A. Magill, M. J. Ash, & F. L. Smoll (Eds.), *Children in sport* (2nd ed.) (pp. 247-278). Champaign, IL: Human Kinetics.

Passer, M. W. (1982a). Children in sport: Participation motives and psychological stress. *Quest*, **33**, 231-244.

Passer, M. W. (1982b). Psychological stress in youth sports. In R. A. Magill, & F. L. Smoll (Eds.), *Children in sport* (2nd ed.) (pp. 153-177). Champaign, IL: Human Kinetics.

Passer, M. W. (1983). Fear of failure, fear of evaluation, perceived competence, and self-esteem in competitive-trait-anxious children. *Journal of Sport Psychology*, **5**, 172-188.

Passer, M. W. (1984). Competitive trait anxiety in children and adolescents: Mediating cognitions, developmental antecedents and consequences. In J. M. Silva & R. S. Weinberg (Eds.), *Psychological foundations of sport and exercise* (pp. 130-144). Champaign, IL: Human Kinetics.

Passer, M. W., & Scanlan, T. K. (1980, May). *A sociometric analysis of popularity and leadership status among players on youth soccer teams*. Paper presented at the meeting of the North American Society for the Psychology of Sport and Physical Activity, Boulder, CO.

Roberts, G. C. (1986). The perception of stress: A potential source and its development. In M. Weiss & D. Gould (Eds.), *Sport for children and youths* (pp. 119-126). Champaign, IL: Human Kinetics.

Scanlan, T. K. (1986). Competitive stress in children. In M. Weiss & D. Gould (Eds.), *Sport for children and youths* (pp. 113-118). Champaign, IL: Human Kinetics.

Scanlan, T. K., & Passer, M. W. (1978). Factors related to competitive stress among male youth sports participants. *Medicine and Science in Sports*, **10**, 103-108.

Scanlan, T. K., & Passer, M. W. (1979). Sources of competitive stress in young female athletes. *Journal of Sport Psychology*, **1**, 151-159.

Seefeldt, V., & Gould, D. (1980). *Physical and psychological effects of athletic competition on children and youth* (Report No. SP 015398). Washington, DC: ERIC Clearinghouse on Teacher Education.

Simon, J. A., & Martens, R. (1979). Children's anxiety in sport and nonsport evaluative activities. *Journal of Sport Psychology*, **1**, 160-169.

Smith, N.J., Smith, R.E., & Smoll, F.L. (1983). Athletic stress: Developing coping skills through sport. In *Kidsports: A survival guide for parents* (pp. 132-148). Reading, MA: Addison-Wesley.

Smith, R. E. (1980). A cognitive—affective approach to stress management training for athletes. In C. H. Nadeau, W. R. Halliwell, K. M. Newell, & G. C. Roberts (Eds.), *Psychology of motor behavior and sport—1979* (pp. 54-72). Champaign, IL: Human Kinetics.

Smith, R. E. (1986). A component analysis of athletic stress. In M. Weiss & D. Gould (Eds.). *Sport for children and youths* (pp. 107-111). Champaign, IL: Human Kinetics.

Smith, R. E., & Smoll, F. L. (1982). Psychological stress: A conceptual model and some intervention strategies in youth sports. In R. A. Magill, M. J. Ash, & F. L. Smoll (Eds.), *Children in sport* (2nd ed.) (pp. 178-195). Champaign, IL: Human Kinetics.

Smith, R. E., Smoll, F. L., & Curtis, B. (1978). Coaching behaviors in Little League baseball. In F. L. Smoll & R. E. Smith (Eds.), *Psychological perspectives in youth sports* (pp. 173-201). Washington, DC: Hemisphere.

Smith, R. E., Smoll, F. L., Hunt, E., Curtis, B., & Coppel, D. B. (1979). Psychology and the bad news bears. In G. C. Roberts & K. M. Newell (Eds.), *Psychology of motor behavior and sport—1978*. (pp. 109-130). Champaign, IL: Human Kinetics.

Smith, T. (1983). Competitive trait anxiety in youth sport: Differences according to age, sex, race, and playing status. *Perceptual and Motor Skills*, **57**, 1235-1238.

Smoll, F. L., & Smith, R. E. (1981). Developing a healthy philosophy of winning in youth sports. In V. Seefeldt, F. L. Smoll, R. E. Smith, & D. Gould, (Eds.), *A winning philosophy for youth sports programs* (pp. 17-24). East Lansing, MI: Youth Sports Institute.

Smoll, F. L., & Smith, R. E. (in press). Coach-parent relationships: Enhancing the quality of the athlete's sport experience. In J.M. Williams (Ed.), *Sport psychology for coaches: Personal growth to peak performance*. Palo Alto, CA: Mayfield.

Smoll, F. L., Smith, R. E., Curtis, B., & Hunt, E. (1978). Toward a mediational model of coach-player relationships. *Research Quarterly*, **49**, 528-541.

Thomas, J. R. (Ed.) (1977). *Youth sports guide for coaches and parents*. Washington, DC: American Alliance for Health, Physical Education, and Recreation.

Vandeweghe, E. (1979). *Growing with sport: A parents' guide to the child athlete*. Englewood Cliffs, NJ: Prentice-Hall.

PART V

Injuries in Youth Sport

Organized competitive sport for children has been immersed in controversy ever since its inception. In particular, critics argue that participation places children under a high risk of injury. Fractures, dislocations, heat disorders, and even death are often cited as injuries associated with children's sport participation. Fortunately, recent statistics reveal that the extent and severity of children's sport injuries have been greatly exaggerated. In a survey of 1.8 million medically attended sport injuries to children 5 to 14 years of age, Rutherford, Miles, Brown and MacDonald[1] found that the majority of these injuries were either relatively minor strains and sprains (39%) or contusions and abrasions (31%). Severe injuries occurred in a much smaller percentage of the sample.

Although the number of severe injuries in youth sport are less than initially thought, this does not imply that severe injuries do not occur in young athletes. Severe injuries do occur and have resulted in increased concern. The effects of injuries to the epiphyseal plate and overuse injuries are both of special significance because they can affect the future growth and development of the child and also are associated with the organization and intensity of the programs in which young athletes participate.

This part contains two papers specifically examining epiphyseal and overuse injuries in young athletes. Both articles are written by physicians extensively involved in the identification, treatment, and rehabilitation of these injuries. First, Ken Singer examines injuries and disorders of the epiphyses, types of epiphyseal injuries and fractures, treatments for these injuries, and the relationship between these injuries and youth sport participation. Second, Jack Harvey discusses overuse syndromes in young athletes and examines plantar fascitis, achilles tendinitis, anterior leg pain, stress fractures, Osgood-Schlatter disease, patellofemoral syndromes, and their treatment.

[1]Rutherford, G.W., Miles, R.B., Brown, Y.R., & MacDonald, B. (1981). *Overview of sports-related injuries to persons 5 to 14 years of age*. Washington, DC: US Consumer Product Safety Commission.

19

Injuries and Disorders of the Epiphyses in Young Athletes

Kenneth Singer
ORTHOPEDIC AND FRACTURE CLINIC OF EUGENE
EUGENE, OREGON, USA

Fear of epiphyseal injury and subsequent permanent deformity have been among the objections raised to the participation of children and adolescents in athletics. Because organized and nonorganized sport participation will continually be with us, our primary goal is to provide a sporting environment that is as safe as possible for our children. In the growing skeleton, the center of growth of each bone is certainly one of the weaker biomechanical links and, therefore, quite susceptible to injury. This paper discusses this link—the epiphyseal plate, its unique anatomic and physiological properties, and various types of epiphyseal problems that children and adolescents might encounter during sport participation. Subsequently, the relationship between athletic participation and epiphyseal injuries is discussed.

The Structure and Function of the Epiphysis

If insight is to be gained about epiphyseal injuries in young athletes, the process of bone formation must be understood. During growth, new bone is formed through primary and secondary centers of ossification. Primary ossification begins at birth because the cartilaginous precursor of the long bone is present at that time. Vascular channels enter this structure, and it then calcifies by a histological sequence known as endochondral ossification. In contrast to primary ossification, secondary ossification develops at the ends of the bone, beyond the epiphyseal plate. Longitudinal bone growth occurs here through a sequence of endochondral ossification. Eventually, the secondary centers of ossification fuse with the primary center and the epiphyseal plate closes. This signals the arrival of maturity.

The ages at which the various secondary centers of each bone appear and subsequently fuse have been studied and well documented (O'Donoghue, 1984). It is while the cartilaginous plate is still present, however, that the child is susceptible to injury and, when injured, the possibility of permanent growth disturbance lurks.

The epiphysis is generally thought of as the entire portion of the bone including the cartilaginous growth plate and the remainder of the bone going toward the joint. The radiolucent line which represents the very specialized cartilaginous cells which are responsible for longitudinal growth is usually referred to as the epiphyseal plate or the physis. Very frequently people will use the term *epiphysis* to mean just the portion of the bone on the opposite side of the growth plate of the metaphysis, hence the term ep-i-physis, or epiphysis. However, generic usage more commonly calls attention to the growth center as the epiphysis. The epiphyseal plate is radiolucent on x-ray and seen as a white cartilaginous zone in the true anatomic specimen (see Figure 1).

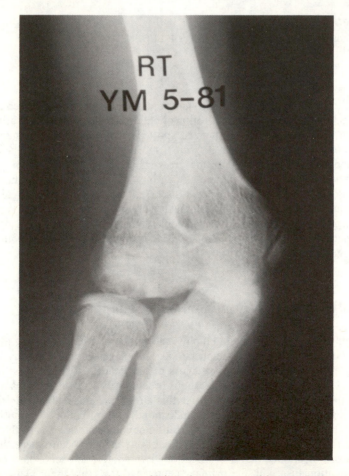

Figure 1. X-ray of the epiphyseal plate (seen as a white cartilaginous zone).

What is it that makes the epiphysis so special? Figure 2 contains a view of the various layers of cartilage cells in the narrow line which is radiolucent on the x-ray. Starting at the portion closest to the secondary center of ossification, an area of very specialized cells that are capable of providing growth can be seen. These cells are in a resting state. Going further toward the diaphysis, the cells start to divide, line up in columns, and then gradually elongate. Just prior to entering the metaphyseal area is a zone of calcification. As can be seen in Figure 2, the ratio of ground substance to cellular material in the epiphysis changes quite radically. Because the ground substances provide more mechanical support, the weakest portion of the epiphysis is in the area of provisional calcification, which is the area most sensitive to shearing injuries. Thus, when an epiphyseal fracture occurs across the line of the epiphysis, the cells that have the capacity for continued growth and bone formation usually go with the secondary center of ossification. This is important in the healing and remodeling of fractures.

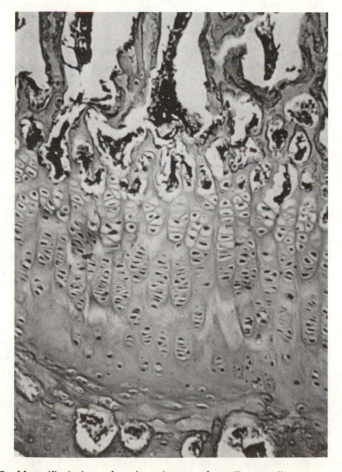

Figure 2. Magnified view of various layers of cartilage cells.

Several types of epiphyses occur throughout the body. The epiphyses present at either or both ends of a long bone are responsible for longitudinal growth. However, epiphyses occurs in other areas near bony prominences that serve as muscle attachments, sometimes called apophyses or traction epiphyses. Examples of these are the insertion of the patellar tendon into the tibial tuberosity; insertion of the psoas tendon at the lesser trochanter or the hip abductors at the greater trochanter; the anterior superior and inferior iliac spines where the sartorius and rectus femorus respectively attach; and the greater tuberosity of the ischium where the hamstrings attach. Nonetheless, they all have the same characteristics of an epiphysis and are potentially susceptible to injuries.

The next section consists of a brief discussion of the types of fractures that can occur and some of the associated problems. Hopefully, the discussion offers an understanding as to the nature of the types of injuries young athletes might incur.

Epiphyseal Injuries

Fractures

The most commonly used classification of epiphyseal fractures is that described by Salter and Harris (1963). This description is useful because it identifies where the fracture is situated with respect to the epiphysis; it also demonstrates that the location of the fracture often determines the prognosis and, therefore, is important when planning treatment.

Illustrated in figure 3 are the five types of epiphyseal fractures classified by Salter and Harris. As can be seen, the typical Salter Type I fracture is a cleavage line across the epiphyseal plate. This is usually a shearing or stress type of injury. The fracture may be displaced or undisplaced. If it is displaced, it is obvious on x-ray and must be reduced. If it is undisplaced, it may be very difficult to diagnose as the x-ray may appear normal and the diagnosis may be missed. There will be tenderness over the end of the bone at the epiphyseal area, and one must be suspect of an epiphyseal injury. If careful examination shows the tenderness is at the epiphysis rather than the joint, a follow-up x-ray 10 to 14 days later may show evidence of healing.

A Salter Type II fracture is basically the same as a Salter Type I fracture with the exception that a small triangular piece of bone goes with it (see Figure 3). Very frequently on the x-ray only the small triangular-shaped piece of bone can be seen if the fracture is undisplaced. Although it appears to be only a chip fracture, the fracture line goes all the way across the epiphysis.

Type I and Type II injuries are the most common and, fortunately, the most benign. They may have to be reduced, but they heal quickly, approximately twice as fast as the same fracture through the adjacent bone. Because the shear plane is through the zone of provisional calcification, the important resting and rapidly dividing cells which are responsible for growth are left undamaged; therefore, growth will continue and remodeling will occur.

The Type III epiphyseal fracture represents a different story. As can be seen in Figure 3, this fracture begins at the joint and extends into the secondary center of ossification and then across the epiphyseal line. The importance of

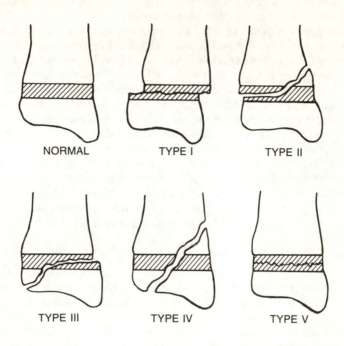

Figure 3. Salter classifications of epiphyseal fractures.

this injury is that the fracture is an intra-articular fracture as well as being an epiphyseal fracture. Fractures extending into the joint must be reduced perfectly and often require surgery. The epiphyseal line must be well aligned also, or a bone bridge may form across a portion of the epiphysis and growth disturbance will result.

The type IV fraction is even more significant in that the fracture line goes across the epiphysis and through the joint (see Figure 3). This definitely requires perfect anatomical repositioning in order to restore the joint congruity and the epiphyseal line. Growth arrest problems in Type III and Type IV injuries are much more common than Type I and Type II: in Type I and Type II about 3 to 4%; Type III and IV about 10 to 20%.

Type V fractures are the most drastic injuries. These represent impaction fractures and result in crushing injuries to the epiphysis. This damages the germinal cells to the point where they might stop growing, and, in this instance, a total growth arrest can occur. An example of such an injury is shown in Figure 3.

Very frequently the injury, although classified on the x-ray as one of the above types, will contain components of multiple types. For example, a child injures her shoulder and sustains an apparent Type I fracture; however, there is also a component of a Type V fracture injury as well, that does not become apparent until a growth arrest has occurred. If a growth arrest does occur, it may lead to significant deformity requiring treatment in the form of multiple operations or even lengthening procedures.

A very common injury in older adolescents is that of avulsion fractures of the traction apophysis. The muscle attached to the apophyses contracts violently and pulls off the apophysis. As these youngsters get bigger and stronger prior to their epiphyses closing, their muscles become much stronger. A violent muscular contraction while the muscle is stretched is the usual mechanism of injury. In Figure 4 is an example of this type of injury which occurred in a young soccer player struck on the anterior thigh while kicking the ball. The psoas contracted, but the hip could not flex, and the epiphysis displaced.

There is some debate concerning treatment of this injury. Most textbooks (O'Donoghue, 1984, p. 465) say that if epiphyses are more than 1.0 cm displaced, they should be replaced. My personal feeling is that almost never do they need to be replaced. There is generally sufficient healing potential and remodeling potential that the epiphyseal fragment will heal, the muscle will reattach, and an appropriate length-tension relationship will occur.

Overuse Epiphyseal Injuries

Another entire category of epiphyseal injuries, relevant in discussions such as this, relate predominately to what are most likely overuse syndromes to the various growth centers. This is the entire family of diseases known as the osteochrondroses. These can occur in several areas such as the elbow in young baseball players, at tendon site attachments such as in Osgood-Schlatter's disease, and at impact sites such as in Sever's disease. Our general perception is that these are caused by vascular abnormalities, and are probably a result of chronic repetitive trauma that in some way affects the blood supply to a

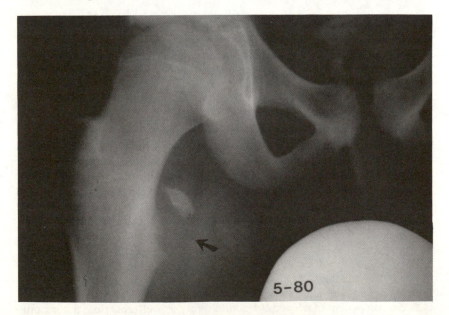

Figure 4. Avulsion fracture of the traction apophysis.

growth center which then undergoes changes. This, however, cannot be clearly proven at this time. The following paper by Jack Harvey discusses some of the more common overuse injuries, but I would like to address in detail the subject of osteochondritis dissecans.

Osteochondritis dissecans is a more significant form of osteochondrosis or osteochrondritis which occurs in areas adjacent to the joint. It begins as a cleavage line in the subchondral bone and then extends further. This eventually can slough off a portion of the joint surface, leaving a loose body in the joint and a crater on the joint surface. The body will attempt to heal the crater, but it cannot completely heal because our bodies are unable to regenerate articular cartilage. Problems similar to this prematurely ended the careers of many individuals involved in throwing activities, for example, Sandy Koufax; this entity was perhaps produced by excessive pitching at a young age. Fortunately, many youth baseball organizations have initiated rule changes limiting the amount of innings pitched and, in turn, have decreased the probability of this type of trauma occurring.

Osteochondritis can also occur in children involved in other popular sports. Figure 5, for example, contains an x-ray of a young basketball player who complained of discomfort in his knee. The x-ray shows osteochondritis dissecans or the area of partial separation of a portion of the secondary center of ossification. If the child is quite young when this develops, the knee has the capacity for healing, but if the child is near the end of growth, a fibrocartilaginous separation will occur between the two areas of bone fragmentation, and with the stresses of normal sporting activity, the piece will eventually separate. We used to remove these fragments, but now we are much more aggressive in attempting to reattach the loose fragment. The results of this treatment seem to be much better in preserving the articular surface.

Figure 6 depicts a similar condition that has occurred in the capitellum of a young gymnast. Gymnasts use their arms as weightbearing extremities and put unusual stress across them. This young girl developed this entity, required surgical excision, and returned to elite competition.

The preceeding discussion represents a survey of the types of injuries that can occur to the epiphyses. Obviously, any and all of the above injuries can occur with practically any and all growth centers, although there are some patterns that exist which are somewhat predictable, such as the elbows of throwers. It is important to understand those patterns and to make athletes, teachers, and coaches aware of them so that they can modify their training programs when necessary and be vigilant of potentially dangerous training procedures.

Epiphyseal Injuries and Youth Sport Participation

The incidence of epiphyseal injuries is not known, but if all of the above entities are included, they are a large number. If one excludes bruises and sprains, epiphyseal problems are perhaps the most frequent injuries that we encounter in dealing with children and adolescents involved in organized athletic programs. Although many of these more traumatic injuries can occur with any sport or activity, certain injuries are sport-specific, such as wrist epiphyseal

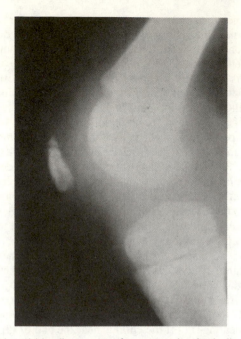

Figure 5. Osteochondritis dissecans of a young basketball player's knee.

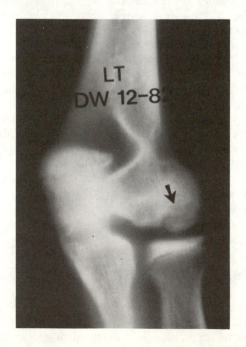

Figure 6. Osteochondritis dissecans of the capitellum of a young gymnast.

injuries in gymnastics and lateral compression injuries to the epiphysis of the capitellum in throwing sports. Most of them will heal with no lasting effects.

Organized sport has involved our youths' playtime with increasing regularity over the last several decades, and societal influences are dictating more than ever the type and duration of these sporting activities. If left to their own devices, the youngsters usually stop playing when something hurts and overuse syndromes such as many of these seldom occur. Now, however, we see team practices and competitive sports occurring more frequently and for a longer duration. Coach, parent, and peer influences dictate the individual's involvement more and more.

In addition, as skill levels improve in general, it takes the individuals longer to develop those skill levels. Fifteen years ago most athletes played many sports. Now even at the high school level many team sports involve year-round involvement. A promising basketball player spends his summer going to one or more basketball camps instead of playing baseball, soccer, swimming, or even fishing. This repetitively stresses the same areas, as most sport activities have some degree of stress specificity to the anatomic structures. The basketball players knees are not allowed the luxury of the summer off as they would have been if he swam, played soccer, or baseball. Therefore, the stresses accumulate and overuse syndromes develop.

Further, we are preoccupied with strengthening our young athletes. Certainly strength training has a role in increasing performance and probably in preventing many injuries. However, when strength training is encouraged for 8- to 12-year-olds, it is probably not very beneficial. Individuals are made artifically strong by these techniques. Because the kinetic energy equals one-half times the mass times the velocity squared, it is easy to see how increasing weight, strength, and speed will increase the energy that must be absorbed by biological structures. Epiphyses are fragile, often have limited blood supply and limited healing potential; therefore, they will more likely be damaged. They are a weak link in the musculoskeletal system.

Most of these conditions will heal with no problems. However, some will not heal, and damage to growth centers involving joints may leave individuals with the possibility of permanent changes that may affect them in later life. In many instances, we do not know what the long-term effects will be.

Conclusion

As a society, we eschew and applaud our champions at the professional and Olympic levels. These standards of excellence filter down to the high school level. Junior high athletes and coaches emulate and imitate their high school counterparts, and before we know it, the younger athletes are obsessed with the same standards of excellence and demands for achievement. It is important for parents, educators, coaches, trainers, and physicians alike to be aware of these problems and to adjust training levels and sessions with the best interests of the athletes in mind.

There has been a great deal of discussion in the medical and lay press regarding whether or not competitive athletics are healthy or deleterious to the immature skeleton. Particular questions arise as to whether or not contact sports are hazardous and at what age children should begin them. We cannot intelligently answer these questions to our satisfaction. In my own experience, injury statistics in seventh and eighth grade contact sports do not seem to be particularly high, probably due to the fact that children are small and have not learned yet the "advantages" of high-speed collisions.

If we all are willing to spend a portion of our time and abilities to help with the formulation and enforcement of strict rules and regulations designed to protect the child from injuries, and to devote a major effort to teaching conditioning and safety, then the healthy aspect of sport can be encouraged and the danger minimized. I emphasize *minimize*, for injuries cannot be eliminated.

References

O'Donoghue, D.H. (1984). *Treatment of injuries to athletes* (4th ed.). Philadelphia: W.B. Saunders.

Salter, R.B., & Harris, W.R. (1963). Injuries involving the epiphyseal plate. *Journal of Bone Joint Surgery, 45*, 587–622.

20

Overuse Syndromes in Young Athletes

John S. Harvey, Jr.
FORT COLLINS SPORTS MEDICINE CLINIC
FORT COLLINS, COLORADO, USA

To excel in sports today, the young athlete is forced to train longer, harder, and earlier in life. Swimmers and gymnasts in junior high can spend 3 to 6 hours a day in the pool or gym. Runners in high school may average in excess of 30 or 40 miles a week. Amateur teenage cyclists may cover well over 200 miles per week in training rides. Beginners in sports, although not training at these intensities, are also subjecting their bodies to the rigors of training throughout the year as they migrate from sport to sport.

The reward for this regimen is an increased level of fitness, better performances, faster times, and the satisfaction of attaining a personal goal. This applies to the neophyte athlete trying to learn a new sport as well as the elite athlete pushing himself or herself to the limit. However, there is a price for this intensity of training. Hours of practicing the same movements produce gradual wear on specific parts of the body. Variations in the athlete's anatomy or technique, hours of practice, and the intensity of training may combine to produce an overuse injury.

Overuse injuries are being seen with increasing frequency by the primary care physician as well as the sports medicine specialist. These injuries are often unfamiliar to the clinician who may not be acquainted with the biomechanics of the sport or the obsession these athletes seem to have in continuing activities that are painful. This may prompt the physician to admonish the athlete to cease the activity for several weeks. Although rest is an important part of treatment, such an absolute dictum is rarely acceptable. This often results in the athlete ignoring the advice and continuing to attempt to train in a manner that aggravates the injury.

An understanding of the pathophysiology of overuse injuries, coupled with a small knowledge of anatomy and biomechanics, and some "training room" techniques is extremely helpful to the physician treating these patients (see Figure 1). The common factor in overuse injuries is the repetitive microtrauma that occurs to a particular anatomic structure. Performing the same activity time and time again may cause one structure to rub against another (chondromalacia), repetitive traction on a ligament or tendon (plantar fasciitis, Osgood-Schlatter disease), or cyclic loading of impact forces (lower extremity stress fractures).

The result of these frictional, tractional, or cyclic loading forces is inflammation of the involved structure. This produces the clinical complaints of pain, tenderness, swelling, and disability.

The history is very important in making the diagnosis of an overuse injury. In 80% of the cases we see in our clinic, the athlete has only recently taken up the sport or has markedly increased his or her training intensity within a few days to a couple of weeks prior to the onset of symptoms. On occasion, he or she may have started participating in a second sport or another activity (for example, weightlifting) that has similar biomechanics that provide added stress, which initiates the injury. Often there is a previous history of these symptoms from a previous year when the athlete participated in the same sport. At that time the pain may have been minor, but now with increased intensity, it is severe and requires attention. Sometimes the athlete may have bilateral symptoms (chondromalacia, Osgood-Schlatter disease, anterior tibialis syndrome), while other injuries (plantar fasciitis, Achilles tendinitis) are usually unilateral.

If the injury is not treated or, as is often the case, the athlete tries to ignore or "run through" the injury, there is a progression of symptoms. Early on, the athlete usually has mild pain for a few minutes after a workout or competition. Often there is little or no tenderness and no disability. If the athlete continues to train at the same intensity, he or she will now notice pain and, perhaps some slight involuntary alteration of biomechanics near the end of the work-out. Continuation of training now gives moderate pain and mild to moderate tenderness at the beginning of the work-out. However, this may disap-

Increased Muscular Forces
+
Increased Rate of Remodeling
↓
Resorption and Rarefaction
↓
Focal Microfractures
↓
Periosteal and/or Endosteal Response
("Stress Fracture")
↓
Linear Fracture
("Stress Fracture")
↓
Displaced Fracture
↓

Figure 1. The pathophysiology of an overuse syndrome as illustrated by the development of a stress fracture.

pear after several minutes ("running through the injury") only to markedly return at the end of the work-out. Pain and disability are now quite evident after the work-out and may appear at other times during the day (walking, going up or down stairs, and so on). Often there is pain and stiffness upon arising in the morning. The final progression is severe pain, tenderness, and disability that are present during most of the day and intense enough to prevent continuation of training or competition. This progression from a mild to severe overuse injury will help the clinician select how aggressively to treat the malady as well as judge the length of treatment and rehabilitation. The sooner the athlete presents with the injury, the more readily it will respond to therapy.

Bursae, tendons, muscles, ligaments, joints, and bones are all subject to overuse. A knowledge of anatomy and the mechanics of the sport with the typical history of a gradual but progressive pain, tenderness, and disability should make the clinician suspicious of the diagnosis. Because most sports involve running, there follows a discussion of some specific overuse syndromes that are commonly encountered. Guidelines for treatment of overuse injuries and some specifics on the common injuries are included to help the clinician deal with the teenage athlete suffering from an overuse syndrome.

Plantar Fasciitis

One of the most incapacitating and prolonged of the overuse syndromes is inflammation of the plantar fascia. This malady occurs from the repetitive stretching of the plantar fascia between its origin at the anterior plantar rim of the calcaneous and its insertion into the metatarsal heads. The athlete usually incurs the injury from marked increases in training duration or frequency. Hill running and speed work are often responsible for irritation of the inflammation because of increased traction to the fascia in these activities.

The patient usually complains of pain in his or her arch (medial arch sprain) or heel pain (stone bruise). The pain is usually located along the medial edge of the plantar fascia on the bottom of the foot in the center of the arch. Frequently, the patient may have pain on the anterior plantar surface of the calcaneus, and occasionally may have pain in both sites. The pain is often intense enough to cause the patient to limp or walk on the lateral surface of the foot.

Examination of the plantar aspect of the foot reveals tenderness to firm deep palpation of the medial edge of the fascia or at its origin on the anterior edge of the calcaneus. Examination may be facilitated by forcibly dorsiflexing the toes and palpating the medial arch. This stretches the fascia and makes its edge readily apparent. On rare occasions, a fascial granuloma may be felt. Asking the athletes to walk on their toes may also reproduce the pain in a few cases.

X-rays do not contribute to the diagnosis. On occasion, they show a traction spur extending from the lip of the calcaneus. It is our feeling that these spurs are not the source of the problem but a result of continued traction and ossification at the origin of the fascia. They are often present in many people who do not have or have previously had the symptoms of fasciitis. On rare occasion, plantar fascial strain may progress to a third-degree rupture. This may be facilitated by prior steroid injection.

Differential diagnosis includes stress fractures of the metatarsals or the more unusual stress fracture of the calcaneus. Apophysitis of the calcaneal growth plate in the young athlete (Sever's disease) produces pain in the posterior calcaneus, especially on its lateral surfaces. The anatomic proximity of the distal part of the peroneus longus tendon in the plantar surface of the foot includes this unusual tendinitis in the differential diagnosis. Lastly, nerve entrapments, or neuromas, can occasionally cause plantar foot pain. These tend to be rare, except for the more easy to distinguish Morton's neuroma, which involves the metatarsal heads and toes.

Achilles Tendinitis

This rather common problem often can be recurring. The etiology is a combination of a short Achilles tendon and repeated forcible traction such as from running, jumping, or standing up while cycling. As with most overuse syndromes, it initially is usually most pronounced after exercise. In more advanced cases it often produces pain and stiffness early in the morning upon arising. The location of the pain in the vast majority of the patients is around the tendon itself at the level of the malleoli. Occasionally, it may be as proximal as the musculotendinous junction or as distal as its insertion on the posterior calcaneus.

Examination reveals tenderness to careful palpation of the tendon between the examiner's thumb and forefinger. In some advanced or chronic cases, gentle palpation of the tendon while the patient dorsiplantar flexes the foot may reveal crepitance. Patients may also experience pain when forcibly plantar-flexing the foot against resistance or upon walking on their toes. As with plantar fasciitis, x-ray does not add to the diagnosis. Chronic tendinitis may rarely show calcification or occasionally display a traction spur extending off the posterior surface of the calcaneus. Again, in our experience these spurs do not merit treatment and are frequently present in the athlete who has never had symptoms of Achilles tendinitis.

The differential diagnosis depends mainly on knowing the anatomy of the area and ensuring that it is the tendon that is inflamed rather than an adjacent structure. This may be difficult when trying to differentiate a retrocalcaneal bursitis from Achilles tendinitis—one may just have to treat these together. Plantar fasciitis, Sever's disease, and stress fractures of the calcaneus occur more anteriorly and distally than the insertion of the Achilles tendon. Peroneal tendinitis and tibial or fibular stress fractures are usually anatomically distant enough to allow easy differentiation. Rupture of the plantaris in the young athlete is rare, and of course usually occurs with instant onset of pain after very forcible plantar flexion. Chronic overuse may proceed to a third-degree rupture of the tendon. This can be ascertained by palpation of a gap in the tendon and the absence of a small amount of dorsiflexion upon forcibly squeezing the involved gastrocnemius (Thompson's test). As with plantar fasciitis, ruptures in young athletes are rare and are usually preceded by chronic overuse and steroid injections (Shields, Kerlan, & Jobe, 1978).

Anterior Leg Pain

Anterior leg pain, or "shin splints," is probably one of the most common overuse syndromes seen in the young athlete. It is usually seen in the unconditioned athlete or the athlete not conditioned to a new sport, for example, a swimmer starting tennis. Coaches frequently accuse shoes, track surfaces, or other situations as the cause of anterior leg pain, but these relationships are unproved. The etiology usually is increased training intensity in athletes who have inflexible and weak anterior or posterior tibialis muscles. The pathophysiology seems to be traction at the origin of either of these two muscles along the edge of the tibia.

The athlete complains of diffuse linear pain along the anterior or medial edge of the midshaft or distal one third of the tibia. Occasionally, they can reproduce the pain by forced contraction of the dorsiflexors of the foot. Examination reveals an area of diffuse tenderness along the origin of either the anterior or posterior tibialis muscles. Again, x-rays are not helpful except perhaps to aid in ruling out a tibial stress fracture. Although stress fractures are usually present with point tenderness, on rare occasions, they may produce tenderness in a more diffuse area, especially if a large muscle mass overlies the fracture or if there are multiple fracture sites. In difficult cases, a bone scan will display the well-defined area of uptake seen in a stress fracture as opposed to the linear uptake along the origin of the musculature in anterior leg pain (Norfray, Schlachter, & Kernahan, 1980). A quite serious condition may be confused with this entity. Anterior compartment syndrome may produce postexercise tenseness, diffuse pain, and tenderness on the anterior leg (Reneman, 1975). Clues to the diagnosis of anterior compartment syndrome include an area of anesthesia in the web space between the first and second toe, a decrease in dorsiflexion strength of the foot, or chronic anterior leg pain not resolved by conventional therapy. Compartment syndroms are important to recognize, as they may exacerbate and compromise the arterial circulation to the anterior leg musculature. Measurement of the pressure in the muscle compartment will rule out or confirm a diagnosis of a compartment syndrome (McDermott, Marble, & Yabsley, 1982; Mubarak, Hargens, & Owne, 1976). This medical emergency requires immediate surgical intervention.

Stress Fracture

With the increased intensity and duration of training, many young athletes suffer stress fractures. Although potentially they can occur in any bone to which sufficient repetitive stress has been applied, more common sites include tibia (50%), metatarsals (18%), fibula (12%), femur (6%), and other sites (less than 1% each) (Orava, 1980).

Patients almost always have a history of high-training intensity and frequently have recently made an increase in their training regimens. Sharp, persistent, progressive pain or a deep, persistent, dull ache located over the bone are the most common symptoms of a stress fracture. On occasion, patients may complain of pain with impact (heel strike). The most important clinical diagnostic sign is point tenderness over a bony surface. On rare occasions, a bony irregularity or callus may be felt. Stress fractures of bones that have a generous amount of overlying soft tissue (such as the femur and pelvis) may produce quite a dilemma in diagnosis, as they do not offer the examiner the typical sign of point tenderness. Usually they present as an apparent chronic muscular problem such as a strain; however, the lack of a typical history for the strain and failure of the injury to resolve may bring the clinician to the diagnosis. Routine radiographs are references as showing between 50% and 60% of stress fractures, with some increase several weeks after onset of the symptoms when callus formation is apparent. In our clinic we feel we have markedly increased our percentage of pickup on radiograph by adhering to the following guidelines:

1. Use of xerography rather than conventional x-ray.
2. Have the patient help the x-ray technician locate a radio-dense marker at the exact site of pain.
3. Include a view exactly tangential to the area of pain to adequately visualize the cortex.
4. Small cracks, callus, or periosteal elevation as well as a disturbance of the subcortical trabecular architecture are the signs to observe. On several occasions bony canals seem to be sites for initiation of the fracture (see Figure 2).

In our clinic we rely on our clinical impression and resort to bone scans only if confirmation of a suspected stress fracture is essential, or the diagnosis obscure. Continuation of training is forbidden when there is a stress fracture, as it may lead to progression to a frank fracture (Brahms, Fumich, & Ippolito, 1980).

Osgood-Schlatter Disease

Traction apophysitis of the tibial tubercle, Osgood-Schlatter disease, is a malady confined to the young athlete. The large forces of the extensor mechanism of the leg are magnified by the patellar mechanism, and repetitive forces transmitted to the insertion of the infrapatellar tendon at the immature tibial tubercle result in a traction apophysitis. Sports involving repeated flexion and forced extension of the knee are the inciting factors.

Athletes complain of pain and tenderness directly over the prominence of the involved tibial tubercle. Pain is enhanced with forcible leg extension or direct pressure to the tubercle. Exquisite tenderness and occasional swelling over the involved tubercle is the best diagnostic sign. The tubercle is often enlarged and in some cases may remain so into adult life. Also, there is usually pain with forced leg extension (for example, in deep knee bends). X-ray evaluation is extensively discussed in the literature, but we have not found it essential to the clinical diagnosis or management. Radiology may be helpful to rule out other rare lesions of the tibia, such as cysts or tumors.

Differential diagnosis will include the relatively unusual stress fracture of the proximal tibia, the more medial pes anserinus bursitis, infrapatellar ten-

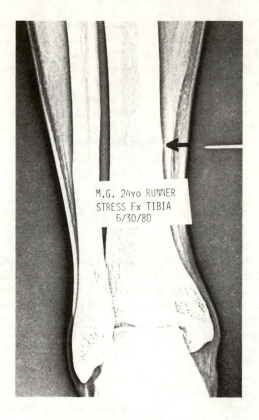

Figure 2. Xerogram of a stress fracture. Arrow shows site of periosteal elevation of an early fracture. Radiodense marker is seen to the right of the arrow, marking the site of the patient's tenderness.

dinitis, and various patellofemoral problems. Usually the strict isolation of signs and symptoms to the tibial tubercle per se is diagnostic.

Patellofemoral Syndromes

Patellofemoral joint pathology can present in a variety of complaints. These complaints may often mimic other specific knee pathologies. Patellofemoral syndromes are the most common cause of chronic knee pain in the young athlete and need to be included in all differential diagnoses of chronic knee pain in teenagers.

The etiology of the patellopathy may be secondary to direct trauma, but most frequently is a combination of malalignment of the extensor mechanism of the leg (increased Q angle, tibial torsion, and pronation of the foot), increased patellar compressive forces (inappropriate exercise, such as full squats), and an increase in training intensity (James, 1979). Occasionally these complaints are found in the recently immobilized knee with muscular atrophy of the knee and poor muscular development (quadriceps insufficiency). The usual presenting complaint is knee pain or a sensation that the knee is "not right" or weak. Often a good history will disclose intermittent bilateral symptomatology of equal or lesser degree.

Pain is usually present after running (especially on hills or during sprints), during forced extension of the leg from a fully flexed position, and often when just sitting with the leg acutely flexed. The location of the pain is varied and diagnosis is often not readily apparent unless the pain is in the unusual retropatellar location. Peripatellar pain, especially on the lateral aspect of the knee, is probably the most common presenting sign. Occasionally, diffuse pain is noted medially, in the back of the knee or just generally inside the knee. The athlete may describe a grinding sensation with forced leg extension, and on occasion swelling may appear. Episodes of "instability" are usually related to pain, which may be sharp on occasion. Careful questioning will usually rule out a suspicion of true instability.

Inspection may give some clues such as vastus medialis atrophy, patella alta, "squinting" patella, and increased "Q" angle, or actual swelling of the knee. Range of motion usually is not impaired but may be uncomfortable in extremes of flexion. Lateral subluxation of the patella and patellar crepitance occasionally may be observed or felt during extension of the leg. Palpation of the retropatellar edge or compression of the patella frequently produces marked discomfort. Mild compression of the patella during quadriceps contraction (Clarke's sign) is occasionally helpful in diagnosis. Careful examination of the ligaments and menisci is essential to rule out pathology of these structures.

Radiography may be helpful to document patella alta, increased "Q" angle, or other radiologic signs associated with patellagia, as well as to rule out other bony pathologies, such as cysts and tumors. If the diagnosis is especially elusive, or the symptomatology severe enough, arthroscopic evaluation of the patellofemoral joint and the internal structures of the knee is indicated.

Differential diagnosis of recurrent knee pain has to include systemic disease (arthritis), infection, tumor, and various internal derangements of the knee. Many unusual internal derangements, such as fat-pad syndromes, discoid meniscus, plicae, or osteochondritis are extremely difficult to differentiate without arthroscopy. Hip pathology, such as Legg-Calve-Perthes disease or slipped capital femoral epiphysis, are also included in the differential of acute or chronic knee pain. Occasionally, patellofemoral syndromes are diagnoses of exclusion.

Treatment

All overuse syndromes have the development of inflammation in common. Therefore, much of the treatment can be addressed in general terms. The goal of the treatment program is to reduce inflammation through rest or alteration of activities, physical modalities, and medication. Using all these techniques in concert usually provides the quickest resolution to the problem. Besides these general guidelines, there are often techniques for specific injuries that expedite their resolution or hold them in abeyance. This section will cover the general guidelines as well as specifics for the common injuries previously mentioned.

Rest is the cornerstone in the treatment program for overuse injuries. We do not mean absolute rest or immobilization by casting. Rest may be relative rest with the athletes altering their training program by decreasing their mileage by 25 to 75% or stopping particularly intense workouts (sprints, etc.). Sometimes a schedule of 1 day of work-out followed by one or two days of rest or alternate activities (cycling, pool running, or swimming) is sufficient. Dividing the work-out into two daily shorter work-outs and therapy sessions rather than one long work-out is also occasionally effective.

The use of alternate exercise is extremely important. By prescribing a form of exercise that allows the athlete to maintain conditioning, but not aggravate the injury, the physician gains the confidence of the athlete, and usually ensures that the athlete will not cheat and continue the aggravating activity. For running sports, we prefer to have the athlete run in the deep end of a swimming pool to provide nonweight-bearing exercise. The advantage of this is that it closely mimics the biomechanics of running and allows intense or long-duration work-outs. Studies in England and our clinic experience have shown pool running to be extremely effective in maintaining cardiovascular and muscular fitness in runners (Gatti, Young, & Glad, 1979). The technique for pool running is for the athlete to tread water in the deep end of the pool and then change the movement of arms and legs to closely resemble running. A few runners may require a flotation belt to maintain neutral buoyancy. The athlete should follow his usual training schedule in terms of intensity, speed, frequency, and duration. As the athlete gets well, he gradually weans himself from pool to land running.

Cycling is another good choice for alternate activity. Most athletes have access to a stationary bike or 10-speed bicycle. The bike should have the seat height adjusted properly and be equipped with toe clips. Pedalling the cycle should concentrate on using very little resistance on stationary cycles and lower gears in the 10 speed. The rider should attempt to maintain a pedal speed of 90 to 110 rpm. This high speed ''spinning'' will enhance the aerobic nature of the ride and not stress the injury. The training duration and intensity should match the running schedule. Patients with Achilles tendinitis or chondromalacia should avoid hills and standing up on the bicycle. As the athlete gets better, he or she should slowly wean him or herself from the cycle to land running.

Other alternate activities may be less desirable, as they do not mimic the biomechanics of running or require special equipment. However, the athlete with a prolonged injury may benefit from the variety. Swimming, rowing, cross-country skiing, or roller skating could all be alternatives. Weightlifting activities involving the uninjured extremities are also acceptable. Any activity that produces discomfort at the injury site should be avoided.

''Playing while hurt'' is a situation that often comes up. The physician may be placed in a position of trying to decide if an enthusiastic young athlete should be allowed to participate in an event that is extremely important to the athlete. If there is any chance of producing a serious injury (such as a stress fracture progressing to a frank fracture), the answer is obviously and emphatically *NO*. However, if the athlete will only have to endure some pain and discomfort and not seriously aggravate the injury, competition may be considered. This decision should involve physician, athlete, parent, and coach. The younger the athlete, the more conservative the decision. If a decision is made to allow the athlete to compete, rest, ice, and mild anti-inflammatory medications should be the only treatment. As much rest or alternate activities as possible before competition will give optimal performance, as forced training sessions usually produce more pain than conditioning in the athlete. Under no circumstance can the use of oral or injectable analgesics to allow competition be condoned! After the competition, the athlete must agree to submit to the treatment program and get well.

Physical modalities such as cold, heat, sound, and electricity have been used for years to treat inflammation. Careful studies comparing the efficacy of these modalities unfortunately are not available. This section will contain some of the bias of our clinic. The goal of these modalities is to promote healing by decreasing pain, swelling, spasm, enhancing blood flow, and perhaps directly affecting the mediators of inflammation.

Cryotherapy, or the use of ice or cold for a prolonged period of time, is the most convenient and perhaps the most effective modality. Unlike the use of ice with compression in acute traumatic injuries (strains and sprains), cryotherapy involves the use of 30 to 40 min of ice over the injury. This is most frequently applied after a workout but can be used at other times during the day as well. Ice cubes contained in a freezer bag and placed over the injury is a most effective method. If the cold pack is very tightly applied with an elastic bandage, frostbite may result. However, ice applied directly but not firmly to an injured site with adequate blood flow is safe for prolonged periods of time. The ice may also be applied with massage if a paper cup of water is frozen and then rubbed over the injury for 20 to 40 min. Mild stretching or contraction of the muscles for a few minutes after the cryotherapy also helps increase blood flow and enhance healing.

Cold whirlpools are often present and may be used, although they offer no real advantage over the ice bag or ice cup. The temperature of the whirlpool should be between 50° to 65° F, and prolonged exposure in the colder temperatures does have a small chance of producing frostbite of the toes or fingers, which have a large surface area.

Contrast therapy, or the alternate cold and heat, has been used effectively by many athletic trainers. Usually the treatment begins and ends with cold, and the cold intervals are longer.

Cold	Hot	Cold	Hot	Cold	Hot	Cold
3 min	1 min	3 min	1 min	3 min	1 min	3 min

We have not been impressed with any superiority of contrast therapy over cryotherapy. However, on occasion we will use it to "buy time" when an anxious athlete feels that our present therapy is not working fast enough and wants to try something different.

Therapeutic heat (hot packs, diathermy, and so on) is still used by many, but seems to have lost ground to cryotherapy. Our experience is quite limited in the use of heat and we prefer cryotherapy in the treatment of overuse injuries.

Electrical current (electrogalvanic stimulation) and sound (ultrasound) are often used by many physical therapists and athletic trainers. Both of these modalities are helpful adjuncts to the treatment of overuse injuries. Our experience with daily cryotherapy in conjunction with electrogalvanic stimulation has been exceedingly good. Specifics on the use of these modalities are readily available at any hospital physical therapy department.

Exercise can be therapeutic on some overuse syndromes—if properly applied. A good example is in the treatment of chondromalacia. By using quadriceps straight leg raising exercise and leg extensions in the terminal 30 of extension, a good conservative result can be obtained. Isokinetic high-speed exercise of the quadriceps muscles has also produced good results. Refractory cases of chondromalacia are often helped by an off-season conditioning program designed to strengthen the anterior and posterior tibialis muscles.

Good stretching is also an important part of many treatment programs once the pain has stopped. Stretching of the Achilles tendon and anterior tibialis are helpful in prevention of recurrence. Stretching and strengthening of an affected muscle often are indicated in recurrent or chronic injury.

Taping, splints, braces, and orthotics are usually very specific for the injury being treated as well as for the accompanying anatomic variations. Plantar fasciitis is one injury that lends itself to a particular tape job. By taping the arch with one-inch tape, the inflamed plantar fascia can readily be supported. This tape application is also very easy for the patient to apply to himself (see Figure 3). Various tape applications of arch, ankle, and leg have been

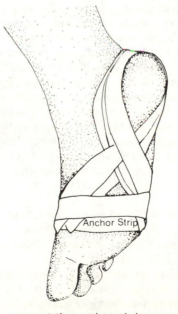

Figure 3. Taping to support the arch and decrease the traction to the plantar fascia for patients with plantar fasciitis.

used for anterior leg pain, but our experience does not support their efficiency.

Orthotics can be helpful in both Achilles tendinitis and in the patient with chondromalacia who is flatfooted and runs with extreme pronation. In the athlete with Achilles tendon inflammation, a firm quarter-inch heel lift is helpful in reducing the tension placed on the tendon when bearing weight. This lift can be made of quarter-inch orthopedic felt or obtained commercially, made of synthetic rubber. Arch supports with a slight varus can't seem to help decrease abnormal tracking of the patella in a pronated athlete. These are best obtained from a commercial source (Spenco) or custom produced by an orthotist or podiatrist. Some running shoes are now produced with this feature as an integral part of the shoe.

A variety of braces are available for the patient with patellofemoral subluxation and chondromalacia. Patient acceptance is marginal and the results erratic. A neoprene brace with a hole for the patella and some felt bracing to "hold" the patella medially is the most effective design. The brace is occasionally helpful but is not a substitute for a good patellofemoral exercise program.

Medication

Medications should directly mediate inflammation. The use of pure analgesic is indicated only in those rare cases when the athlete is in severe pain. Athletes on these analgesics for intense pain should not be allowed to train or compete.

Aspirin is one of the most effective and popular sports medicine drugs and at adequate doses is a very efficacious anti-inflammatory agent. It is important that the athletes understand the effectiveness of aspirin and that they follow the dosage schedule. Two to three tablets four times a day is often a good starting dose and may be "pushed" upward in severe cases. Be alert for symptoms of toxicity in using high-dose aspirin therapy. For less severe cases sporadic use of aspirin (such as before a work-out) is often adequate.

If aspirin proves to be ineffective or unacceptable to the patient, one of the other nonsteroidal anti-inflammatories may be prescribed. Patients respond differently to these medications and have different tolerances, allergies, and preconceived notions ("Motrin cured my friend with this injury"), and trials of different medications may be indicated in many cases. Medications with fewer dosage schedules (once or twice a day) usually give the best compliance in athletes.

Although frequently used, documentation of any efficacy with topical medications (rubs, ointments, etc.) is lacking. Our experience is that these often take precedence over more conventional and effective therapy, so we do not promote their use.

The use of steroid injections is discouraged in our clinic. Frequently, repeated injections are necessary, and documentation exists of weakening of tendons and actual rupture after a series of injections (Shields, Kerlan, & Jobe, 1978). The indication for steroid injection is rare in a pediatric sports medicine practice.

Some patients may have tried or are using dimethyl sulfoxide (DMSO). Studies have shown inconclusive results on the efficacy of this medication in the treatment of overuse injuries. The use of industrial grade solvent with impurities carries risks, and some evidence about reduction of tensile strength of tendons is present. Further, well-controlled studies are necessary before the drug can be recommended for sports injuries.

Conclusions

With the increased interest and intensity in athletics, physicians can expect to see an increasing number of overuse injuries. A knowledge of anatomy and biomechanics coupled with a good history and clinical examination should provide the diagnosis in most cases. Treatment should center on a combined approach of relative rest (alternate exercise), physical modalities, and, occasionally, medication.

References

Brahms, M. A., Fumich, R. M., & Ippolito, V. D. (1980). Atypical stress fracture of the tibia in a professional athlete. *American Journal of Sports Medicine*, **8**, 131-132.

Gatti, C. J., Young, R. J., & Glad, H. L. (1979). Effect of water-training in the maintenance of cardiorespiratory endurance of athletes. *British Journal of Sports Medicine*, **13**, 161-163.

James, S. L. (1979). Chondromalacia of the patella in the adolescent. In J. C. Kennedy (Ed.), *The injured adolescent knee*. Baltimore: Williams and Wilkins.

McDermott, A. G., Marble, A. E., Yabsley, R. H., & Phillips, M.B. (1982). Monitoring dynamic anterior compartment pressure during exercise. *American Journal of Sports Medicine*, **10**, 83-89.

Mubarak, S. J., Hargens, A. R., Owne, C. A., Garetto, L.P., & Akeson, W.H. (1976). The Wick catheter technique for measurement of intramuscular pressure. *Journal of Bone and Joint Surgery*, **58a**; 1016-1020.

Norfray, J. F., Schlachter, L., Kernahan, W. T., Arenson, D.J., Smith, S.D., Roth, I.E., & Schlesman, B.S. (1980). Early confirmation of stress fractures in joggers. *Journal of the American Medical Association*, **243**, 1647-1649.

Orava, S. (1980). Stress fractures. *British Journal of Sports Medicine*, **14**, 40-44.

Reneman, R. S. (1975) The anterior and lateral compartmental syndrome of the leg due to intensive use of muscles. *Clinical Orthopedics*, **113**, 69-80.

Shields, C. L., Kerlan, R. K., Jobe, F. W., Carter, V.S., & Lombardo, S.J. (1978). The Cybex II evaluation of surgically repaired Achilles tendon rupture. *American Journal of Sports Medicine,* **6**, 369-372.

Stanitski, C. L., McMaster, J. H., & Scranton, P. E. (1978). On the nature of stress fractures. *American Journal of Sports Medicine*, **6**, 391-396.

PART VI

Game Modifications in Youth Sport

Many adults falsely assume that children are actually miniature adults, scaled down in size but otherwise possessing adult capacities for learning and executing skills. In the same respect, children are often expected to conduct themselves as and play like adults in athletic contests. They are expected to (a) play on fields and courts with dimensions similar to those used by adults; (b) use equipment of the same size and weight as adults; and (c) abide by many of the same rules that govern adult games. However, children are not mini-adults; they are smaller in size, have lower strength levels, and are cognitively less mature. The difference in children's size, strength, and maturity is a clear indication that sports should be adapted or modified according to the child's maturity and skill level.

The major objectives of youth sport programs can be more easily achieved by scaling the game down to a child's level or by simply changing some rules to ensure maximized skill development. The primary benefit of rules and game modifications is that children experience more success in participation by learning skills faster and more proficiently. In situations where playing areas are smaller and a team is comprised of fewer players, young athletes have more opportunities to participate, resulting in a sense of achievement which leads to positive self-esteem. Modifications also reduce hazardous situations and thus promote a more physically safe environment. Prohibiting metal cleats and head-first slides in baseball, for example, reduces injuries.

Enjoyment is the third objective that can be accomplished through game modifications. Under the present structure of organized youth sport competition, winning is often emphasized at the expense of skill and fun objectives, and typically, high attrition rates occur during the early adolescent years. When 8- to 9-year-old children were asked how their sport could be made more fun, frequent responses were (a) making the game easier, (b) cutting down the length of the game, and (c) increasing actual playing time for everyone[1]. Thus, children themselves are telling us that fun is an important reason for their participation.

Terry Orlick begins Part VI with a convincing argument for the need to eliminate the professional sport model that exists and to bring children's sport back to "playfulness." He highlights the need to offer alternatives to highly competitive programs so that children are more playful, more in control, and more cooperative. The immediate new frontier in children's sport, Orlick says, is stress control.

Following Orlick, Kathy Haywood provides empirical evidence from the growth and development and biomechanical areas to justify changes in youth basketball. The growth status and skill level of children of varying ages provide a rationale for modifying youth sport rules, equipment, and court or field dimensions.

Then John Pooley criticizes the highly competitive model of youth sport from the standpoint that too much pressure is placed on children. Furthermore, he argues that average and lower level athletes are denied equitable opportunities for instruction and praise which leads to drop out and burnout and encourages physical aggressiveness. Pooley presents his own developmental model of activities and organizational structures for different levels of growth and development based on empirical research and practical experience.

In his article, Don Morris presents a games analysis model that maximizes the inclusion of all children in activities commensurate with their physical and psychological maturity levels. He suggests that leaders willing to shift the locus of control or share decisions for making game modifications with children will build confidence in young athletes.

From the Canadian sport system, Terry Valeriote discusses the design of sport programs using development models that focus on the physical, psychological, social, and cognitive maturity levels of children of various ages when designing sport programs. These models purport to provide parents, coaches, and administrators with realistic expectations with regard to skill development, and coaches with specific information for drills and skills to be emphasized during certain age periods. Further, Valeriote suggests that professional organizations need to place pressure on governmental bodies, sport-governing bodies, and recreation departments to implement such models in programs under their charge.

Finally, Monta Potter presents a practitioner's viewpoint of the game modification issue in youth sport. She expresses the desire youth sport agencies have to modify according to maturity levels, but notes that realistically, there are barriers to modifying children's games that agency-sponsored programs cannot neglect. Potter lists these barriers as (a) parental beliefs in the traditional sport models, (b) existing inappropriate facilities and equipment, and (c) communication gaps perceived between researchers and practitioners (which is an obstacle in information flowing in either direction). Potter appeals to all individuals involved in children's programs to join hands and devise programs to meet both children's needs and those that are realistic for agencies to implement.

---

[1]Orlick, T. (1973). Children's sports—A revolution is coming. *CAHPER, 39*(3), 12-14.

21

Evolution in Children's Sport

Terry Orlick
UNIVERSITY OF OTTAWA
OTTAWA, ONTARIO, CANADA

Three Olympics ago, Canadian children were making recommendations about modifications they wanted to see in children's sport (Orlick, 1972). Many of their recommendations and perspectives were written in an article entitled, "Children's Sport—A Revolution is Coming," (Orlick, 1973) and subsequently in *Every Kid Can Win* (Orlick & Botterill, 1975) and in Level I of the Canadian Coaching Certification Program. Children wanted three basic changes:

1. They all wanted to play (not just sit around and watch the good guys play).
2. They wanted sports to be scaled down to their level (e.g., to have adaptations within the game to make the challenge and requirements more appropriate for children).
3. They wanted less emphasis on winning and more emphasis on having fun.

These were their hopes and dreams and they wanted change now—immediate and dramatic change. They were seeking a revolution in children's sport, and after speaking with them, so was I.[1] Did their recommendations fall upon deaf ears? We have not had the revolution for which we were hoping, but we have had some evolution over the past 5 or 10 years.

In preparation for this paper, interviews were conducted with representatives of 27 of the more established (or developed) Canadian sports governing bodies representing children's sports. Twenty-six of those national sports associations reported that some modifications had been implemented for children in their sport over the past 10 years. These sports included Alpine skiing, badminton, baseball, basketball, boxing, canoeing, cross-country skiing, fencing, figure skating, field hockey, football, gymnastics, ice hockey, lacrosse, rhythmic gym-

---

[1]Appreciation is extended to Ms. Lori Hansen for her assistance in providing background research material from various sports associations for use in this paper.

nastics, ringette, rowing, rugby, soccer, softball, speed skating, swimming, track and field, volleyball, waterpolo, and wrestling.

Implemented Game Modification

The modifications generally fall within the children's recommendations for more equal playing time and for scaling down the sport. For example, many team sports have implemented rules to ensure that all team members play a fair share of the game (see Appendix A for specific all play rules). Many sports also have implemented changes within the game itself and/or with equipment to make it more suitable for children. For example, some sports have cut down on the length of the game, the size of the playing area, and have made adjustments in size and type of equipment (see Appendix A for specific examples).

The introduction of a noncontact rule in children's ice hockey is one of the best examples of a rule change representing children's best interests. In many interviews with children, one of the commonly expressed dislikes about playing hockey was the roughness (e.g., getting pushed around, hit, body checked, boarded). Rule 50b in the *1983-1984 Canadian Amateur Hockey Association (CAHA) Hockey Rulebook* now states that ''In categories of Pee Wee and below (12 and under), a minor penalty shall be assessed any player who, in the opinion of the referee, intentionally body checks, bumps, shoves or pushes any opposing player.'' That single rule, introduced to a sport steeped in tradition, changed the playing experiences of thousands of boys and girls across this country.

It is interesting to note that before this rule was changed for children, many ''old-timers'' hockey leagues were sprouting up across the country, and the players themselves agreed upon noncontact rules. They were out to have a good time and did not want to sustain injuries or have their bodies crushed into the boards unnecessarily. Ironically, adults were discovering that they did not want to play in the type of system that had been thrust on children. They, too, wanted to have fun, and so we have come full circle: old-timers hockey for children.

Obstacles to Playfulness

We are winning the battle with adapting games (structures, equipment, rules) to make them more appropriate for children. However, when it comes to the children's recommendation of de-emphasizing winning and reemphasizing fun, we are not faring as well. Children's games and lives are still being killed by the importance of numbers. In my view, we are losing the battle to keep winning in perspective. You cannot introduce a rule that says winning is not important, kids are important, and have it followed. It is a much more difficult task than that.

The Canadian Coaching Certification Program promotes a philosophy which centers around what they feel is best for a child's overall development. However, that does not guarantee the positive implementation of that philosophy in the real world. It does not guarantee more fun, more playfulness, or less pressure to win.

Children, coaches, and parents bring to the game a history that is influenced by home, school, peers, and television. This history is sometimes difficult to change. Try telling a 6-year-old who watches his or her father go crazy in front of a TV game, and who is told to go out and win and is rewarded for that win, that winning is not important. Adults may be able to "accept" the general viewpoint that winning is not that important in children's games, but when it gets down to "my" child or "my" team, perspectives and actions can change. You can walk into an arena, gym, pool, or onto a field any day of the week and still see abuses in children's sport. Adults still scream at kids, and in many programs, winning is still a priority in children's games.

Recently, a parent told me about how his daughter's soccer coach cheated on line calls to win a close game. Coaches had been asked to make out-of-bound calls on their respective sides of the field. The parent had been standing on the line watching and noticed that his daughter's coach made several "out" calls against the opposing team when the ball clearly was not out. These were teams of 8-year-olds and under. Furthermore, the parent heard one little boy's father continously yelling at his son to keep his eyes on the ball. During a break in the game, the father firmly told the wide-eyed little boy, "Don't take your eyes off the ball for the rest of the game!" The little boy trotted back on the field and watched the ball for the rest of the game. He never went near the ball or tried to kick it; he just watched it, wherever it went.

Perhaps the most enlightening incident that occurred at the game was when one little boy went with the wrong team during the break at halftime. When an embarrassed parent later walked over and asked him what he was doing, he replied, "They have oranges here, we only have water." Now, that child had things in perspective.

Thus, we have changed the field, the size of the ball, the length of the game, and have introduced rules to ensure that everyone plays and nobody sits. These have been very positive adaptations and have been implemented on a wide scale. However, we have not been able to influence wide-scale change in the emphasis on outcome, on scoreboard victories, even for the youngest age levels. Why not?

We are fighting against enormous odds in this quest.

> The evidence of an emphasis on competitiveness as the predominant mode of behavior in our society is overwhelming. Western industrialization set the stage, and urbanization provided the impetus for competition to spread throughout the land and permeate the disparate areas of education, social life, industry, athletics, and scientific research. Even religion has not remained immune . . . the prevailing mode of competition in American culture thus continues despite convincing evidence that it is damaging to physical, spiritual, emotional, and social health (Elleson, 1983, pp. 197).

We are operating in a culture where high values are placed on winners and low values are placed on "losers" in professional sport, amateur sport, schools, elections, and in many other phases of life. Ninety-nine percent of media sport coverage is focused on professional sport, which is geared to winning and material profit. Once very 4 years, there is a 2-week blitz on amateur sport (the Olympics), and here again, the focus is on worshiping winners.

It is difficult to prevent adults (and in some cases, children) from bringing this orientation into children's programs, even if it is undesirable, inappropriate, and counter-productive in terms of children's development and enjoyment. This past year, while working with 4- and 5-year-olds in preschools, it was clear that some of those children were already oriented toward winning, as opposed to playing. I often heard "I wonned, I wonned." If you cannot be free to enjoy the process of "just playing" the game (or modified sport) as a child, will you ever be free to enjoy it?

The elimination of professional sport or the professional sport model (which continually glorifies winners and shames "losers") would be one of the most useful steps taken to bring children's sport back into a playful perspective. Of course, that is not likely to happen. Playful, humanistic values are "bought out" by money, power, exposure, and by people succumbing (or bowing) to the systems within which they are housed.

Alternatives to the Competitive Model

If we look back at our original (Canadian) people (e.g., the Inuit), we have a long road to travel in regaining our playfulness in games and as people. Games originally freed people to be playful and to come together in joy and harmony. That can, and still does, occur in our society, but mostly within alternative structures (i.e., outside the realm of competitive games and sport). Some significant steps have been taken over the past 10 years toward the development (or redevelopment) of alternatives to the commonly known competitive games and sports (e.g., the cooperative game movement). Several books have addressed this issue and have presented some practical alternatives which most children really enjoy. (For specific activities and further references, see Michaelis & Michaelis, 1977; Morris, 1980; Orlick, 1978a, 1978b, 1982; Weinstein & Goodman, 1980).

Cooperative Games

Some sport programs for children have drawn upon these cooperative and fun-oriented activities and tied them into their overall development program. For example, the Canadian Volleyball Development Model ties in several cooperatively structured volleyball activities where players on both sides of the net play toward a common (collective) goal. The Canadian Canoe Association has integrated a series of innovative, fun activities as a part of the general skills training program (see Sample, 1984). Students in my classes have integrated cooperative games into children's programs in figure skating (e.g., parachute activities on ice), as well as in cross-country and Alpine skiing. Well-selected cooperative, fun-oriented activities have helped to keep the spark and joy in many children's programs.

We should continue to seek out ways to keep competitive games (and the preparation for them) playful. To do this, we need to shift the emphasis away from winning and constant evaluation because it kills playfulness. Commodore Longfellow, the originator of the Red Cross Water Safety Program, offered good insight when he said that children learn best if they are "entertained hugely" while being "educated gently."

Adults spend too much time trying to get children to achieve mastery over adult goals, rather than letting children become absorbed in their own goals (e.g., through play and playfulness). When children function outside the limitations of competition, they are usually most playful, more in control, and more cooperative. They can change things freely and are not restricted in terms of their creativity.

How often in our society are children free from competition, from having to put forth their best effort, or from evaluation? What became of a child's right to play in a child's (or childlike) way? Where can a child play when nothing is at stake? Must we always think of "best," even in domains which originally served the unique purpose of freeing us from the distress of having to think about best?

Should we teach children to strive and to be satisfied only with a best effort in all domains (e.g., in school, work, social situations, sport, games, and in "recreation")? If children's lives are turned into child's work and worry, what becomes of play? Where is the time for relaxation, for stepping away, for playfulness, for living the present moment?

Freedom from Evaluation

By turning everything into a competition or a quest for mastery, we rob children of an important balanced life perspective. As much as we can gain from mastery, we can lose from not having a place free from the need for mastery. Even as adults, somewhere in our lives we need some space free from evaluation, free from having to perform or live up to the expectations of others. We need this for psychological health and psychological balance. Where will this be for children and youth if they are castrated from play and games and "recreational" activities? Where is the alternative? Is it in bodiless or mindless spectator pursuits, in television, in chemical stimulants, in dropping out?

Children who are funneled through a high-achievement system often learn to live for the future, to evaluate their overall worth by numbers, to accept that there is no place or play free from evaluation. They learn that they are always being judged, must always do their best or suffer the consequences of being "a failure."

When evaluation is stressed, children can lose their playfulness at a very early age and carry the void with them for life. Perspectives which can enhance or destroy the quality of living begin at an early age. The push to hurry or eliminate the playfulness of childhood and to turn children into achieving machines as fast as possible is by no means limited to sport. It has become a pervasive societal "value."

School is one of the worst offenders. A 5-year-old neighbor girl leaves on the school bus at 7:15 a.m. and arrives home at 5:15 p.m. She is on the school bus or in school for 10 hours a day. Soon, in addition to this, she will come home with a couple of hours of homework. Who in their right mind would set up a system like this for children? Where is the time for play and for being a child when such an orientation extends to nonacademic pursuits as well (e.g., infant exercise classes and music programs)?

Just prior to my daughter's fifth birthday, she started to express an interest in playing the violin, so we contacted a music conservatory to find out about lessons. When the director asked if she had any musical experience, I replied that my daughter had grown up with music and dance in the home but had not yet had any formal education in either. (I remind you she was not yet 5 years old.) We were granted "an interview" (a brief "evaluation" session) to see if she had the "right stuff" to be admitted to the program. The rejection letter arrived about 3 weeks later, explaining that the school was seeking 5-year-old experienced musicians ("with preconservatory training"). I had seen advertisements in the newspaper for 8-year-old "experienced" hockey players, but 5-year-old experienced musicians was new to me!

Had my daughter been accepted into that program, any real love for music that she had would more than likely have been destroyed in that atmosphere of early perfection. I had hoped to give her an opportunity to develop an expressed interest and a skill which she might carry with her and which might bring her joy for the rest of her life—not for her to become a professional musician, at least not as a 5-year-old.

Mechanisms for Value Changes

Certified Leaders

In the absence of parent certification and media certification, it is difficult to know how effective a Coaching Certification Program can be in terms of modifying children's values and behaviors. We have no precertification baseline measures for the Canadian Coaching Certification Program, so it is difficult to make accurate statements about its effect. I suspect that it has been effective in some ways and with some people, but that it has not been effective enough to counter the many other societal forces pulling in other directions. We would likely be in much worse shape without it, but we are still far from ideal with it. The basic values taken into competitive games do not appear to have been affected in any significant or large scale way. They are probably not likely to improve dramatically until some very basic societal values and media projections are changed (e.g., the societal compulsion to be number 1, to be biggest, better than, best, to have more of everything—from money to missiles).

We can change game structures and game rules and, in some cases, coaches' feedback; but when it comes to changing basic values about something as central as the importance of my kid or my team winning, we are faced with a very formidable obstacle. Large scale changes in basic orientations to winning and losing with respect to how people treat each other as human beings are difficult to implement; that is why we are still struggling with humanistic change.

These kinds of changes are not likely to be effectively dealt with unless we approach them from multiple mediums of intervention. Children's games, lives, and values are influenced by the people who design and occupy all of the environments to which children are exposed. The way we parent, what children see and hear on TV and films, and what teachers and coaches transmit are all critically important, primary mediums of intervention. (For suggestions on how to effectively utilize the mediums of parental education, TV programming, and teachers and coaches, see Orlick, 1983.)

If ever we could implement an effective program of people certification for all people who influence children, we would take a giant step forward. If children's teachers, coaches, media people, leaders, and so on, could be selected based upon how they interact with children and how they function as human beings, many present and future realities would be dramatically improved.

Coping with Competitive Stress

The immediate new frontier in children's sport will be stress control, or the modification of the child's capacity to constructively cope with the competitive (or nonplayful) situation. In some ways, it may seem ridiculous to prepare children to cope with the stress of "playing" a game, when clearly the game and emphasis within the game should be adapted to meet the child's needs. However, this is the real situation with which we are faced. As we continue to work on solutions (e.g., alternative game structures, modifications in existing sports, and values change), we should also begin preparing children to cope with what many of them must now face in the realm of competitive sport.

Stress control programs for children in sport will be an innovative and progressive step, but only needed as a result of society's inability to allow children to live and grow playfully as children. The perceived level of stress and the importance attached to the outcome of children's games, to our knowledge, did not exist among our ancestors.

Today's children, like elite athletes, often need strategies to cope with the stress of games, errors, unmet goals, wins and losses. This would have been an absurd concept among our original people (e.g., children having to prepare to face the stress of playing a game). Although it may not represent progress in one sense (i.e., the state of our games and our world), it represents progress in another sense. The state of children's emotional control while engaged in a game can be improved in this way, and the learning of life skill strategies through games can be used to help children cope with stress in various phases of life, such as in school, at home, on the playground, and on the street.

The inability to manage stress and competition in a healthy way can result in some serious problems for people of all ages. Fortunately, children are capable of learning a variety of coping strategies and self-control procedures if these are adapted in their content and presentation. Some of the basic psychological skills outlined in *In Pursuit of Excellence* (Orlick, 1980) and in *Olympic Psyche* (Orlick, in press) can be adapted for use with children and youth (see Sample, 1984).

This past year I did some preliminary experimentation with 5-year-old preschool children and found that they could follow a basic relaxation procedure and "think" relaxation into various parts of the body. These children had a surprisingly good capacity to engage themselves in various sorts of mental imagery. For example, they could see themselves doing physical things in imagery and could call up the images of other people in their imagination (with eyes closed and open). Some were capable of readily changing unwanted images. For example, with minimal instruction, my 5-year-old daughter was capable of changing "scary" presleep images by replacing them with joyful images as she closed her eyes and tried to fall asleep.

I discussed the concept of not worrying about what is beyond our control with my daughter and her 5-year-old cousin. I attempted to communicate the idea that if something is already past, we cannot control it, so it does not help us to worry about it. One day my daughter, my nephew, and I were out walking next to a lake. My nephew slipped off a log and his foot fell into the water, soaking his shoe and sock. Looking up with that sheepish look hinging on terror, he glanced over to see if I had noticed. I had glanced away as if I had not in order to spare him unnecessary anguish. My daughter, however, said quite clearly, "Alex got his feet wet" and immediately followed up by providing him with a comforting coping strategy. "But it doesn't matter. It's already did, we can't do anything, we can't do magic." Alluding to the concept of "magic" was all hers. She was telling him in her own words that we cannot do magic and control the past, so we should not worry, for we cannot do anything about it. Her comment seemed to calm him as he breathed a sigh of relief.

I have thought of her "can't do magic" coping strategy in other situations. For example, when a child's game is over and done, we also "can't do magic" and control the past, so we are best to set it aside ("tree it") and move on without unnecessary anguish.

In closing, I would like to share with you a significant question, posed by Vera Elleson (1983, p. 197). "Are we creative agents of cultural change or are we dispensers of bandaids to the injured and facilitators of adjustment to the way things are?" I hope that we are both. We continue to push for creative and positive change for children, and at the same time, we help children to cope with the imperfect world in which they live.

Appendix A

Rule Modifications in Children's Sports

(Sample mini-programs being implemented in Canada)

Mini-Soccer

All play—Team consists of maximum of 11 players, 7 players on the field at a time. Each player must participate a minimum of 50% of the total playing time.

Game modifications—Size of playing area, height, width, and type of goal and size of ball adapted to age level; length of game shortened to 4 periods of 12 minutes each; no off-side rule; unlimited substitution; field markings adapted to age level (e.g., penalty kick line); referee explains any infractions to offending players.

Mini-volleyball

All play—Team consists of 5 players, 3 players on the court at once. Every player dressed gets fair (equal) share of time on the court.

Game modifications—Reduction in number of players on court, height of net, size of court, size and weight of ball (so it is easier to hit over the net), and use of cooperative games for developing game skills.

Mini-basketball
All play—Team consists of 10-12 players; 5 players play the first quarter, and 5 different players play the second quarter. No player plays more than 2-1/2 quarters per game to ensure that all receive a fair share of playing time.
Game modifications—Lower basket, adapted court dimensions (e.g., length and width of court, free throw line), smaller, lighter ball, shorter game duration (4 quarters of 6 min each).

Program adaptations have also been made in some individual sports such as the "run, jump, and throw program" to introduce young children to track and field and the "Can Skate" and "Can Figure Skate" recreational figure skating programs (part of which includes fun games on ice). Also, the children's program in rhythmic gymnastics has been adapted to include different size apparatus for children and a separate set of rules and technical programs for each age group. There have been many good adaptations in the size and quality of equipment for children (e.g., better and safer skis, modified racquets, protective equipment, etc.).

References

About stress (1979). Cryptographic booklet, Greenwood, MA: Channeling L. Bete.
CAHA model programs (1984). Ottawa, Canada: Canadian Amateur Hockey Association.
Canadian volleyball annual and rule book (1982-83). Ottawa, Canada: Canadian Volleyball Association.
Elleson, V. J. (1983, December). Competition: A cultural imperative? *The Personnel and Guidance Journal,* **62**(4), 195-198.
Hockey rules (1983). Ottawa, Canada: Amateur Hockey Association.
Michaelis, B., & Michaelis, D. (1977). *Learning through noncompetitive activities and play.* Palo Alto, CA: Learning Handbooks.
Mini-basketball rules. Ottawa, Canada: The Canadian Basketball Association.
Mini-Soccer: A mighty good program. Ottawa, Canada: Canadian Soccer Association.
Mini-volleyball is fun. (1976). Canadian Volleyball Association, Ottawa, Canada: Colban of Canada.
Morris, G.S. (1980). *How to change the games children play* (2nd ed.). Minneapolis: Burgess Publishing Co.
Orlick, T.D. (1972). *A Socio-psychological analysis of children's sport participation.* Doctoral Dissertation, University of Alberta, Edmonton, Canada.
Orlick, T.D. (1973, January/February). Children's Sport—A revolution is coming. *CAHPER Journal,* **39**(3), 12-14.
Orlick, T.D. (1978a). *The cooperative sports and games book.* New York: Pantheon.
Orlick, T.D. (1978b). *Winning through cooperation—Competitive insanity: Cooperative alternatives.* Washington, DC: Acropolis Press.
Orlick, T.D. (1980). *In Pursuit of Excellence.* Association of Canada Ottawa, Canada: Coaching Association of Canada; Champaign, IL: Human Kinetics.
Orlick, T.D. (1981). Positive socialization via cooperative games. *Developmental Psychology,* **17**(4), 426–429.

Orlick, T.D. (1982). *The second cooperative sports and games book*. New York: Pantheon.

Orlick, T.D. (1983, June). Enhancing love and life mostly through play and games. *Humanistic Education and Development*, pp. 153–164.

Orlick, T.D. (in press). *Olympic psyche*. Champaign, IL: Human Kinetics Publishers.

Orlick, T.D., & Botterill, C. (1975). *Every kid can win*. Chicago: Nelson Hall.

Orlick, T.D., Partington, J., & Salmela, J. (1982). *Mental training for coaches and athletes*. Ottawa, Canada: Coaching Association of Canada.

Partington, J.T. (1982). The murder of play. In J.T. Partington, T.D. Orlick, & J. Salmela (Eds.), *Sport in perspective*. Ottawa, Canada: Coaching Association of Canada.

Play female hockey. (1983). Ottawa, Canada: CAHA.

Run, jump, throw: Elementary orientation handbook. (1979). Ottawa, Canada: Canadian Track and Field Association.

Run, jump, throw: Awards program handbook. (1979). Ottawa, Canada: Canadian Track and Field Association.

Sample, B. (1984). *Its gotta be fun. Sport psychology and the young paddler*. Ottawa, Canada: Canadian Canoe Association.

Setterlind, S., & Patriksson, G. (1982). Teaching children to relax. In T. Orlick, J. Partington, & J. Salmela (Eds.), *Mental training* (pp. 35-36). Ottawa, Canada: Coaching Association of Canada.

Smoll, F., & Smith, R. (Eds.). (1978). *Psychological perspectives in youth sport*. Washington, DC: Hemisphere.

Weinstein, M., & Goodman, J. (1980). *Play fair: Everybody's guide to non-competitive play*. San Luis Obispo, CA: Impact.

22

Modification in Youth Sport: A Rationale and Some Examples in Youth Basketball

Kathleen M. Haywood
UNIVERSITY OF MISSOURI—ST. LOUIS
ST. LOUIS, MISSOURI, USA

Few adults involved in youth sport doubt that *some* rule adaptations are needed in their programs. Who would attempt to put a baseball team of 8-year-olds on a major league diamond? Many of the players could not hit the ball past second base, much less throw across the diamond for a put-out at first! At issue, then, is not whether rules, including equipment and distances, should be changed, but how extensive the changes should be.

The reluctance of youth sport organizers, volunteers, and parents to change rules is *not* because they care little about the children in their programs. In fact, many adults resist changes because they do not want to put their young athletes at a disadvantage years later. They believe that playing a modified game takes away from the experience an athlete needs when later "trying out" for the elite team, going for the college scholarship, and so on. This athlete, they fear, will be uncomfortable with the official ball or the official distances after playing with modified equipment and distances.

Although adults may realize that just a few of these children will go on to the college varsity or the professional ranks, they are nevertheless willing to maintain the "official" rules for these few prospects. Consequently, the rule changes that youth sport organizers make are typically the obvious ones (e.g., shortening the basepaths). Other, more subtle changes are rarely considered, and some games often remain untouched.

Youth league organizers are often willing to adapt their rules for children if a reasonable adaptation is proposed to them with a rationale for the change. Physical education, recreation, and athletic professionals cannot expect league officials to accept a change merely on their word. The suggestion must be tied to something known about the nature of children or empirical evidence showing the benefits of the change. For this reason, it is helpful to review briefly what we know of the physical growth of children before discussing specific changes for youth league basketball, the sport with which this paper is concerned.

Children's Growth

Several aspects of children's growth have implications for the performance of sport skills. First, children do not grow linearly; that is, they do not grow the same amount each year of their lives. Rather, they experience periods of rapid growth and periods of relatively slow growth. The adolescent growth spurt, of course, is the most dramatic period of rapid growth. This means that children just a few years apart in chronological age are often quite different in physical size which necessitates the grouping of children into age categories, at least for those sports where bigger size is an advantage.

Children enter these periods of faster and slower growth at different ages. We can generalize to say that all children will experience a given growth-spurt period, but each child is on his or her own time line. Again, the adolescent growth spurt is a good example. Although girls tend to enter it sooner than boys, the ages at which children begin their growth spurt are quite variable. When we couple this individual timing with the fact that some children will simply be taller or shorter than average by virtue of their genetic inheritance, it is obvious that even children of the same chronological age will be of different sizes. Some youth leagues deal with this variability by grouping children into height or weight categories.

Several other aspects of growth demonstrate that even this strategy does not work perfectly. First, children might be equal in body weight but completely different in body composition. That is, differing amounts of fat weight and lean body weight, including muscle mass, make up the body weight. So, while one child weighs 95 lbs because of excess fat weight, another weighs 95 lbs because of leanness and muscle mass.

Second, although the same height, children may vary considerably in strength. True, children do tend to become stronger as they grow bigger, but the peak gain in strength comes after the peak gain in muscle mass. In a study, Asmussen and Heeboll-Nielsen (1956) measured the strength of boys who were equal in height but about 1.5 years apart in age: The older boys were stronger than the younger boys of the same height.

Lastly, adults often assume children are merely scaled down adults. In fact, young children are proportioned differently. They tend to be short-legged so that the legs have to grow relatively faster than the trunk during childhood to reach adult proportions. Differences in proportion, however, are probably not very significant after the age of 7 (Asmussen, 1973, p. 68). There are differences in breadth as well as length. For example, during their teens, boys undergo broadening of the shoulders to achieve adult body proportions.

These characteristics of children's growth have several implications for youth sport programs. One is that rule adaptations are certainly in order to accommodate children's small body size and lower strength levels. Another is that league organizers can expect a good deal of variation in body size among children. Age is also a factor of size and strength. Thus, in light of children's size and strength, the biggest changes in rules and equipment are needed for young children. Then as young athletes approach adolescence, rules and equipment only need to be slightly modified. This natural but gradual transition from modified sport games to the official game seems to match the pattern of children's growth.

The Biomechanics of Children's Sport Performance

In addition to children's growth status, their skill performance also might provide a rationale for changing game rules. The problem is that we know very little about the repercussions of children's growth status on skill performance. It seems that children's differing limb and body proportions would affect the mechanical parameters of skill performance, such as the center of gravity, moments of inertia, resistance and force "arms", and so on. However, we just do not know if these subtle differences are large enough to affect performance in a significant way. Remember that many aspects of motor learning and control such as hand-eye coordination, attentional factors, and motor memory as yet might be unperfected in children. Skill performance in children may reflect these factors more than the subtle differences in mechanical efficiency due to children's growth status.

What is obvious when we observe children, however, is that they do not execute the basic skills of throwing, jumping, running, kicking, and so on, very efficiently. But as children get older, they tend to perform these skills more efficiently. Many of the motor development texts used today give the impression that this process is complete in all children by 6 or 7 years of age. Halverson, Roberton, and Langendorfer (1982) examined 12- and 13-year-olds, among others, for the efficiency of their overarm throwing skill. This was done by categorizing boys and girls into previously identified stages. They found that some aspects of the boys' performance were quite efficient, but at least one aspect of efficient arm motion was attained by only 41% of the boys. The girls were quite inefficient; for example, none used the most efficient trunk action with her throw. This study reminds us that many children by age 13 have not yet attained mature, efficient skill levels, and this will affect the distance and speed they can throw, kick, or strike, the speed they can run, the height they can jump, and so on.

Rule Modifications

The point is, we do have a factual basis for suggesting modifications in sport rules for youth leagues. We can document a number of ways that children are different from adults. Yet, there is an additional point to be made in the rationale for adapting rules and equipment: Given that children are different from adults, a rule adaptation might result in a modification of a single skill or a whole game for the *young players* that makes the game more like the adult version than it is without the adaptation.

Let us consider an example: A 10-year-old basketball player is two thirds of his or her potential adult height and has two thirds of the strength of the average adult. What are we challenging him or her to do when we provide a 10-foot high basket and a regulation size and weight basketball? Is it reasonable to expect one-handed jump shots that go right into the basket, or rather two-handed pushes from chest level that barely get to the basket? Looking at the problem another way, imagine giving an adult a substantially heavier and larger basketball than we do now and putting the basket at a height at least double the player's stature. One wonders how much fun the adult player would find this game!

We might not be able to scale down every dimension and every piece of equipment on a direct, meter-for-meter basis. Certainly, there is room for many changes and adaptations. We are more likely to provide children with games that contain skills mechanically similar to the adult version than those without such changes. The equivalent of an adult's one-handed jump shot with official equipment might be executed by a child *only* with a smaller, lighter ball and a lower basket. Thus, the only way a young child can learn to execute many of the skills of the adult game is with adapted dimensions and equipment!

One wonders whether it will be easier for a child to make the transition to longer distances and a bigger ball as his or her size and strength increase or to break the habit of taking a two handed chest shot in favor of a one-handed set or jump shot. There is little scientific data to give a definitive answer, but there is no evidence to indicate the longer distance transition is more difficult than learning a new skill. If rule adaptations provide a more enjoyable game for young children, sufficient justification exists for modifying official rules.

Examples of Basketball Modifications

Consider applying some of the aforementioned rationale to youth league basketball. Possible rule modifications can be placed in two broad categories: *quantitative* changes and *qualitative* changes. The quantitative changes will be discussed first, some of which have been examined systematically in controlled research studies.

Quantitative game modifications

An obvious quantitative change to make for young children in basketball is to scale down the ball itself. Haywood (1978) tested two aspects of children's basketball performance with a regulation basketball and a junior basketball, 5 cm (2 in) smaller in circumference and 57 g (2 oz) lighter in weight. Prior to testing, the 31 boys and 31 girls between 9.0 and 12.7 years of age were measured for first-to-fifth finger (one hand) maximum spread. The average spread for children was 19.1 cm, or 25% of the circumference of the regulation ball and 27% of the circumference of the junior ball. When the average collegiate player picks up a regulation ball, the one-hand spread is 31% of the circumference for a man and 28% for a woman. Thus, children come closer to putting as much hand surface on the ball as an adult when they use the junior ball.

Two aspects of basketball performance tested were ball handling, as measured by the Speed Pass Test; and shooting, as measured by the Front Shot Test (*AAHPERD Skills Test Manual: Basketball for Boys,* 1966). The children performed the ball handling test significantly better with the junior basketball than the regulation ball. The younger children in the study shot better with the junior ball while the older children shot better with the regulation ball. This could reflect the greater experience and practice the older children had with the larger ball, a factor important to performance of an accuracy task. It is interesting to note that studies on the use of a slightly smaller ball for interscholastic and intercollegiate women's basketball yielded similar results: The use of the smaller ball was associated with better ball-handling skills and with slightly better shooting (Husak, 1983).

Another possible modification is lowering the basket for young children. Isaacs and Karpman (1981) tested 8- to 9-year-olds on shooting at both 8-foot high and 10-foot high baskets. Boys and girls were five times more likely to make a shot at the 8-foot basket than the 10-foot basket. Note that the logic of this result can be related both to the shorter stature of children and their lower level of absolute strength. Of course, the basket height might be beyond the control of youth league officials, but this study demonstrates the benefits of such an adaptation.

Additional quantitative changes might include reducing the court size and shortening the official game time. Again, league officials often must work with whatever physical facilities are available, and making the court too small sometimes encourages children to crowd around the ball. However, some changes in distance, such as shortening the free throw line distance, are easy to make. Nearly all youth leagues shorten the playing time, some by use of a running clock. Challenging children to be at a fitness level to play longer is a worthy objective, but most youth league teams do not practice long and often enough to incorporate much conditioning time. Without a guarantee that children are physically prepared for longer games, shorter ones might be better. In addition, this keeps the games in perspective as one of many things children do, rather than as events consuming whole evenings or half a weekend.

Qualitative game modifications

Aside from quantitative changes in rules, it is possible to make qualitative changes, wherein whole segments of a sport game are set aside, for example, elimination of "stealing" bases in youth league baseball. The jusification of such changes might come from the status of children's growth or from other considerations. It might simply be unreasonable to teach young children all the rules and skills of a complex game in a limited time. Also, some aspects of a game are easily seized by a slightly bigger and more skilled team and turned into a very large difference in score.

One of the qualitative changes often made in youth league basketball is the "no press" rule. This change requires the defensive team to wait on the offensive half of the court, allowing the offensive team to throw the ball inbounds and advance it up the court unpressured. Youth league officials found through experience that one team could press another to the point that the ball was in one half of the court almost the entire game and the outcome was an extremely lopsided score. The "no press" rule simplifies the teaching of rules to first- and second-year players and helps to keep games more balanced.

Another qualitative change might be to eliminate jump balls and instead trade possession on tie balls. This simplification of the rules and formations taught might decrease the incentive for children to crowd around the ball and "tie it up." There are probably several other ways to qualitatively change basketball rules for young children. As children gain playing experience, these other aspects of the game can be introduced with the proper formations and strategies.

Summary

The growth status and skill level of young children provide a rationale for modifying youth sport rules. Professionals who suggest rule modifications to youth league officials might point out characteristics of children to justify the adaptation. Professionals can assure league officials that rule and equipment modifications will not handicap young athletes but will rather assist them to learn skills that are mechanically similar to those used by adults. The collection of data on performance with modified equipment and rules provides evidence of the benefits of these adaptations. Unfortunately, not enough data has been collected to demonstrate the range of benefits that potentially exists. More of such studies would encourage rule modifications when it can be shown that they are beneficial.

References

Asmussen, E. (1973). Growth in muscular strength and power. In G.L. Rarick (Ed.), *Physical activity: Human growth and development* (pp. 60-79). New York: Academic Press.

Asmussen, E., & Heeboll-Nielsen, K. (1956). Physical performance and growth in children. Influence of sex, age, and intelligence. *Journal of Applied Physiology*, **8**, 371-380.

Halverson, L.E., Roberton, M.A., & Langendorfer, S. (1982). Development of the overarm throw: Movement and ball velocity changes by seventh grade. *Research Quarterly for Exercise and Sport*, **53**, 198-205.

Haywood, K.M. (1978). *Children's basketball performance with regulation and junior-sized basketballs*. St. Louis, MO: University of Missouri-St. Louis. (ERIC Document Reproduction Service No. ED 164 452).

Husak, W.S. (1983). *Ball size effects on the competitive performance of women basketball players* (Phase I and II Report). Mission, KS: National Collegiate Athletic Association.

Isaacs, L.D., & Karpman, M.B. (1981). Factors effecting children's basketball shooting performance: A log-linear analysis. *Carnegie Research Papers*, pp.29-32.
Skills test manual: Basketball for boys. (1966). Washington, DC: American Association for Health, Physical Education and Recreation.

23

A Level Above Competition: An Inclusive Model for Youth Sport

John C. Pooley
DALHOUSIE UNIVERSITY
HALIFAX, NOVA SCOTIA, CANADA

Dettmar Cramer, a world renowned coach from the Federal Republic of Germany, visited the United States in the early 1970s as a guest of the National Soccer Association. During a Saturday afternoon minor competition for boys aged 8, 9, and 10, he observed that there was a pleasant atmosphere until the matches began.

> Then the coach of one team started marching up and down one sideline. The coach of the other team, wisely enough, walked up and down the other sideline! Then they starting shouting, ''Get him, hit him. Get that big boy, hit him.'' You can picture those beautiful children who are so shy, and the coach is so big, and he has such a very loud voice. Now he shouts, ''Hustle, hustle, chase that ball.''
>
> You see, boys of that age want to have fun first, but we have quite a different opinion about life and about the important things of life. For us, victory is so important, success is so important. For little boys, fun is more important than to win the match . . . . Play is more important than victory, and skill is also more important than fitness for this age group. A little boy is more or less fit, and what we have to give him initially is technique, and secondly skill and everything else comes later. We must remember to build gradually. A boy of 10 years is not a little adult. At his age of development at the age of 10, a boy is ready to be introduced to skill activities. He is a perfect human being of 10 years. His way of seeing things is different from the adult way of seeing things, and therefore, we must not judge boys with our adult concepts. (D. Cramer, personal communication, 1971).

Cramer's advice to youth leaders is clear and forms a suitable introduction to this paper, whose purpose is to propose an inclusive model for youth sport.

An organizational structure for youth sport is preceded by brief sections which include a criticism of the current highly competitive model and alternatives to the status quo competitive model.

Criticism of the Highly Competitive Model of Youth Sports

We may assume that many individuals believe that the present competitive structure, which consists of a highly selective process based upon innate skill and intense coaching from a young age, is desirable. Unquestionably, this model prevails in North America and perhaps in other parts of the world as well.

Results of implementing such a model are that (a) average or moderate performers are discriminated against, mostly because their performance is negatively reinforced, and skilled leadership (in the form of instructional advice) is denied them; (b) too much early pressure in training or competition for the skilled leads to burn-out and subsequent withdrawal from sport; and (c) skill development is inhibited because the pressure to win takes precedence over the development of technique.

Each outcome of the highly competitive sport model could form the basis of a separate paper, although more empirical research is needed to substantiate conclusions drawn from personal experiences. While the relationship between stress and competitive involvement has aroused much interest (Hendry & Thorpe, 1977; Scanlan & Passer, 1978; Watson, 1977), there is increasing concern about the harmful effects stemming from youth sport competition. This concern is typified by Leonard Koppett (1981), a sports reporter of the *New York Times*, who said that overorganized games have at least four harmful effects on children: (a) Competitive outcomes are overemphasized too early; (b) children are segregated by athletic ability at ages when they should be interacting at a high level with children of various abilities; (c) children are robbed of the opportunity to learn things independently of external sources; and (d) competition elicits physically aggressive acts from children. Koppett concludes that organized competitive sport for youth seems to turn off children more than it turns them on.

Alternatives to the Highly Competitive Model[1]

Valid alternatives appear to the prevailing North American model of highly competitive youth sport which take into account theories of skill acquisition, socialization, growth and development, empirical studies relating to cross-cultural settings, and pragmatic considerations. A few examples are cited here.

In the Federal Republic of Germany, interschool competition has been stimulated by two broadly based programs: the "Jugend trainert für Olympia" (begun in 1969), and the "Bungesjugent-Spiele" (Federal Youth Games)

---

[1]The author thanks Margo Gee for assistance in this section.

which are held twice each year. Specialization with emphasis on achievement in sport contests is uncommon within these programs; rather, it is left to the elaborate system of sport clubs to develop competitive sport (Rehbein, 1984).

Elsewhere, in Australia, researchers found that when analyzing juniors in an adult-rules cricket game, players whose batting technique was less developed were found to bat less often, bat less time in each inning, occupy lower order positions, have less of the strike (face fewer balls), and score fewer runs (Evans & Davis, 1980). The authors recommended modifications in order to provide equitable involvement. The two other techniques of bowling and fielding were treated the same way; that is, modifications were recommended.

Subsequently, a trial modified game was played, and comparisons were made with the adult game. Results showed that the "team score in the modified game was higher by 50 runs than the average team score in the normal game" and "the team generally had almost double the catching and throwing opportunities in the modified game, while fielding opportunities varied only marginally" (p. 28). The authors concluded that not only did the modified game generate more opportunities for each player in the techniques of bowling and fielding, but run scoring opportunities were greater. As shown in this study, "the introduction of modified rules clearly created the opportunity for more players to be involved in all aspects of the game" (p. 31).

Similarly, an earlier study by Gibson (1977) on boys aged 10 to 13 years who participated in Junior Australian Rules football showed that one third of the players did not get an opportunity to develop their skills during adult-style games. Further, the games were dominated by only 10% of players in each skill area. He also found that there was no system or pattern in the play and that packs continually formed around the ball, with physical size determining participation. The author concluded that this led to deteriorating skill levels, a decrease in players' level of interest (supported by motivation scores collected during the season), and ultimately to attrition. The author subsequently put forth two models for the development of under 10 and under 14 age football (see also Brayshaw, 1978).

These studies are very important because they provide empirical evidence for the efficacy of modified conditions in major team sports. The methodology needs to be replicated with different age groups and different sports in a variety of countries. Moreover, if possible, a longitudinal study should be initiated to compare the consequences of modified approaches in team games with the "adult approach" under a variety of disparate conditions.

Australian studies are not restricted to the aforementioned two cases. A report prepared by Gillian Winter in 1980 for the Division of Recreation in Tasmania and the Tasmanian State Schools Sports Council centers upon modified approaches to sport for Australian children. The report also presents a series of guidelines to assist organizations concerned with the process of modifying major games. It should be noted that modified approaches are also being incorporated in the sport of netball (Brown, 1980), and for a number of years, "Little Athletics" (track and field in North American language) and modified rugby have been widely practiced.

Finally, a strategy to reduce competitiveness in sport for youth in Canada, with special reference to soccer, was advocated by Pooley (1978). It met with considerable interest and sympathy by those who administered youth soccer.

Subsequently, increasing support for mini-soccer occurred, resulting in a de-escalation of interprovincial play for the younger age groups.

A Model for Youth Sport

The model proposed here is predicated upon the results of research, the author's experience as a teacher of physical education, as a coach of a number of sports in six countries for 30 years, and finally, as an enthusiastic athlete for 40 years. The activities and organizational structure are designed for children and youth at different levels of growth and development.

The following are objectives of the program:

1. To provide maximum opportunities for all youth to *participate* in sport
2. To *develop* the *motor skill potential* of all youth irrespective of their ability levels
3. To provide opportunities for youth to *learn leadership roles* as team captains, coaches, administrators, and officials

The language used here relates more to team sports. However, the structure is also applicable to individual sports. A synopsis of the model is seen in Table 1.

Unstructured Play (Under 7 years old)
- Provide opportunities (facilities, equipment) without formal direction.
- Encourage a variety of activities which are spontaneous and self-determined games.

Intersquad Activity (About 7 to 9 years old)
- Arrange neighborhood intersquad activity with some adult leadership.
- Give all an opportunity to take part.
- Change teams frequently, keeping groups small.
- Teach major techniques for no more than one third of the available time.

House League (About 9 to 11 years old)
- Combine adult and youth leadership; adults are formally qualified.
- Incorporate "mini" form of sports.
- Choose teams at any given meeting; all must play.
- Record no results.
- Teach techniques and principles of games no more than one half of the time available in practice sessions; use remaining time for games comprised of small teams.

Mini Leagues (About 11 to 13 years old)
- Use smaller than adult-size teams, facilities, and equipment where appropriate.
- Allow young people to share in team selection, coaching, and administrative tasks with adult leaders.
- Avoid publicity, sponsorship of teams, unhealthy rivalry between teams.
- Permit only best qualified coaches to be responsible for each club.

Table 1. Activities and organizational structure at different levels of growth and development

ACTIVITY	STRUCTURE	LEADERSHIP	SELECTION
Unstructured Play 0 to 7 Years	None	Spontaneous from youth	None
Intersquad Activity 7 to 9 Years	Scaled down Frequent changes	Adult organized Youth involved	"Pick-up" Teams
House Leagues 9 to 11 Years	Mini-form Decided on day	Adult and youth	Decided on day, loosely structured.
Mini Leagues 11 to 13 Years	Small-sided teams	MOST Qualified coaches	Separate leagues based on ability.
Leagues-Two Levels 13 to 15 Years	Modified games/sports	Qualified coaches	Better and keener players get additional practice.
Leagues-Two Levels 16 to 18 Years	Adult form	Qualified coaches	

- Arrange a minimum of two carefully structured practices to one game per week, each to be about an hour's duration.
- Balance league games with training sessions in which at least 50% of the training is in game-like activities, and at least 50% of all activity is in practice conditions.
- Encourage end-of-season dinners and/or socials where either every player is honored or no players are honored.
- Encourage each player to take responsibilities as team or squad leaders, administrators, coaches, and officials.
- Select the better players from each club to meet for two or three sessions per week under an independent coach.

Leagues Catering for Two or More Levels of Ability (About 13-15 years old)

- Use modified elements of the sports dependent upon the abilities and experiences of the players.
- Permit only qualified and experienced coaches to be responsible for each club (best does not mean most technical).
- Ensure that youth with different abilities are encouraged to continue playing through the structure of separate leagues.
- Use a "round-robin" format for all leagues without end-of-season play-offs.
- Avoid publicising league standings, club or team sponsorships, and league trophies.
- Encourage end-of-season dinners and/or socials where either every player is honored or no players are honored.
- Arrange a minimum of two carefully structured practices to one game per week, each to be about an hour's duration.
- Encourage all players to take responsibilities as team or squad leaders, administrators, coaches, and officials.
- Select the better and keener players from each club to meet for two or three sessions per week under an independent coach.

Leagues Catering for Two or More Levels of Ability (About 16 to 18 years old)

- Practice the adult form of the sport.
- Permit only well-qualified coaches for each team.
- Ensure that youth with different abilities are encouraged to continue playing through the structure of separate leagues.
- Arrange a minimum of two carefully structured practices to one game per week, each to be about 1-1/2 to 2 hours duration.
- Encourage youth who show special abilities as administrators, coaches, and officials to practice these skills in their club and the leagues with which they are associated.
- Encourage end-of-season dinners and/or socials where either every player is honored or no players are honored.

Conclusion

The Olympic Motto, *Citius Altius Fortius* (faster, higher, stronger) may be interpreted as achievement of those qualities as a personal goal or as achievement in the Olympic setting (McIntosh, 1983). Although only the best in the world are allowed to compete in the Olympics, we must not apply the same constraints at all levels of development. Yet many do. For years, concerned and dedicated coaches, teachers, administrators, and parents have been saying that sport programs must cater to all, but those who actually practice this principle are in the minority. We must continue to strive toward alternative modes of competition until the majority feel this way. In fact, we can be guided by another Olympic principle: It is an honor to take part, irrespective of the outcome.

If coaches are concerned with the development of human potential, it is their ethical responsibility to help all members of the sport club or team, not just the most gifted. The model proposed in this paper has promise, not only because it treats all athletes or potential athletes alike, but also because it recognizes and promotes other roles in sport such as administrator, coach, and official.

References

Brayshaw, I. (1978). Cricket and kids. *Sports Coach*, **2**(1), 18-19.

Brown, J. (1980). Netball is catching. *Sports Coach*, **4**(4), 48-52.

Evans, J., & Davis, K. (1980). An analysis of the involvement of players in junior cricket. *Sports Coach*, **4**(3), 26-31.

Gibson, B. (1977). Participation in Junior Australian Rules football. *Sports Coach*, **1**(3), 15-25.

Hendry, L., & Thorpe, E. (1977). Pupils' choice, extracurricular activities: A critique of hierarchial authority? *International Review of Sport Sociology*, **12**(4), 39-40.

Koppett, L. (1981). *Sports illusion, sports reality*. Boston: Houghton Mifflin.

McIntosh, P. (1983). Carnegie Golden Jubilee Lecture 1983: Physical education in the crystal ball. *Carnegie Research Papers*, **1**(5), 4-9.

Pooley, J.C. (1978). *An alternative model to reduce competitiveness in sports for youth: The case of soccer*. Paper presented at the AGM of the Canadian Soccer Association, St. John's, Newfoundland.

Pooley, J.C. (1981, April). *Drop-outs from sport: A case study of boys' age group soccer*. Paper presented at the American Alliance for Health, Physical Education, Recreation and Dance National Conference, Boston, MA.

Rehbein, E. (1984). *Physical education in schools in the Federal Republic of Germany*. Paper presented at the Fourth International Symposium for Comparative Physical Education, and Sport, Kiel, FRG.

Scanlan, T.K., & Passer, M.W. (1978). Factors related to competitive stress among male youth participants. *Medicine and Science in Sports*, **10**(2), 103-108.

Watson, G.G. (1977). Games, socialization and parental values: Social class differences in parental evaluation of Little League baseball. *International Review of Sport Sociology*, **12**(1), 17-48.

24

Developing A Sense of Competence in Children Through Game Modifications

G.S. Don Morris
CALIFORNIA STATE POLYTECHNIC UNIVERSITY
POMONA, CALIFORNIA, USA

> Pitting children against one another in games where they frantically compete for what only a few can have guarantees failure and rejection for many. Children's games and programs are in fact designed for elimination. Many ensure that one wins and everyone else loses, leaving sport "rejects" and "dropouts" to form the vast majority of our North American population. (Orlick, 1978, p. 3)

Orlick's description of activities common to most children is accurate indeed, for most games and sports in our culture are designed to exclude the majority of participants rather than include them. Sport programs also are designed to produce a single victor. As one observes the phenomenon of an enthralled crowd chanting, "We're number 1, we're number 1," one begins to understand our culture's passion to be the best by eliminating the most!

The Concept of Inclusion

This paper does not intend to discuss the virtues of losing, nor does it attempt to convince anyone that striving for "number 1" is deleterious to one's development. Others have done that for us. Rather, the focus will be upon the concept of *inclusion*: what, why and how. This is not to sell a product or an idea; rather, it is to share with those who value the concept of inclusion a procedure that not only grants permission, but also promises everyone a feeling of belonging, a feeling of control, a feeling that everyone truly does count! Inclusion means that skills of individuals are appropriately matched to the movement task and strategy demands of a game or sport. For this to occur, one needs to know how to adjust task and strategy demands; therefore, it becomes important to understand that the structure of any game or sport can be altered to accomodate every child within a single activity framework.

A reasonable question presents itself at this point: Why should we move towards inclusion? Our pluralistic society is home for many different people. Represented within our society are individuals possessing a multitude of skills and abilities. Similarly, each child brings to us his or her own personal needs and desires. These same children learn and develop skills at different rates. As a consequence, our educational programs are asked to address everyone's unique status within a single movement environment. Rather than direct our attention to one single group of children, we must accomodate a full spectrum of abilities. Reality for our teachers and coaches finds the program participants falling along an ever-lengthening skill continuum. Therefore, given our role and responsibility to ensure that every child has an equal opportunity for participation, inclusion of all becomes a mandate. With these beliefs firmly in place, it is incumbent upon us to create an environment that permits congruity between our educational intent and our educational action.

Inclusion occurs when a child's personal "comfort zone" is created within the movement environment. To accomplish this, teachers and coaches must be prepared to examine the design of their activity structures as well as their modes of presenting these structures to the sport participants. Such an examination permits coaches to create an environment that helps players to feel more confident about themselves as human movers. Confidence in moving is defined as "the sense or feeling of perceived competence in relation to perceived challenge in a movement situation" (Griffin & Keogh, 1979, p. 3). Furthermore, one can suggest that confidence is a mediating factor in determining whether a child chooses to participate in a movement activity and the degree to which he or she perseveres with the movement experience. Likewise, children's confidence levels are the outcome of participation in movement activities. A true confidence cycle exists. Promising work by individuals in physical education (Feltz, Landers, & Raeder, 1979; Feltz & Weiss, 1982; Morris, 1983; Weinberg, Gould, & Jackson, 1979) suggests that confidence and competence do indeed mediate behavior within a movement environment.

To help children accommodate this need to feel competent, Harter (1978, 1980) suggests that children have the opportunity to experience successful performance. Harter argues that these accomplishments produce intrinsic pleasure and joy within children, thus motivating them to continue with their participation. By creating a movement environment that permits all children to be included in the development of an internal sense of well being, one may find children are willing to attempt certain movement tasks and persevere with the task. This alone would permit all children to develop their maximum potential.

How does a coach or teacher design an environment founded upon this inclusion concept? First, one must be willing to examine the design of an activity. Morris' (1980; Morris & Stiehl, 1985) games analysis procedure provides us with a mechanism to alter, modify, and/or adapt to the *design* of any game or sport in order to accommodate individual differences. By applying this procedure with effective teaching methods, coaches and teachers can indeed create a comfort zone within the movement environment for all participants.

Games Analysis Procedure

Games analysis is a process-oriented approach to game modification. It can serve as a blueprint or guide for modifying any type of game or sport and consists of three basic steps.

1. The teacher or coach becomes acquainted with the games analysis model (see Figure 1). The model identifies the decisions that must be attended to when designing a game. Specifically, it can be seen in Figure 1 that decisions must be made about the number of players involved, organizational patterns, movements used, equipment, game limitations, and purposes.
2. With experience, a teacher or coach learns how to adjust one or more of the aforementioned decisions. For example, Figure 2 visually depicts the options available regarding decisions which can be made in formulating the movements to be used in games and sport.
3. The coach or teacher shifts the locus of control for game modifications by permitting alternative game or sport designs. This shift can rest with the coach or teacher and/or the participants themselves. (see Figure 3).

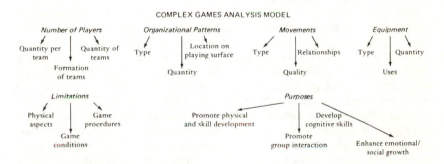

Figure 1. Games analysis model.

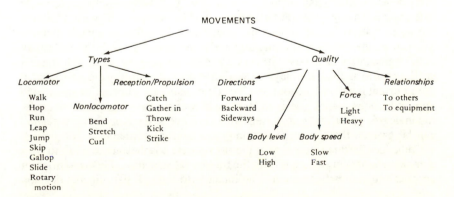

Figure 2. Movements in games analysis.

DECISION-MAKING

Game Designed By	Players	Organizational Pattern	Movement	Equipment	Limitations	Purpose
G.L.	G.L.	G.L.	G.L.	G.L.	G.L.	G.L.
G.L.	G.L.	G.L.	G.P.	G.L.	G.L./G.P.	G.L.
G.L./G.P.	G.L./G.P.	G.L.	G.P.	G.P.	G.L./G.P.	G.L.
G.P.	G.P.	G.P.	G.P.	G.P.	G.P.	G.P.

G.L. = game leader makes decision; G.L./G.P. = decisions are shared; G.P. = game players make decisions.

Figure 3. Decision-making in games analysis.

The third step is especially important because it allows the opportunity to program game designs. That is, anyone (the adult leader or the children involved) can design and then alter a game structure. Moreover, by permitting the participants to begin assuming responsibility for the development of a game, a new game awareness by children occurs. As the children gain control over their own sport design, a sense of competence and confidence emerges. This last procedural step is actualized when the participants assume control over all game design decisions.

Step three, then, permits children to actively make decisions and to assume responsibility for the game/sport design. Thus, the locus of control shifts toward the participants. This shift in locus of control is important because recent research (Morris & Dufour, 1984) provided preliminary data indicating that children's self-confidence and feelings of competence are positively affected when they are permitted to gain control of their game environment. Much more work is needed, however, before more definitive statements can be made.

Employing the game analysis approach permits the game designer to alter the degree of difficulty for each game task. This can occur for each game participant, thereby accommodating each participant's developmental skill level. Indeed, a match can now exist between game requirements and an individual's ability to perform. For example, let us assume that the children's movement skill level in basketball precludes them from displaying efficient evasive dribbling behavior when confronted in the back court by several defenders. A simple rule change denying back-court guarding would be in order. Likewise, changing the size of the ball, the geographic boundaries, and the number of players allowed on the court at one time might also permit more children to display better ball control. The possibilities are endless and are the result of a coach's willingness to analyze the players' needs and alter the activity design to match their current level of functioning. Over time, using the concept of successive approximations with the design of each subsequent activity gradually increasing in degree of difficulty consistent with the players' development, all players can be granted the opportunity to improve their performance.

Embedded in this discussion is the notion that coaches are willing to play a game in a manner different from the traditional structure. This is a different approach to games instruction. The intent is to help all participants develop to their maximum ability. Coaches simply have to ask themselves a series of questions as they compare each child's ability to the description of the game found within the games analysis model. In other words, some preconceived game or practice activity construct is initially created. The coach, through a series of questions focused upon the game model, compares his or her players' performance to the demands of the game. For example, soccer practice activity, by design, calls for the children to "hold their positions" while the ball advances down the field. The resultant action, however, finds 20 players herded about one ball in play. Is the problem with the children's desire to directly move the ball? Do the players have the physical skill to dribble the ball down the field? Is the ball too large, too small for the children to control? As anyone can now observe, a series of questions regarding various categorical decisions within the games analysis model must be asked. A coach's response(s) dictates the nature of the activity adaptation.

The games analysis procedure is not the panacea for the inclusion concept. Rather, it represents but one approach that has been found to be successful. It must be accompanied with the appropriate teaching methods if the entire environment is to meet all the children's needs.

Conclusion

In summary, ample evidence points toward sport as a human construct that promotes many different kinds of personal interaction. Furthermore, evidence abounds that suggests participation alone in these activities does not necessarily result in favorable interactions for all involved. Children are emerging human beings who do not have the benefit of our life experiences. However, they are learning, growing, and acquiring skills that permit them to interact favorably within a society. Games and sport represent a small part of their world, and yet much can be learned by them as they participate. If one believes that part of childhood ought to be spent gaining a sense of self, gaining a sense of competence, and gaining skills that will allow us all to coexist, then our game and sport environments ought to help all children, not just those who motorically excel. As John Denver (1982) recently observed,

> It's about time we realize it
>   we're all in this together
> It's about time we find out
>   it's all of us or none
> It's about time we recognize it
>   these changes in the weather
> It's about time
>   it's about changes
>   and it's about time.

Maybe it's about time we ask why we do what we do with our children's games.

References

Denver, J. (1982). *It's about time* (song lyrics & recording). New York: RCA Records.

Feltz, D.L., Landers, D.M., & Raeder, V. (1979). Enhancing self-efficacy in a high-avoidance motor task: A comparison of modeling technique. *Journal of Sport Psychology*, **1**, 112-122.

Feltz, D.L., & Weiss, M. (1982). Developing self-efficacy through sport. *Journal of Physical Education, Recreation and Dance*, **53**, 23-26.

Griffin, N.S., & Keogh, J. (1979, April). *A model for movement confidence*. Paper presented at the Iowa Symposium on Motor Development, Iowa City, IA.

Harter, S. (1978). Effectance motivation reconsidered. *Human Development*, **21**, 34-64.

Harter, S. (1980). The development of competence motivation in the mastery of cognitive and physical skills: Is there still a place for joy? In G.C. Roberts & D.M. Landers (Eds.), *Psychology of motor behavior and sport* (pp. 3-29). Champaign, IL: Human Kinetics.

Morris, G.S. (1980). *How to change the games children play* (2nd ed.). Minneapolis: Burgess.

Morris, G.S. (1983). *Application of games analysis: Its impact upon elementary children's confidence*. Unpublished manuscript, California Polytechnic University–Pomona.

Morris, G.S., & Dufour, K. (1984). *Games analysis: Can children's sense of competence really be modified through games?* Unpublished manuscript, California Polytechnic University–Pomona.

Morris G.S., & Stiehl, J. (1985). *Physical education—From intent to action*. Columbus: Charles E. Merrill.

Orlick, T. (1978). *The cooperative sports and games book*. New York: Pantheon Books.

Weinberg, R.S., Gould, D., & Jackson, A. (1979). Expectations and performance: An empirical test of Bandura's self-efficacy theory. *Journal of Sport and Psychology*, **1**, 320-331.

25

The Development Model in Canadian Sport

Terry A. Valeriote
COACHING ASSOCIATION OF CANADA
OTTAWA, ONTARIO, CANADA

> Sport is the continuum from the local club level to the national Team at the apex of its discipline. Success at the highest level depends upon the strength of the whole continuum. (Canadian Federal White Paper on Sport, 1979)

Since 1969, Canadian sport has been fortunate to receive financial support from both federal and provincial governments. At the federal level, this support has enabled approximately 65 national sport and recreation associations to base themselves in one central location, Ottawa—the nation's capital. Similar full-time associations with paid employees have been created at the provincial level, but in varying degrees, depending upon finances. For example, the Province of Ontario has a large sport budget and is able to assist sport to employ many full-time executive and technical directors. In contrast, the Province or Prince Edward Island, with a very small sport budget, has relatively few full-time people working in any sport.

In essence, an administrative structure has been created. This administrative structure, however, does not mean that a sport system exists. An essential element is missing, namely a federal/provincial development plan to determine how to produce and deliver sport programs to our youth participants. The plan would give clear direction to administrators, coaches and parents as to the best program to offer participants as they proceeded through sport from the beginning to elite level. It would enable everyone to play by the "same ground rules" to maximize individual participation, learning, and growth.

The creation of a development model implies that because of patterns of growth and development, participants in sport have different needs at various stages of development. In the development model, the appropriate skills, modifications of the game, degree of competition, and other developmental activities for participants are set forth for each stage of development. The model thus provides a blueprint for action for all groups involved in the development and delivery of sport skills and knowledge, including administrators, athletes, coaches, parents, and officials.

Among other things, a development model suggests alternatives to the ways in which we now develop and implement sport programs. For example, instead of developing coaching education programs based upon a level system (e.g., Levels 1 to 5), which is still a general approach because a level can apply to coaches working with any age group, we might develop a system geared specifically to developmental stages of the participants, namely, children, adolescents, and adults. Furthermore, a development model uses a holistic approach which addresses the physical, mental, emotional, and social needs of participants. Consequently, in children's sport, which is a developmental phase and not a time for emphasizing winning, children would be exposed to fun, relaxation, and concentration procedures. These skills are required not only for future success in sport, but also for success in coping with life. Finally, although research in the sport sciences often takes a generalist approach, the application of the development model directs research specifically to children, adolescents, and adults; this is a more appropriate approach for the organized delivery of sport skills: For example, what strength-training programs are appropriate for children as compared to adolescents and adults?

Current Status of Development Models

The first development model was produced in a pilot project with volleyball. Field hockey and basketball now also have development models, and organizers of soccer, alpine skiing, rowing, and others are starting to create such models. Each of these models addresses various phases of development starting from the child level, 6 years of age, to the mature participant, 55 years of age. For each phase, specific recommendations are made to coaches, administrators, and parents as to the appropriate skills (physical, cognitive, and social psychological) to be learned by participants, the type of games and competitions in which they should engage, and other activities that would meet the total development of the participant.

The federal government has also produced a document entitled, *Growing in Sport, a Handbook for Creating a Sport Development Perspective*. This document has broadened the concept of the development model by including both recreational and competitive streams and providing guidelines for participants from 3 to 53 years of age. It states,

> There are many inconsistencies and contradictions both within and between sport programs in Canada today; in addition, many of these programs have emerged with a single emphasis on high performance. As a result of this emphasis, many Canadian athletes, both amateur and professional, lack good basic skills and techniques and many participants with a great deal of potential have dropped out of sport early. These "dropouts" have not enjoyed the social and health benefits of a lifetime of participation in sport, nor have they gone on to represent Canada as high performance athletes. In essence, they did not have the opportunity to mature within a sport program which encouraged optimal social and physical experiences through sport participation. (Kent & Strachan, 1984, p. 2)

Sport Canada and its consultants will soon be working with sport in Canada towards the development and implementation of development models. The next step will be the initiation of a cross-country promotional campaign similar to our successful "ParticipAction" campaign for fitness in which the values of a healthy and developmental sport environment are presented.

The Future of Development Models

The creation of development models is thus gradually increasing. However, because many people at all levels of participation are concerned with immediate success, gold medals and being number one, persistence is needed to keep the concept in the forefront. Constant support and lobbying from all groups in the sport sector are required. For example, people in the university system have long written about the ills in youth sport. It would be extremely useful if their professional organizations went the extra step and created organized lobby groups to place pressure on any institutions (governments, sport organizations, recreation departments) that ignored or violated the development principles of youth.

International sport organizations might provide direction by recommending youth development schemes, based upon needs of participants, for their sport. This recommendation was emphasized by the German Sports Federation in a statement of principles regarding children in competitive sport. The Federation states,

> With this Statement of Principles the German Sports Federation wishes to underscore the positive effects of children's competitive sport by pointing out at the same time the necessary limitations. The German Sports Federation and its member organizations will push for the acceptance of the Statement in the rules of competition and the organization of training for children's sport. It will also concern itself with getting these principles recognized by the international federations. (Children in Competitive Sport, 1983, p. 44)

The International Olympic Committee might show leadership by establishing reasonable minimum age requirements for participants, particularly those in sports such as women's gymnastics and figure skating. If athletes are allowed to compete at too young an age, a worldwide ripple effect that results in highly competitive situations for the very young is created. This third recommendation is particularly important. Rushall and Lavoie (1983) have cited examples of sports (e.g., swimming, track and field) in which one country's success at the Olympics prompted other countries to model their training programs. They state,

> An underlying message that has been embraced . . . is that the "harder" one trains, the better will be the resultant performace . . . . What is important for a nation's sporting development is that all potentially good athletes are retained in the system long enough to realize their potential. Currently, this doesn't seem to be done since hard work eliminates those who do not have anything but the toughest work tolerance capacities. The "hard work ethic" is still eliminating many potentially good athletes from participating at the highest levels of sport. (p. 4)

The concept of a sport development model is not new. Fortunately, in Canada, some action is occurring. There is no doubt that guidelines need to be developed and implemented. Equally important are the courage, persistence, and organization to tackle the real problem, namely, the sport system itself or, more appropriately, the lack of such a system.

References

Children in Competitive Sport. (1983). *International Journal of Physical Education*, **20**(3), 44.

Kent, J., & Strachan, D. (1984). *Growing in sport, a handbook for creating a sport development perspective*. Ottawa: Fitness and Amateur Sport.

Rushall, B., & Lavoie, N. (1983, May). A Call to Re-focus Serious Sport Training. *Sports,* pp.3.

Canadian Federal White Paper on Sport. (1979). Fitness and Amateur Sport Branch, Government of Canada, Ottawa.

26

Game Modifications for Youth Sport: A Practitioner's View

Monta Potter
EUGENE SPORTS PROGRAM
EUGENE, OREGON, USA

As an associate director of the Eugene Sports Program (Eugene, Oregon), one of the major challenges that my colleagues and I continually face is the question of how to modify sports in order to maximize the success and confidence of our young participants. The purpose of this paper is to address the issue of game and sport modifications from the perspective of the administration behind the success of organized programs. To achieve this purpose, the background of the Eugene Sports program, modifications implemented by the program, and barriers to modifying children's sports will be discussed.

Background of the Eugene Sports Program

The Eugene Sports Program was formed in 1953 as the Eugene Boys Athletic Association (EBAA) when a group of 10 fathers formed an organization so that their sons would have a chance to compete in youth sports. In that first year, 90 5th and 6th grade boys participated in the sports of basketball and baseball.

By 1957, the EBAA had grown to include more than 2,000 boys, and a part-time staff was hired to handle recruiting, registration, scheduling, and organization. The association became a year-round program with the addition of football in 1960.

Girls were allowed as participants in 1974, and the EBAA was thereafter called the Eugene Sports Program (ESP). Fall soccer and volleyball were added in the 1975 program and spring soccer was added in 1981. In 1983, ESP enrolled 9,100 boys and girls in the total program, comprising 725 teams across all sports and including 1,151 volunteer coaches. Now, after 31 years of operation, ESP is self-governed by a Board of Directors who are elected from and by the volunteer coaches and an 11-member, full-time staff.

Three major components form the basic philosophy which guides the operation of six sports: These are (a) required playing time for every youth in each contest; (b) all participate—no cuts; and, (c) no all-star or out-of-town competition. Organized competitions do include, however, championship games, end-of-season tournaments, and placement on A, AA, or AAA teams based on try-outs for teams.

Modifications Implemented by ESP

The four categories in which sports are modified for children and youth are equipment, dimensions of the playing area, length of the contest, and rules changes in particular sports. A summary of the changes employed by ESP in these specific categories by sport is displayed in Table 1.

In general, equipment changes include reduced ball size and lower barriers (hoops in basketball and nets in volleyball). In addition, T-ball is enjoyed by the first and second grade children to ensure maximum batting success with this "closed skill" version of the games of baseball and softball.

In some cases, dimensions of the playing area are reduced as well as restraining lines for particular skills such as serving in volleyball, shooting free throws in basketball, and pitching in baseball or softball. In all of the sports, the length of the contest is shortened until at least the middle school grades. Finally, various rules changes are implemented to meet the needs of particular sports, for example, weight limits in tackle football, no-press defense in basketball, and no stealing in baseball and softball.

Barriers to Modifications in Children's Sport

Many youth sport researchers would like to see additional changes in children's sport. For example, there is a good deal of discussion about implementing game modifications which would control the over-emphasis placed on keeping score and declaring winners in youth sport. These are worthy objectives, but are often difficult to implement. I would like to share, from a practitioner's point of view, what I believe to be barriers which limit the implementation of those and other changes throughout the entire system of youth sport.

The first barrier is what could be labelled, "It's always been done that way." From our experience, people generally oppose change. Parents want their children to experience what they experienced themselves. We frequently hear phrases such as, "I was able to hit a pitched ball when I was 8 years old, so I want my son to have this opportunity." Youth sport agencies, most of which are nonprofit and run largely by volunteers, must be responsive to

Table 1. Game modifications used in the Eugene Sports Program

Sport	Equipment	Dimensions of playing area	Length of contest	Rules of the game
Volleyball	Smaller & softer ball Lower nets	Court size is the same Shorter serving lines	Shortened (sudden victory)	
Soccer	Smaller ball (grades 1 to 6)	Smaller (length and width)	Grades 1 to 2: two 20-min halves Grades 3 to 4: two 25-min halves Grades 5 to 6: two 30-min halves	Less players per side; Corner kicks moved in
Basketball	Smaller ball Grades 3 to 4: 27" circumference Grades 5 to 6: junior size Grades 7 to 8: regulation size	Smaller court Closer free-throw lines	Grades 3 to 5: running quarters Grades 6 to 8: stopped clock	Alternate possessions (no jump ball) No zone defense until 8th grade No full-court press until 8th grade
Flag Football/ Tackle Football	Junior size football	Regulation size	Shortened	No fumble recovery (ball is dead) Weight limits (tackle) Grade 7: 75 to 160 lbs Grade 8: 105 or more lbs
Baseball/ Softball	T-ball for grades 1 to 2 (also use Incrediball)	Shortened base paths for grades 1 to 8 Shorter pitching distances	Grades 1 to 2: 8 innings Grades 3 to 6: 6 innings Grades 7 to 9: 7 innings	No stealing until 7th grade T-ball: no strikeouts; bat around the order

volunteer boards of directors and to the people who pay for participation. Change does come but often at a "snail's pace." For instance, the Eugene Sports Program operated for 20 years before a change in policy allowed girls to participate as well as boys.

A second barrier to change is in the use of existing facilities. Our organization is dependent in all its sport programs on the facilities and equipment of the local school districts. When soccer goals are placed in the ground 100 yards apart, it is difficult to modify the size of the playing surface. Shorter basket heights in basketball and lower nets in volleyball necessitate changes where equipment is not always adjustable. Last year's purchase of 100 regulation size soccer balls may make a modification of ball size economically unlikely for this season.

The last barrier is what I perceive as a barrier between researchers and administrators. The growing amount of research being conducted in youth sport has no reliable medium of communication between those who study youth sport issues and those who run the programs. Information is largely inaccessible unless the program is in or near a university town that has good community involvement. This lack of access to information is partly the responsibility of youth sport administrators who must begin asking questions and seeking the answers.

These barriers imply that change in youth sport will not come quickly. Certainly, not everything needs to change. The point is, however, that before researchers or governing boards implore agency-sponsored programs to make drastic modifications in their sports, the barriers to change should be considered. It is the responsibility of practitioners in youth sports, including parents, coaches, administrators, and researchers, to join hands and together formulate ideas which are not only appropriate for the developmental needs of our young participants, but also realistic within the operating structure of youth sport programs.

PART VII

Elite Young Runners: An Interdisciplinary Perspective

Clearly, great advances have been made in our understanding of young athletes and the effects of sport participation on children. But to keep moving forward, further research is needed, especially longitudinal, multidisciplinary research. Although complex physical, psychological, and social effects of athletic competition on children are best understood by this kind of research, longitudinal, multidisciplinary research is rare and difficult to conduct.

However, the Youth Sports Institute housed at Michigan State University has initiated multidisciplinary, longitudinal studies on young athletes in an effort to understand the effects of athletic competition on children. Specifically, a team of over 35 investigators from the Departments of Health and Physical Education, Food Science and Human Nutrition, and the Colleges of Osteopathic and Human Medicine have collaborated to design several 5-year longitudinal studies of children involved in the competitive sports of long-distance running, wrestling, and ice hockey.

This part of the proceedings includes papers reporting the status of the data collected in the first year of one of these studies—the interdisciplinary assessment of elite young distance runners. Chapter 27 begins with an introduction to the study, while chapters 28 through 36 discuss parts of the study including the areas of young runners' training habits, psychological characteristics, dietary habits, physiological and perceptual responses to work exhaustion, anthropometric assessments of body size and shape, serum alkaline phosphatase activity, temporal and kinematic characteristics of gait patterns, serum lipid and lipoprotein levels, and motor ability measures. Comparisons on these measures were made between the sample of young male and female runners and matched male and female control subjects. Finally, the last paper gives a summary of the first year findings.

27

Introduction to an Interdisciplinary Assessment of Competition on Elite Young Distance Runners

Vern Seefeldt
MICHIGAN STATE UNIVERSITY
EAST LANSING, MICHIGAN, USA

Peggy Steig
EASTERN MICHIGAN UNIVERSITY
YPSILANTI, MICHIGAN, USA

Intensive training has been an accepted procedure for adults who wish to excel in competitive sports. The revolution in training programs during the 1960s, which emphasized greater intensities and durations of activity than had previously been advocated or condoned, now pervades the athletic experiences of high school youth and elementary school children. Despite the short history of intensive training programs in children's sports, there are indications that both beneficial and detrimental effects can accrue from such experiences (Martens, 1978; Orlick & Botterill, 1975; Sayre, 1975).

In the absence of sound scientific evidence upon which to construct training programs for children, individuals in charge of such programs have relied upon experimental and experiential information obtained from adults. Reports that children respond to exercise stress in much the same way as adults on certain physiological parameters may encourage the extrapolation of these results to other biological, as well as psychological and biomechanical functions. The assumption that children thrive on adult training regimes must be questioned in many sports, but especially in running, where much of the activity is of an individual nature without the constant guidance of a qualified adult supervisor. Under unsupervised conditions, a young athlete may assume that greater dedication and more intensive training will enhance performance, unmindful of the limitations that nature sets on the various functions of a developing organism.

The present investigation was conducted for the purpose of examining the effects of competitive-distance running on children and youth. Specifically, this assessment was conducted on the premise that if beneficial and/or detrimental effects of long-distance running were measurable, they would be most apparent in children whose training and performance were markedly different from those of their age peers. For this reason, the runners were identified as those whose performance consistently placed them among the winners of races for their age and gender.

The investigators are aware that sampling the extremes of a distribution ignores the possibility that equally beneficial effects may occur in runners who did not possess the credentials of this sample, or conversely, that detrimental effects may have caused numerous children to drop out of running because of various undesirable experiences. Nevertheless, the findings in this study are likely to be good indicators of changes that occur when children train and compete intensively in long-distance running.

Sample

Runners

Boys and girls were selected on the basis of their performance in races held in Michigan during the 1981 racing season. Results of races, printed in the *Michigan Runner* (May-August, 1981), were scrutinized. Runners, within the age restriction of 9 to 15 years, who consistently placed within the top five finishers in races of 10 Km or over for their age and gender were identified and contacted about becoming subjects in the study. These criteria isolated 13 boys and 15 girls, all of whom agreed to participate in the study on a longitudinal basis.

Of the 28 runners, 27 resided in Michigan, and one subject, who routinely ran in the Michigan-based races, lived in Ohio. All of the boys and 12 of the 15 girls were Caucasian; three girls (sisters) were of Spanish-American descent. Seven of the runners were members of a track club where they trained under the direction of a professional coach; all others trained on their own or ran under the supervision of a parent. The age-gender distribution of the runners is shown in Table 1.

Controls

The control subjects were randomly selected from a large pool of participants in the Motor Performance Study, an ongoing program at Michigan State University designed to teach motor skills to children who function within the normal range in mental and physical skills. Motor skills tests have indicated that children in the Motor Performance Study do perform within the range expected of children in the United States (Branta, Haubenstricker, & Seefeldt, 1984). Each of the control subjects was randomly drawn from age appropriate subsamples that had been established by 6-month increments from those participants

Table 1. Subjects classified according to chronological age and gender

Chronological age (CA)		Boys N = 26		Girls N = 27	
Year	Range (months)	Runners	Controls	Runners	Controls
10	115 to 126	2	2	1	1
11	127 to 138	1	1	2	2
12	139 to 150	4	4	2	1
13	151 to 162	4	3	3	1
14	163 to 174	2	3	5	4
15	175 to 186	0	0	2	3
Total N		13	13	15	12
Mean CA (months)		148.2	146.4	154.9	158.4

in the Motor Performance Study who were within 1 $SD \pm M$ in standing height for their age, according to growth records provided by the American Medical Association (1975). Although each runner was initially matched with a control by gender, age and height, one child in the control sample declined to be tested while on site, another could not complete all the tests, and a third refused to permit the venous blood sample to be taken during the treadmill test. These three subjects were excluded from additional involvement, thereby contributing to the disparity in numbers between the runners and the control group.

Slight differences in numbers of runners and controls will be reported in the papers which follow this introductory paper. These differences are due to the within-test disposition of the subjects and were unavoidable under the conditions of the testing procedure. Chronologically, the female controls are oldest ($M = 158.4$ months), followed by the female runners ($M = 154.9$ months), followed by the male runners ($M = 148.2$ months), while the male controls were youngest, with a mean age of 146.4 months (see Table 1). Because both the within-gender group mean differences (males = 1.8 months; females = 3.5 months) and the between-gender group mean differences (4.3 months) are small, the chronological ages of the subjects should not be a contributing factor to the results.

Method

Although the comprehensive battery of tests administered to the runners and controls is not completely represented by the following papers, the total battery is shown in Table 2 so that readers may be aware of the array of tests conducted within a 1-day period. Due to extensive travel distances on the part of some subjects, all tests were administered to all subjects on the same day. Subjects fasted during the evening and arrived at the laboratory early the following morning. Immediately after a blood sample was taken, they ate breakfast and proceeded through the test battery on a random basis. The only restriction to the random order of testing was that rest intervals were imposed between

Table 2. Battery of tests and assessments administered to runners and control subjects

Test battery items
Anthropometry (47 bodily sites)
Blood sample (KDA profile and serum lipids)
Cinematographic recording of gaits
Densitometry
Electro- and echocardiograph
Hand-wrist x-ray (biological maturity)
History of illness and injuries
Motor performance battery (8 tests)
Muscular endurance (Cybex)
Nutritional profile
Physical examination
Psychological profile
Reaction time and movement time
Review of activity and competitive history
Treadmill test of work capacity

tests that required an exhaustive effort. Protocols and conditions of testings are described within the papers that are specific to the parameters under investigation. All runners were tested near the end of their competitive season to take advantage of the accumulated training effect. All controls were tested within a 3-month period after the runners had been tested. With the exception of the delay in testing dates for the control subjects, all other conditions for runners and controls were identical within the limitations of human variation at the test sites.

The next few chapters present information about the similarities and differences in physiological, psychological, motor, and biomechanical parameters between the male and female runners and the matched sets of male and female control subjects who participated in this study. The significant results obtained on many of these assessments, despite the small sample size, indicate that children who train and compete as long-distance runners are markedly different than their nonrunning age peers. At this time, we cannot determine whether these differences were caused by the specific nature of the running program or by the runner's predisposition to this activity. The present study will continue over several years, however, and with subjects of this age range will permit a more precise answer to this question in subsequent years.

References

American Medical Association. (1975). *Height weight interpretation folder for boys-girls*. Chicago, IL: AMA.

Branta, C., Haubenstricker, J., & Seefeldt, V. (1984). Age changes in motor skills during childhood and adolescence. In R.L. Terjung (Ed.)., *Exercise and sport science reviews* (Vol. 12, pp. 465-520). Lexington, MA: Collamore Press.

Martens, R. (1978). *Joy and sadness in children's sports*. Champaign, IL: Human Kinetics.

Michigan Runner, **3** (1981, May, June, July, August).

Orlick, T., & Botterill, C. (1975). *Every kid can win*. Chicago: Nelson-Hall.

Sayre, B. (1975). The need to ban competition sports involving preadolescent children. *Pediatrics*, **55**, 564.

28

Training and Racing Involvement of Elite Young Runners

Paul G. Vogel
MICHIGAN STATE UNIVERSITY
EAST LANSING, MICHIGAN, USA

Large numbers of children are currently involved in long-distance road racing. Although running has been called a family activity (Sheehan, 1983), many of the children who participate are engaged in extensive training and racing schedules. Lopez and Pruett (1982) report incidences of 6-year-old children running 10 to 15 miles per day and up to 80 miles per week while training for marathon races. The fact that children between the ages of 4 to 16 years have performance times listed for the marathon also suggests that many of them are engaged in extensive training (Young & Hejda, 1978).

Long-distance training appears to elicit desirable cardiovascular adaptations similar to those which occur in adults (Brown, Hanover, & Decter, 1972; Chausow, Riner, & Boileau, 1984) and does not appear to have long-term negative effects on the cardiovascular system (Rarick, 1978). Many physicians, educators, and exercise physiologists believe that running in moderation is not contraindicated, but they voice concern about heavy, prolonged distance running (Gordon, 1983-84; Taunton, 1980).

Among the voiced concerns is the way in which bone adapts to exercise and its vulnerability to injury. Although exercise may support normal or hypertrophic bone growth (Alekseev, 1977; Malina, 1969), the borderline between too much and too little stress has not been defined (Caine & Lindner, 1984). According to Aegerter & Kirkpatrick (1975), bone structure is altered in accordance with function. It also appears that bone sacrifices its growth zone to retain function in the presence of strong continuous forces (Adams, 1976; Malina, 1969 & 1972).

The vulnerability of the young runner to injury is increased with incremented training loads. Reportedly, maturing bone is especially susceptible to trauma and chronic overload, which in turn is associated with stress fracture, inflammation, and epiphysitis (American Academy of Pediatrics, 1981; Larson, 1973; Lascari, 1980; Malina, 1969; Peterson & Peterson, 1972). Also, the epiphyseal site has been estimated to be 2 to 5 times weaker than the surrounding fibrous capsule and joint ligaments (Ehrlich & Strain, 1979; Schwab, 1977). This weakness has important implications for complete and/or balanced growth.

Lopez (1982) argued that another important reason why a child is more vulnerable to overuse injury than adults is that the ratio of contractile muscle strength and tendon strength to bone length is lower because bone growth preceeds the development of muscular strength. In addition, there have been no longitudinal studies investigating the effects of long-term running on the incidence of degenerative disease of the involved joints (*Physician and Sportsmedicine*, 1982).

Interest in the well-being of young runners in light of these concerns has prompted many groups involved with running to develop policy statements designed to protect young participants. The American Academy of Pediatrics (1982) made no recommendation regarding how much total mileage is appropriate, but indicated that "Under no circumstances should a full marathon be attempted by immature youths" (p 86). To deter the excessive involvement of children in running, *Runner's World* (1983) has refused to accept or maintain marathon records for runners under 12 years of age and advocates maintaining no records for children under the age of 5. Also, a position statement from the International Athletes Association Federations Medical Committee on Long-Distance Training and Competition for Young Children declared,

> Training and competition for long distance track and road running events should not be encouraged. Up to the age of 12 it is suggested that not more than 800 m be run in competition . . . a maximum of 3,000 m for 14-year-olds. That marathon races are not open to boys and girls under the age of 18 years seems eminently sensible to the committee. (*Sports Medicine Bulletin*, 1983)

According to Baxter (1983), some European countries prohibit runners who are less than 16 to race any distance beyond 3,000 m.

Some individuals have placed the blame for early burnout on running too many miles at young ages. However, Baxter (1983) suggested the real reason may be more psychological than physiological. He stated that an overemphasis on winning, rather than focusing on improvement, a sense of accomplishment, and/or personal bests in effort and performance could lead to premature dropout. Sheehan (1983) agreed, noting that with competition, children will run too many miles, run too many races, and will deny that they are hurting and need to stop.

Because both beneficial and detrimental effects of long-distance running on children are supported, the need to clearly identify and determine the degree to which children are involved in long-distance training and racing and, more importantly, to determine the effects of such involvement is eminent. Micheli highlighted this need with this incisive statement: "We are essentially experimenting with whole groups of children" (Lincoln, 1982, p. 55). This need to document involvement is further underscored by the fact that current published policy statements have been designed to protect children from an overemphasis on running long distances in races rather than cautioning them about both racing and training distances. Therefore the purpose of this aspect of the young runners study was to clearly describe the degree to which children are involved in long-distance training and racing. Although this paper is limited to the initial task of describing training and racing activities, subsequent papers will report the effects of such involvement.

Method

Training and racing information was collected on 28 elite young runners (13 male and 15 female) as part of the young runners' study (Seefeldt, 1986) The data were collected using a combination of log, questionnaire, and interview methods. Subjects, with the assistance of their parents, coaches, and/or training records, completed a questionnaire which included annual estimates of the number of weeks involved in training, the average number of training days per week, minutes per day, and miles per day. Estimates of exercise intensity and involvement in other sports were also obtained but are beyond the scope of this paper and are, therefore, not included. Similar information was collected relative to the number of races run at distances ranging from .8 km (.5 miles) to 42.3 km (26.2 miles).

Results and Discussion

The mean values reported by age and gender describe both the training and racing involvement of runners in the 7- to 14-year-old age range. The mean number of years involved in racing for the 7- to 8-, 9- to 10-, 11- to 12-, and 13- to 14-year-old age groups was 1.75, 2.14, 3.11, and 3.75 years, respectively. Standard deviations for these same age groups were 1.05, 1.12, 1.5, and 1.83 years.

The weeks per year, days per week, km per day, and km per year are reported in Table 1 for females and males across each of the previously listed age groups. With one exception in the days per week of training in the 7- to-8 year age group, females were much more involved in training than the males.

For the 7- to 8-year-old age group, the females' 241 km per year is 209% greater than the mean distance of 78 km per year run by the males. In the 9- to 10-, 11- to 12-, and 13- to 14-year-old age groups, the females' training involvement is 64, 83, and 108% greater, respectively.

In racing, a similar pattern of involvement emerged. As can be seen in Table 2, the females ran more races and logged more race kilometers than the males in all age divisions except in the 7- to 8-year-old group. In this age group, the females ran more races, but the distances were somewhat shorter; thus, in total kilometers raced, they ran slightly less (10%) total kilometers than the males. In the 9- to 10-, 11- to 12-, and 13- to 14-year-old age groups the

Table 1. Mean values for weekly, daily, and yearly involvement in training for young male and female runners

	Age Groups (years)							
	7 to 8		9 to 10		11 to 12		13 to 14	
Group	n	M	n	M	n	M	n	M
Females								
Weeks/Year	5	25.2	18	36.6	21	40.3	11	42.8
Days/Week	5	2.7	18	5.0	21	5.2	11	5.4
Km/day	3	3.5	11	6.1	15	7.3	11	8.1
Km/year		241.0		1119.0		1517.0		1859.0
Males								
Weeks/Year	7	13.1	16	32.4	17	30.3	8	32.3
Days/Week	7	3.1	17	4.1	17	4.6	8	4.4
Km/day	7	2.0	15	5.1	16	6.0	7	6.3
Km/year		78.0		684.0		830.0		892.0
Combined								
Weeks/Year	12	18.2	34	32.6	38	35.8	19	38.4
Days/Week	12	2.9	35	4.5	38	4.9	19	4.9
Km/day	10	2.4	26	5.5	31	6.6	18	7.8
Km/year		127.0		803.0		1157.0		1453.0

Table 2. Mean number of races run (RR) and kilometers raced (KR) annually within six race distance categories

	Age groups (years)							
Distances	7 to 8		9 to 10		11 to 12		13 to 14	
Raced (k)	RR	KR	RR	KR	RR	KR	RR	KR
Females[a]								
.8 to 3.2	4.5	8.5	14.8	29.8	14.1	33.1	15.1	34.4
4.8 to 10.0	2.3	20.2	11.2	88.4	18.0	143.9	29.4	229.8
11.3 to 16.0	.5	6.5	1.1	14.0	2.3	33.0	2.5	33.4
20.0 to 24.1	0	0	.6	12.1	1.3	28.6	.8	17.7
30.0 to 32.3	0	0	1.4	3.8	.1	1.5	.3	9.6
42.3	0	0	0	0	.2	8.0	.1	3.2
Total	7.3	35.1	29.1	146.6	36.0	248.1	48.2	328.1
Males[b]								
.8 to 3.2	2.8	6.3	8.5	19.8	8.0	19.2	8.5	20.8
4.8 to 10.0	2.0	15.6	8.7	68.0	10.4	89.4	10.4	80.0
11.3 to 16.0	.6	9.0	1.0	14.7	1.0	14.4	2.0	30.7
20.0 to 24.1	.3	7.7	.8	18.7	7.3	16.7	1.1	25.6
30.0 to 32.3	0	0	.2	6.1	0	0	.4	11.5
42.3	0	0	.1	3.0	.1	0	.1	5.2
Total	5.7	38.6	19.3	130.3	26.8	145.3	22.5	173.8
Combined Totals	6.5	36.9	24.2	138.5	31.4	196.7	35.4	251.0

[a] n = 4, 18, 21, and 13 for ages 7 to 8, 9 to 10, 11 to 12, and 13 to 14 respectively.
[b] n = 9, 15, 15 and 8 for ages 7 to 8, 9 to 10, 11 to 12, and 13 to 14 respectively.

Table 3. Mean yearly distances run (km) for males and females involved in training and racing

Group	Age groups (years)			
	7 to 8	9 to 10	11 to 12	13 to 14
Females				
Training	241	1119	1517	1859
Racing	35	147	248	328
Total	276	1266	1765	2187
Males				
Training	78	684	830	892
Racing	39	130	145	174
Total	117	814	975	1066
Combined				
Training	160	902	1174	1376
Racing	37	139	197	251
Total	197	1041	1371	1627

number of kilometers raced by females was 13, 71, and 89% greater than the kilometers raced by the males, respectively.

As would be expected, based upon the training and racing involvement data (see Table 3), the combined running and racing data indicate that the female runners were more involved in every age group. The magnitude of the difference is 136, 56, 81, and 105% for the 7- to 8-, 9- to 10-, 11- to 12-, and 13- to 14-year-old age groups, respectively.

Based upon these data, it is apparent that very young children are involved in high levels of training and racing, with the involvement of the females exceeding that of the males. The data appear to be consistent with the data reported by Feltz & Albrecht (1986) which show a psychological tendency of the females in this investigation to be more committed to running than their male peers The mean training values reported above are far below the extreme case reported by Lopez and Pruett (1982) but are comparable to the 25 miles per week of training that Butts (1982) reported for female high school runners in their early teens.

References

Adams, J.E. (1976). The Little League survey: The Eugene study. *American Journal of Sportsmedicine*, **4**(5), 207–209.

Aegerter, E., & Kirkpatrick, J.A. (1975). *Orthopedic diseases* (4th ed.). Philadelphia: Saunders.

Alekseev, B.A. (1977). The influence of skiing races on the hand and foot skeleton of young sportsmen. *Archives d'Anatomie, d'Histologie et d'Embryologie*, **72**, 35-39.

American Academy of Pediatrics (1981). Injuries to young athletes. *Physician and Sportsmedicine*, **9**(2), 107–110.

American Academy of Pediatrics. (1982). Risks in long-distance running for children. *The Physician and Sportsmedicine*, **10**(8), 82, 86.

Baxter, K. (1983, November). When children are pushed to run too soon. *Runner's World*, pp. 90–92.

Brown, C.H., Hanover, J.R., & Decter, M.F. (1972). The effects of cross-country running on pre-adolescent girls. *Medicine and Science in Sports*, **4**, 1–5.

Butts, N.K. (1982). Physiological profiles of high school female cross-country runners. *Research Quarterly for Exercise and Sport*, **53**(1), 8–14.

Caine, D.J., & Lindner, K.J. (1984). Growth plate injury: A threat to young distance runners? *The Physician and Sportsmedicine*, **12**(4), 118, 120–122, 124.

Chausow, S.A., Riner, W.F., & Boileau, R.A. (1984). Metabolic and cardiovascular responses of children during prolonged physical activity. *Research Quarterly for Exercise and Sport*, **55**(1), 1–7.

Ehrlich, M.G., & Strain, R.E. (1979, January). Epiphyseal injuries about the knee. *Orthopedic Clinics of North America*, **10**, 91–103.

Feltz, D.L., & Albrecht, R.R. (1986). Psychological implications of competitive running. In M. Weiss & D. Gould (Eds.), *Sport for children and youths* (pp. 225-230). Champaign, IL: Human Kinetics.

Gordon, J.C. (1983-84, December/January). Stress of running, other activities, can lead to heel injuries. *The First Aider*, pp. 16–17. Gardner, KS: Cramer.

Larson, R.L. (1973). Physical activity and the growth and development of bone and joint structures. In G.L. Rarick (Ed.), *Physical activity/human growth and development*. New York: Academic Press.

Lascari, A. (1980). Intensive training and skeletal development. *Recreation Research Review*, **2**, 61–64.

Lopez, R., & Pruett, D.H. (1982). The child runner. *Journal of Physical Education, Recreation and Dance*, **53**(4), 78–81.

Malina, R. (1972). Anthropology, growth, and physical education. In R.N. Singer (Ed.), *Physical education: An interdisciplinary approach* (pp. 237–309). New York: Macmillan.

Malina, R.M. (1969). Exercise as an influence on growth. *Clinical Pediatrics*, **8**, 16–26.

Lincoln, E. (1982). Sports in childhood: A round table. *Physician and Sportsmedicine*, **10**(8), 52–60.

Peterson, C.A., & Peterson, H.A. (1972, April). Analysis of the incidence of injuries to the epiphyseal growth plate. *Journal of Trauma*, **12**, 275–281.

Rarick, G.L. (1978). Competitive sports in childhood and early adolescence. In R.A. Magill, M.J. Ash, & F.L. Smoll (Eds.), *Children in sports: A contemporary anthology* (pp. 113-128). Champaign, IL: Human Kinetics.

Runner's World (1983, November). RW's Advice for Adults. *Runner's World*, **18**(11) 92.

Schwab, S.A. (1977). Epiphyseal injuries in the growing athlete. *Canadian Medical Association Journal*, **17**, 626–629.

Seefeldt, V. (1986). Introduction to an interdisciplinary assessment of competition on elite young distance runners. In M. Weiss & D. Gould (Eds.), *Sport for children and youths* (p. 213-217). Champaign, IL: Human Kinetics.

Sheehan, G. (1983). Children running? Why not? *The Physician and Sportsmedicine*, **11**, 51.

Not kids' stuff. (1983, January). *American College of Sports Medicine Bulletin*, **11**.

Taunton, J.E. (1980, September). *Children and running*. Paper presented at the Vancouver Marathon Symposium.

Young, K., & Hejda, A. (1978). Marathon times. *Runner's World*, **13**, 98–105.

29

Psychological Implications of Competitive Running

Deborah L. Feltz and Richard R. Albrecht
MICHIGAN STATE UNIVERSITY
EAST LANSING, MICHIGAN, USA

The psychosocial implications of athletic competition for children have caused much controversy among coaches, parents, and sports administrators. Proponents of youth sports maintain that athletic participation has positive effects on a child's psychosocial development, whereas critics claim that athletic participation is psychologically detrimental to children because they are placed under excessive emotional stress.

There is a particular concern about the pressure placed on young runners as evidenced by a recent article in *Runner's World* (Baxter, 1983). Baxter stated that pressure from parents and coaches who place winning above fun and enjoyment is discouraging many young runners from participation. He reported incidents of children crying after races where they did not perform up to their parents' expectations, of children being forced to finish marathons just to set age-group records, and of children running in races as early as 1 year of age. As a result of this evidence, *Runner's World* has recommended that parents keep their children out of competitive running events until the age of 12. Unfortunately, this recommendation is not based on strong research evidence that competitive running is emotionally stressful for young children. Research pertaining to the psychological stress in youth sports suggests that most children do not find competition highly stressful (Scanlan & Passer, 1978, 1979), though some children (i.e., high competitive trait anxious children) perceive sports competition as an anxiety-inducing experience (Scanlan & Passer, 1978). Competitive athletics also have been found to produce no more anxiety than physical education classes, band competitions, or academic tests (Simon & Martens, 1979; Skubic, 1955).

Further research is needed to determine the extent and types of emotional stress involved in competitive running in children. The purpose of this aspect of the investigation, therefore, was to examine the psychological characteristics of a group of young long-distance runners. The specific research questions which guided the study were as follows:

- How committed are young runners to running?
- What is the level of competitive trait anxiety among young runners?
- How often do young runners worry about their races? and
- What types of stress do young runners typically experience prior to and during races?

Method

All runners were measured individually in a structured interview setting. The questionnaire used in the interview consisted of 110 items and was designed to assess commitment to running, anxiety, sources of stress typically experienced by runners, involvement of significant others, socialization into running, and socioeconomic status. Most of the items contained in the questionnaire were derived from previous inventories (Carmack & Martens, 1979; Gould, Horn & Spreemann, 1983b; Martens, 1977; Weiss & Knoppers, 1982).

The questionnaire was subdivided into four separate sections. The first section was composed of items taken from the revised form of the Female Sport Socialization Questionnaire (Weiss & Knoppers, 1982) and will not be reported in this paper. The second section consisted of Carmack and Martens' (1979) Commitment to Running Scale, which contained 12 items. Section three contained Marten's (1977) Sport Competition Anxiety Test (SCAT), a 15-item sport-specific competitive trait anxiety measure. The last section of the questionnaire was composed of 28 items designed to assess sources which may create competitive stress in runners. These items were taken from the Gould, Horn, and Spreeman (1983b) questionnaire which assessed 33 sources of stress in junior wrestlers.

Five items from the Gould et al. questionnaire were not included in this section because they were not applicable to running. The excluded items were "I worry about falling for a sucker move"; "I worry about bad calls by the officials"; "I worry about not being mean enough"; "I worry about hurting my opponent"; and "I worry about not making weight." Runners were asked four additional questions in this section which assessed the percentage of races in which they became nervous, how often this nervousness hurt their performance, how often it helped their performance, and how much trouble they had sleeping the night before competitions.

Results and Discussion

How Committed Are Young Runners to Running?

On a scale that ranged from 12 to 60 (the highest score attainable), the young runners appeared to be highly committed to their running ($M = 48.89$, SD

= 6.40). This level of commitment was higher than the level of commitment found by Carmack and Martens (1979) for adult road racers ($M = 48.0$), high school track competitors ($M = 48.0$), and Olympic athletes ($M = 48.2$). Correlational evidence also indicated that the better the runners' performance on the treadmill test (as measured by max VO_2), the higher their commitment to running score (r for males $= .54$, r for females $= .49$). There was a tendency ($p < .065$) for females to be more committed to running ($M = 51.00$, $SD = 5.33$) than males ($M = 46.46$, $SD = 6.85$). This contradicts the results Carmack and Martens reported with adult runners, where males were significantly more committed than females (males, $M = 48.3$, $SD = 6.3$; females, $M = 45.7$, $SD = 7.1$). This suggests that at some point, female runners may decrease their commitment to running as they become older, whereas male runners may increase their commitment. We will be able to examine this possibility as we observe the runners over the next few years of this study.

What Is the Level of Competitive Trait Anxiety Among Young Runners?

The runners appeared to have somewhat higher levels of competitive trait anxiety than Martens' (1977) scores for norm samples of comparable age and gender groups; however, they are consistent with Gould, Horn, and Spreemann's (1983a) scores with junior elite competitors in wrestling. The mean SCAT score for males was 21.85 ($SD = 3.91$) which was not significantly different than for females ($M = 20.47$, $SD = 4.03$). Younger runners (ages 9 to 11 years) had a mean SCAT score of 20.78 ($SD = 3.35$), and older runners (ages 12 to 15 years) had a mean score of 21.12 ($SD = 4.37$). These scores were also not significantly different from each other. At this point in our longitudinal study, we cannot draw any conclusions about the relationship between runners' involvement in running and their predisposition toward competitive anxiety. Continuation in running may decrease competitive A-traits, or runners with high A-traits may discontinue their competitive running.

Young runners also reported that they became nervous and worried in 41% of their races on the average. This represents a substantial number of races for these runners who are the best in their age categories. Results also revealed, however, that 50% felt that this nervousness helped their performance. These findings support the Gould et al. (1983a) research with elite young wrestlers. The majority of elite young competitors do not perceive competition as stressful, and some athletes view this stress as an arousal that facilitates their performance.

What Types of Stress Do Young Runners Typically Experience Prior To and During Races?

The runners rated each of the 28 sources of stress that typically made them nervous or worried on 7-point Likert scales (1 = always, 7 = never). The top 10 ratings by rank order summed over all 28 runners are contained in Table 1, along with the percentage of the sample who indicated that a particular source of stress contributed highly (a lot, almost always, always) to their feelings of nervousness and worry prior to competition.

The most important sources of stress, as revealed in Table 1, concerned a fear of failure and feelings of inadequacy. These results are consistent with those of previous investigations with elite young wrestlers (Gould et al., 1983b) and elite young hockey players (Feltz, 1984). The only gender differences that were found involved worrying about getting mentally ready to run and worrying about improving on their last performance. Girls were more worried about getting mentally ready to run ($M = 3.33$, $SD = 1.80$) than boys ($M = 4.92$, $SD = 1.44$) and were more worried about improving their last performance ($M = 3.13$, $SD = 1.19$) than boys ($M = 4.38$, $SD = 1.04$).

Although a substantial number of young runners (46% to 54%) indicated they often experienced the first five sources of stress listed in Table 1, an equally large number indicated these sources of stress were not very important to them. Finding similar results, Gould et al. (1983b) noted these findings support the view that substantial individual differences exist concerning the sources of stress experienced in young athletes.

Correlation coefficients were computed separately for males and females on runners' commitment to running, SCAT, and the five highest ranking sources of stress scores and years of competitive running experience for ex-

Table 1. Ten most important sources of stress among elite young runners

Source of stress	Rank	M rating	SD	Percentage of sample who experienced this type of stress a lot, almost always, or always.
Performing up to my level of ability	1	3.54	1.69	53.6
Improving on my last performance	2	3.71	1.27	46.4
Participating in championship races	3	3.82	1.56	42.9
Not performing well	4	3.96	1.81	40.7
Being able to get mentally ready to run	5	4.07	1.80	46.4
My physical condition before matches (e.g., yawning too much, always going to the bathroom, tightness in the neck, sore muscles)	6	4.18	1.56	28.6
Losing	7.5	4.43	1.81	32.0
My physical appearance	7.5	4.43	1.50	25.0
Running out of gas— my physical condition	9	4.54	1.48	25.0
Because I don't feel right (e.g., upset stomach, throwing up)	10	4.57	1.53	14.3

ploratory purposes. Significant relationships were found for males and females between commitment to running and worry about improving their last performance; however, the relationship for males was in the opposite direction than the relationship for females. The more committed female runners worried more about improving their performance ($r = -.44$); the more committed male runners worried less ($r = .53$).

The longer runners had been running, the more they indicated they worried about not performing well (males, $r = -.49$; females, $r = -.68$) and about participating in championship races (males $= -.63$; females $= -.46$). These findings appear to be inconsistent with those found by Gould et al. (1983b). They found that less experienced wrestlers worried more about fear of failure and feelings of inadequacy items. This discrepancy may be due to the larger (sample size), older, and more experienced sample reported by Gould et al. Or the discrepancy may also be due to the higher visibility of performance outcome in wrestling. In addition, significant relationships were found between SCAT scores and the top five sources of stress for males. The more competitive trait anxious males also worried more about their performance. For females, the only source of stress that significantly correlated with SCAT was worry about participating in championship races.

From our initial findings, it appears that these young runners were highly committed to their running, did not have extremely high competitive anxiety levels, and worried about less than one half of their races. When they worried, they were concerned about performance failures and feelings of inadequacy. At least one half of the runners did not perceive this worry to hurt their performance. The question of whether competitive long-distance running is emotionally harmful to children of this age group will remain unanswered, however, until we have observed their continued or discontinued involvement over a period of several years.

References

Baxter, K. (1983, November). When children are pushed to run too soon. *Runner's World*, pp. 90–92.

Carmack, M.A., & Martens, R. (1979). Measuring commitment to running: A survey of runners' attitudes and mental states. *Journal of Sport Psychology, 1*, 25–42.

Feltz, D.L. (1984). *Psychological assessment of elite young hockey players.* Unpublished manuscript, Michigan State University, Institute for the Study of Youth Sports, East Lansing.

Gould, D., Horn, T., & Spreemann, J. (1983a). Competitive anxiety in junior elite wrestlers. *Journal of Sport Psychology, 5*, 58–71.

Gould, D., Horn, T., & Spreemann, J. (1983b). Sources of stress in junior elite wrestlers. *Journal of Sport Psychology, 5*, 159–171.

Martens, R. (1977). *Sports competition anxiety test.* Champaign, IL: Human Kinetics.

Scanlan, T.K., & Passer, M.W. (1978). Factors related to competitive stress among male youth sports participants. *Medicine and Science in Sports, 10*, 103–108.

Scanlan, T.K., & Passer, M.W. (1979). Sources of competitive stress in young female athletes. *Journal of Sport Psychology, 1*, 151–159.

Simon, J.A., & Martens, R. (1979). Children's anxiety in sport and nonsport evaluative activities. *Journal of Sport Psychology, 1*, 160–169.

Skubic, E. (1955). Emotional responses of boys to Little League and Middle League competitive baseball. *Research Quarterly, 26*, 342–352.

Weiss, M.R., & Knoppers, A. (1982). The influence of socializing agents on female collegiate volleyball players. *Journal of Sport Psychology, 4*, 267–279.

30

Comparison of Dietary Habits and Nutrient Intake of Competitive Runners with Age- and Gender- Matched Controls

Rachel A. Schemmel, Marianne Stone, and Carole Conn
MICHIGAN STATE UNIVERSITY
EAST LANSING, MICHIGAN, USA

Determining the nutritional intake of U.S. children has been a topic of recent concern for dietary researchers (United States Department of Health, Education, and Welfare [USDHEW], 1977; 1979; United States Department of Agriculture [USDA], 1980; Morgan, Zabik, Cole & Leveille, 1980). For example, data from the Hanes study (USDHEW, 1977) showed that U.S. children on the average consumed adequate amounts of energy, protein, vitamins A and C, thiamin, riboflavin, preformed niacin, and calcium. A similar conclusion was also drawn by Morgan et al. (1980) who evaluated 7-day food diaries of 657 U.S. children from families who were representative of the U.S. population. Thus, the research shows that U.S. children, on average, receive adequate nutritional intakes.

Although these studies have provided important dietary information, it is unfortunate that individual differences have not been examined. That is, averaging data obscures the fact that some children may have excessive intakes of some nutrients while other children may have low intakes. Similarly, few studies have examined the nutritional intakes of subgroups of children such as elite young athletes.

The purpose of this study was to determine whether or not the diets and nutrient intakes of elite young runners were similar to age- and gender-matched control subjects who were not runners.[1] Nutrient intake information could also be used to document whether or not results reported in other aspects of the elite young runners study were confounded by or were nonrelated to dietary factors.

Method

Twenty-eight male ($n = 13$) and female ($n = 15$) runners between the ages of 9.5 and 15 years, as well as nonrunners (13 males; 12 females) of similar age, sex, and height, were asked to keep a 3-day dietary record of foods eaten, which they brought with them on the day they arrived for testing. At that time, trained personnel interviewed each subject about his or her food records for information such as amounts of food eaten, specific foods used in recipes, brand names of foods, or other factors which would help to clarify the dietary record. In many cases, controls only brought a 1-day food record and could not remember foods eaten on the other 2 days. In those cases, only a 1-day record was used for the initial phase of the study. Although subjects will be tested over a 5-year period of time, only the first year is reported here. Information was also obtained on use of dietary supplements and special foods.

Each subject's food records were coded for use in the Michigan State University Data Bank 1.[2] For this study, 29 nutrients are reported. Male and female data are reported separately for both elite runners and controls. Where appropriate, the t-test was used to determine statistical differences between runners and controls. A recommended daily dietary allowance (RDA) (National Research Council, 1980) has been established for many nutrients. Mean values for male and female runners and controls were compared with the RDA as well as with each other.

Results

Energy Intake

The 15 female runners had a mean energy intake of 2258 $\pm$ 134 kcal and the age- and gender-matched controls consumed a mean of 2200 kcal $\pm$ 279. Eleven of the 15 female runners and 10 female controls consumed over 100% of the RDA for energy. Four elite female runners consumed less than 100% of the RDA for energy. In general, there was a trend for older, 14- to 15-year-old

[1]This investigation was supported in part by an All-University Research Initiation Grant.

[2]Michigan State University Data Bank is a modified form of Highland View Hospital-Case Western Reserve University Nutrient Data Bank.

females to consume a lower percentage of RDA for energy than 11- to 13-year-old females. One 15-year-old control ate only 46% of the RDA for kcal. She indicated she was trying to lose weight. However, her weight was at the 50th percentile of National Center for Health Statistics (NCHS) charts (Hamill et al., 1979). All other subjects consumed over 82% of the RDA.

Male runners consumed 2684 ± 165 kcal while controls consumed 2886 ± 276 kcal per day. The 202 kcal difference was not significant. The larger *SE* for kcal reported for the controls (both males and females) than for the runners represents the fact that three 24-hour dietary records were available for runners whereas only 1 day was available for controls. All males except an 11-year-old control consumed at least 80% of the RDA for kcal. This 11-year-old control subject consumed only 44% of his RDA, but the diet represented an atypical day. Because the body weight for this subject was at the 50th percentile (NCHS Growth Charts), it suggests that his energy intake was adequate.

Regardless of the group, the percentage of energy obtained from carbohydrate, protein, and fat was similar among groups and similar to the average American diet: Forty-eight to 50% of the energy came from carbohydrate, 14- to 15% of the energy came from protein, and 35- to 36% of the energy came from fat.

Both female runners and age-matched controls consumed a mean 277g carbohydrate per day. In general, males ate more carbohydrate per day than females. This was also true for total energy. The trend for male controls to eat more carbohydrate per day than male runners was not significant. For both female runners and controls, 17% of the carbohydrate came from refined carbohydrate such as sugar. For male elite runners, 21% of the carbohydrate was eaten as refined carbohydrate, and for male controls, 25% of the carbohydrates came from refined carbohydrate. Seventy percent of the young runners ingested pasta at their evening meal on the day before they planned to race competitively.

Protein

Female elite runners ingested a mean of 78 g protein while controls ingested a mean of 89 g protein per day (Table 1). Males ate 10 to 15 g more protein than females. These findings were not significant, however.

All females and males except one 15-year-old female control subject ate 100% or more of the RDA for protein. The one female who ingested only 46% of her energy intake ingested 50% of the RDA for protein. Twenty-eight out of the entire 53 subjects (53%) ate over 200% of their recommended daily allowance for protein. For the four groups of subjects, a range of 49% to 69% of the protein came from animal sources such as milk, eggs, and meat, and a range of 19% to 31% of the protein came from plant sources such as cereals, vegetables, and legumes (see Table 1). The source of the protein was not identified in some foods; therefore, the summation of plant and animal protein is not 100%.

Fat and Cholesterol

Female runners ate an average of 88 ± 7 g fat per day. Control female subjects age 93 ± 16 g fat per day (see Table 1). Male runners and male controls

Table 1. Dietary intakes of energy, protein, and fats by elite runners and by controls

Source	Females		Males	
	Runners	Controls	Runners	Controls
Energy (kcal)	2258 ± 134[a]	2200 ± 279	2684 ± 165	2886 ± 276
Protein total (g)	78 ± 6	89 ± 16	88 ± 9	106 ± 10
Protein (% of RDA)	209 ± 20	219 ± 41	218 ± 21	226 ± 28
Protein, animal (% of protein intake)	56 ± 6	49 ± 7	69 ± 5	54 ± 10
Protein, plant (% of protein intake)	25 ± 2	31 ± 9	26 ± 4	19 ± 2
Fat total (g)	88 ± 7	93 ± 16	113 ± 13	109 ± 10
Saturated fat (g)	29 ± 2	28 ± 4	42 ± 3	38 ± 5
Polyunsaturated fat (g)	15 ± 2	11 ± 2	14 ± 3	10 ± 2
Oleic acid (g)	24 ± 2	24 ± 4	37 ± 4	27 ± 4
Cholesterol (mg)	253 ± 38	250 ± 49	369 ± 48	348 ± 62

[a]Means ± SE.

ate 113 ± 13 and 109 ± 10 g fat per day, respectively. There was a trend for males to eat more fat then females. This was also reflected in the higher energy intakes of males versus females.

Daily intake of saturated fat, polyunsaturated fat, and oleic acid are also reported in Table 1. Values for these fats do not add to the value for total fat intake because monounsaturated fats other than oleic acid are not included, and some foods have not been analyzed for individual fatty acids. For all female elite runners, the ratio of saturated to polyunsaturated fats was 1.9 to 1.0, whereas for female controls, the ratio of saturated fat to polyunsaturated fat was 2.5 to 1.0. For males, the ratio of saturated to polyunsaturated fat was 3.0 to 1.0 for male runners, and 3.8 to 1.0 for male controls. Male and female runners ate the same amount of polyunsaturated fat per day. Control male and female subjects also ate the same quantity of polyunsaturated fat. However, male subjects (both the runners and controls) ate approximately 33% more saturated fats than females.

Female runners and controls consumed 253 ± 38 and 250 ± 49 mg cholesterol, respectively ($p > .10$). Male runners and controls consumed 369 ± 48 and 348 ± 62 mg cholesterol, respectively. There were no dietary differences in cholesterol intake between runners and controls. Male runners consumed 46% more cholesterol than female runners and male controls consumed 40% more cholesterol than female controls (see Table 1). The higher intake

Table 2. Dietary intakes of vitamins and minerals by elite runners and by controls

Source	Females		Males	
	Runners	Controls	Runners	Controls
Thiamin, % of RDA	115 ± 11[a]	124 ± 13	143 ± 9	136 ± 10
Preformed Niacin, % of RDA	122 ± 8	116 ± 14	124 ± 8	83 ± 12
Riboflavin, % of RDA	168 ± 22	146 ± 15	142 ± 10	164 ± 16
Pyridoxine, % of RDA	86 ± 9	84 ± 16	90 ± 12	88 ± 14
Vitamin B_{12}, % of RDA	127 ± 16	155 ± 27	143 ± 16	211 ± 52
Vitamin A, % of RDA	114 ± 13	148 ± 30	112 ± 8	160 ± 40
Vitamin C, % of RDA	247 ± 45	267 ± 43	291 ± 61	319 ± 73
Supplemental Vitamin C, Number	1[b]	4	4	6
Multiple Vitamin Supplement, Number	11[b]	5	4	6
Iron, % of RDA	88 ± 43	79 ± 8	98 ± 9	105 ± 31
Calcium, % of RDA	94 ± 11	124 ± 29	106 ± 8	123 ± 30
Phosphorus, % of RDA	120 ± 12	116 ± 19	147 ± 9	168 ± 22
Magnesium, % of RDA	92 ± 8	103 ± 31	84 ± 11	93 ± 11
Zinc, % of RDA	64 ± 4	64 ± 11	89 ± 8	89 ± 15

[a]Mean percentage ± SE of the recommended dietary allowances (RDA).
[b]Indicates the number of subjects from the group who ingested a supplement.

of cholesterol is similar to the higher kilocalorie, carbohydrate, fat, and saturated fat intake in males compared to females.

Vitamins

Intakes of vitamins are presented in Table 2. Vitamin intake is expressed as a percentage of the RDA. There were no differences in thiamin, preformed niacin, or riboflavin dietary intake between age- and sex-matched runners and controls. There was a trend for males to have slightly higher intakes of thiamin than females. One female control ingested less than 67% of the RDA for thiamin. She did not take supplements. All other subjects ingested adequate dietary thiamin. One male control and 1 female control ingested less than 67% of the RDA for niacin. Neither took supplements. Eleven subjects ingested 200% or more of the RDA for riboflavin. No one ingested less than 67% of the RDA for riboflavin.

Mean intakes of pyridoxine ranged from 83% to 90% of the RDA for the four groups. There were no significant differences among groups. Seven female runners, 4 male runners, 6 female controls and 2 male controls ingested less than 67% of the RDA for pyridoxine. Mean intakes of vitamin B_{12} were adequate for all groups. Eleven subjects ingested over 200% of the RDA for vitamin B_{12}. One female control ingested less than 67% of the RDA for vitamin B_{12}. She did not take vitamin supplements.

Mean intakes of vitamin A were above 100% of the RDA for all four groups (see Table 2). Three control male subjects and 2 control female subjects ingested over 200% of the RDA for vitamin A, whereas no runners ingested over 200% of the RDA for vitamin A. The very large variability for control subjects negated any statistical differences between age- and sex-matched runners and controls. Six controls and 2 runners ingested less than 67% of the RDA for vitamin A. Mean intakes of vitamin C represented more than 200% of the RDA for all four groups. However, individually, there were 3 subjects out of 53 who had less than 67% of the RDA for vitamin C. One of the 3 subjects was a female runner and 2 subjects were male controls. None of the 3 subjects took supplemental vitamin C, but 2 of the 3 subjects took multiple vitamins. Thirty-five of the 53 (66%) subjects received over 200% of the RDA for vitamin C through their diets. Ten of the 53 subjects took supplemental vitamin C (see Table 3). For each group, these 10 (19%) subjects also had higher dietary intakes of vitamin C than the 42 subjects who did not take supplemental vitamin C (see Table 3).

Sixteen runners (57%) and 10 (40%) controls took daily supplemental multivitamins. However, subjects who were borderline in nutrient intake were not the same ones who took multivitamins.

Minerals

Iron intakes were similar between sex-matched runners and controls (Table 2). Males ingested a higher percentage of the RDA for iron than females. Six female runners and 4 female controls ingested less than 67% of the RDA for iron. Only 1 male, a control subject, ingested less than 67% of the RDA for iron. Two male controls ingested over 200% of the RDA for iron.

Mean intakes of calcium and phosphorus ranged from 94% to 124% and 116% to 168% of the RDA, respectively, for the four groups of subjects (see Table 2). There were no differences in intakes between age- and gender-matched runners and controls. There was a trend for males to ingest a higher percentage of the RDA for both calcium and phosphorus than females. No

Table 3. Dietary and supplemental vitamin C intakes of runners and age/sex-matched controls

Group	Vitamin C Intake			
	Dietary plus supplemental		Dietary only	
	n	% RDA	n	% RDA
Runners				
Females	1	672	14	216 ± 32
Males	4	456 ± 141[a]	9	218 ± 38
Controls				
Females	3	250 ± 132	8	236 ± 44
Males	2	410 ± 176	11	298 ± 83

[a]Means ± SE.

males ingested less than 67% of the RDA for calcium or phosphorus. Three female runners and 3 female controls ingested less than 67% of the RDA for calcium. Three female controls and 1 female runner ingested less than 67% of the RDA for phosphorus.

Mean intakes of magnesium and zinc were below 100% of the RDA in all cases except 1 female control for magnesium. Sex- and gender-matched intakes for runners and controls were similar (see Table 2). In general, females ingested a higher percentage of the RDA for magnesium than males, and males ingested a higher percentage of the RDA for zinc than females. Three female runners and 3 female controls ingested less than 67% of the RDA for magnesium. Two male runners and 1 male control ingested less than 67% of the RDA for magnesium. Nine female runners and 5 female controls had less than 67% of the RDA for zinc. One male runner and 4 male controls had less than 67% of the RDA for zinc.

Discussion

Recently, Farris and colleagues (Farris, Cresanta, Frank, Webber, & Berenson, 1984) investigated fat, fatty acids, and cholesterol intakes of 10-year-old and 13-year-old children in the Bogalusa Heart Study. They found total daily fat intake of the children was 101 ± 50 g for 10-year-olds and 107 ± 54 g for 13-year-olds. These values are similar to the ones reported in the present study. However, unlike the Farris study, data were reported for each gender. The trend for males to ingest more total fat, saturated fat, and cholesterol (but not polyunsaturated fat) than females will be further investigated during the 5-year time span of this study. Males, in general, consume more kilocalories than females, so not only fat, but carbohydrate and protein are consumed in greater quantities by males.

RDAs (National Research Council, 1980) have been determined for some nutrients for which nutrient composition of foods are inadequately known. Nutrients for which food composition data are incomplete include vitamins B_6 and B_{12}; magnesium and zinc (Pao & Michle, 1981). Thus, the tendency for subjects not to meet 100% of the RDA for these nutrients must be evaluated with restraint due to incomplete nutrient composition data.

References

Farris, R.P., Cresanta, J.L., Frank, G.C., Webber, L.S., & Berenson, G.S. (1984). Dietary studies of children from a biracial population: Intakes of fat and fatty acids in 10- and 13-year-olds. *American Journal of Clinical Nutrition, 39,* 114–128.

Hamill, P.V.V., Prizd, T.A., Johnson, C.L., Reed, R.B., Roche, A.F., & Moore, W.M. (1979). Physical growth: National center for health statistics percentiles. *American Journal of Clinical Nutrition, 32,* 607–629.

Morgan, K.J., Zabik, M.E., Cole, R. & Leveille, G.A. (1980). *Nutrient intake patterns of children ages 5 to 12 years based on 7-day food diaries.* East Lansing, MI: Research Report #06, Michigan State University Agriculture Experiment Station.

National Research Council. (1980). *Recommended dietary allowances* (9th ed.). Washington, DC: National Academy of Sciences.

Pao, E.A., & Michle, S.J. (1981, September). Problem nutrients in the United States. *Food Technology, 35*, 58–69.

United States Department of Agriculture. (1980). *Food and nutrient intakes of individuals in one day in the United States, spring, 1977: USDA Nationwide Food Consumption Survey, 1977–78* (Preliminary Report Number 2). Hyattsville, MD: U.S. Department of Agriculture, Consumer Nutrition Center, Human Nutrition, Science and Educational Administration.

U.S. Department of Health, Education and Welfare. (1977). *Dietary intake findings, United States, 1971–1974. Vital and Health Statistics* (Series 11, Number 202. DHEW Publication Number (HRAA) 77-1647), Washington, DC.

U.S. Department of Health, Education and Welfare. (1979). *Dietary intake source data, United States, 1971–1974.* (DHEW Publication Number (PHSO) 79-1221). Washington, DC.

31

Physiological and Perceptual Responses of Elite Age Group Distance Runners During Progressive Intermittent Work to Exhaustion

Wayne D. Van Huss, Kenneth E. Stephens, Paul Vogel, David Anderson, Theodore Kurowski, Jo Ann Janes, and Carrie Fitzgerald
MICHIGAN STATE UNIVERSITY
EAST LANSING, MICHIGAN, USA

The factors which limit endurance performance in children and adolescents have not been established as yet. It is clear in adult athletes that aerobic capacity is closely related to endurance performance, but in children and adolescents there is little support for this position. For example, Mayers and Gutin (1979) found no correlation between running performance and aerobic capacity in elite prepubertal cross-country runners. Also, it is a matter of controversy as to the extent endurance training during the growth years can increase aerobic capacity. Stewart and Gutin (1976), for instance, were unable to demonstrate any training effects on the $\dot{V}O_{2\,max}$, whereas other investigators have shown improvements of about 10% as a result of endurance training (Eriksson, 1972; Lusier & Buskirk, 1977).

In a comparison of elite male endurance runners aged 12 to 16 years with a group of control subjects of the same age, Sundberg and Elovainio (1982) found that the runners 12 to 14 years weighed less, were leaner, and had higher $\dot{V}O_{2\,max}$/kg body weight. Otherwise, the groups were rather similar. At the age of 16 years, however, the runners differed significantly from the controls, with lower resting heart rates and higher $\dot{V}O_{2\,max}$, PWC_{170}, heart volumes, vital capacities, and maximum ventilations. At 16 years of age, the runners more closely resembled the adult runner. The similarity in the results of the 12- and 14-year-old controls and runners tends to be supported by the longitudinal data of Rutenfranz et al. (1982) on the development of maximal aerobic power. They observed that the increase during the prepubertal years was mainly an effect of growth in body size with little or no additional effect of other factors. A higher level of maximal aerobic power was observed at the end of adolescence. In both studies, energy metabolism was measured during work on bicycle ergometers.

The aerobic capacities of endurance trained 12-year-old boys and 17-year-old adolescent runners were compared by Lehmann, Keul, and Hesse (1982). The $\dot{V}O_{2\,max}$ values of 60.3 and 65.0 ml/kg/min, respectively, were not significantly different. Relative heart sizes of 13.2 and 12.5 ml/kg, respectively, were also not significantly different. They concluded that the young boys, in regard to trainability and endurance capacity as reflected by the relative heart volumes and relative aerobic capacity, show no disadvantage to the adolescents. The $\dot{V}O_{2\,max}$ values observed in this study were very similar to those observed by Sundberg and Elovainio (1982) for endurance runners of 12 (59.3 ml/kg/min) and 16 (66.0 ml/kg/min) years of age.

The present study permitted collection of the aerobic capacity and related measures in elite young runners and control subjects to further study the magnitude of the training adaptation in youngsters. Because little information is available on relative perceived exertion (RPE) for youngsters 8 to 15 years of age, this study presented the opportunity to collect such data. RPE has been exhaustively reviewed by Pandolf (1983). The interest in the present study is to describe the RPE's associated with common measures of physiological strain (HR and $\dot{V}O_2$) to determine the nature of the differences in the RPE of runners and control subjects.

Method

The subjects consisted of 28 elite runners ages 8 to 15 (15 female, 13 male) and 25 control subjects (12 female, 13 male) of the same ages and heights as the runners. The control subjects were healthy and physically active but untrained *as runners*. An intermittent treadmill protocol was utilized which consisted of progressively more intense 3-min work intervals with intervening 3-min rest periods until the subject was exhausted. A 15-min recovery period followed. The work intensity progression was as follows: Level 1, 6 mi/hr at 0% grade; Level 2, 6 mi/hr at 5% grade; Level 3, 7 mi/hr at 6% grade; Level 4, 8 mi/hr at 7% grade and continuing to increase 1 mi/hr and 1% grade for each additional level.

The oxygen uptake was measured using the traditional Douglas bag method. Throughout work, rest intervals, and the first 5 min of recovery, the gas collections were fractionated into 1-min bags. The electrocardiogram was monitored continuously using the CM-5 lead. Minute values were recorded for the heart rate from strip counts. The blood pressure was measured by sphygmomanometer immediately following each work level and at 5, 10, and 15 min of recovery. Blood lactate was measured by taking 20 ml arterialized blood samples at the same time the blood pressure was being measured. The blood samples were taken from a prewarmed finger tip, and the whole blood sample was analyzed in the Roche 740 Analyzer.

The data are presented with all runners compared with all control subjects and the male and female runners compared with their respective control subjects. The results have been analyzed utilizing the Sign test and the t test where indicated.

Results and Discussion

The $\dot{V}O_2$ of the runners was consistently ($p < .05$) higher during the work intervals and lower during the rest intervals (see Figure 1).

Work capacity and the $\dot{V}O_{2\ max}$ were greater in all groupings ($p < .05$) for the runners (61.8, 63.3, and 60.2 ml/kg/min respectively for combined, male, and female) when compared with the control subjects (51.9, 54.5 and 49.4 ml/kg/min respectively for combined, male, and female). The $\dot{V}O_{2\ max}$ values for the female and male control subjects are quite similar to the values reported by Rutenfranz et al. (1982) for Norwegian and German boys and girls of comparable age. It is not possible to make exact comparisons as the Rutenfranz et al. results are reported in reference to growth in peak height velocity (PHV).

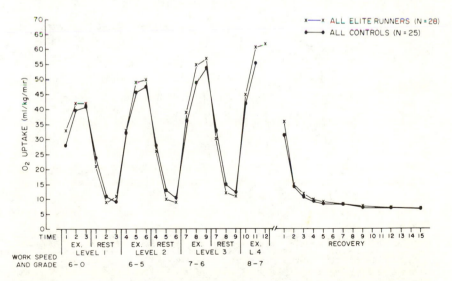

Figure 1. Runners' and control subjects' oxygen uptake responses during and following exhaustive intermittent work.

In the present sample, the PHV had not yet occurred for most of the subjects. The $\dot{V}O_2$ max values for the male runners of 63.3 ml/kg/min were similar in magnitude to that observed by Sundberg and Elovainio (1982) for children 12 years old (59.3 ml/kg/min) and 14 years old (63.7 ml/kg/min), and to that of Lehmann et al., (1982) for 12-year-old boys (60.3 ml/kg/min). It is evident that the $\dot{V}O_2$ of young runners is greater than for nonrunners, but to date none of the studies have resolved whether the differences are the result of training adaptation or whether the differences are hereditary. Longitudinal studies initiated prior to involvement in such endurance training are required to resolve this question.

To our knowledge, no previous studies have reported data on endurance trained females of these ages. It was of interest that the $\dot{V}O_2$ max of the female runners was not different from that of the males. Burke and Brush (1979) studied 13 successful teenage female distance runners (age $M = 16.2$ yrs). The mean $\dot{V}O_2$ max was 63.2 ml/kg/min. These results are comparable to the present study, even though the subjects were older. In addition, a large sample ($N = 127$) of female cross-country runners was studied by Butts (1982) who found a mean $\dot{V}O_2$ max of 50.8 ml/kg/min, and recently Palgi, Gutin, Young, and Wejandro (1984) reported mean $\dot{V}O_2$ max values (42.9 ml/kg/min) for young untrained females 10 to 14 years of age ($M = 11.9$ yrs). Although these studies were not conducted on elite performers, they reflect the capacities of healthy young female competitors.

The HR results (see Figure 2) show that the runners' heart rates were lower both during work and during the rest phases and recovery ($p < .01$). This expected result was consistent in both the male and female comparison.

At the same levels of work the females' HR were slightly higher than for

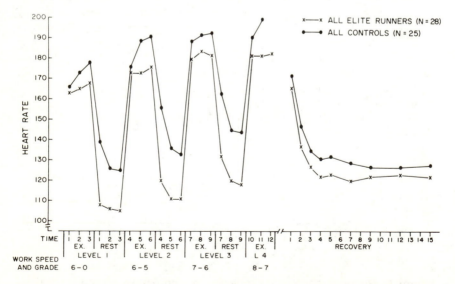

Figure 2. Runners' and control subjects' heart rate responses during and following exhaustive intermittent work.

males. (Level 1, females = 172.1, males 169.4; Level 2, females = 181.5, males = 179.6; Level 3, females = 189.0, males 187.3; and Level 4, females = 194.9, males = 188.6). The maximum systolic blood pressure (BP) attained by the runners and control subjects were not different (Figure 3). The blood pressures reached at each level, however, were quite different. The runners, both male and female, attained lower blood pressures (systolic and diastolic) following each level in which comparisons could be made ($p < .01$). The mean maximum systolic BP was 164 mm Hg for the combined runners and approximately the same for the control subjects. The diastolic BP for the runners ranged from 70 to 75 mm Hg across all levels, and the control subjects' values ranged between 78 and 82 mm Hg. This difference ($p < .05$) is not interpretable because post exercise diastolic blood pressure measured by auscultation is of doubtful validity.

The lactate values for the runners were consistently lower at each exercise level ($p < .05$) following the pretest sample (see Figure 4). The runners were either not producing the lactic acid, or it was being metabolized. Two points are clear: (a) The lactate values are lower for the runners at comparative levels, and (b) the maximum lactate values for the two groups are not significantly different (9.5 and 10.1 mMol/1 for runners and controls, respectively).

The relative perception of exertion (RPE) results are portrayed in Figures 5 and 6. The findings are consistent with those reported in the literature in that there is a strong relationship between RPE and physiological work. When RPE ratings are plotted against HR, the results for the females are linear, but

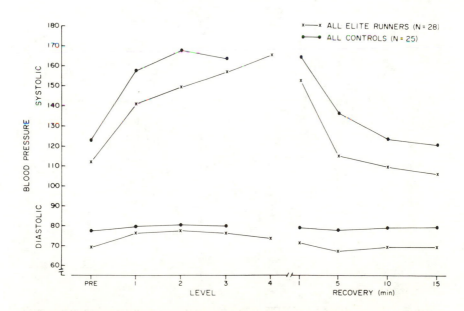

Figure 3. Runners' and control subjects' blood pressure responses following graded intermittent work to exhaustion.

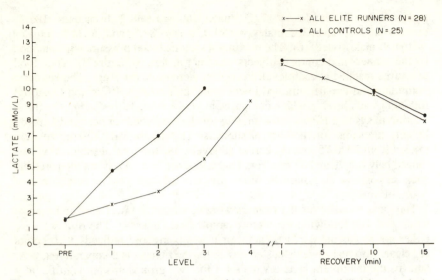

Figure 4. Runner's and control subjects' blood lactate values following graded intermittent work to exhaustion.

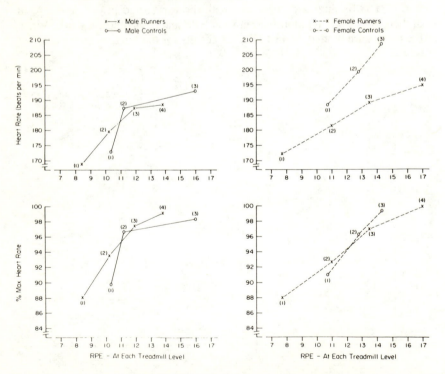

Figure 5. The relationship of RPE to heart rate and the percent of maximum heart rate in male and female runners and control subjects following graded intermittent work to exhaustion (the numbers in parenthesis indicate work level).

at two distinct levels and different slopes. The male ratings, which are slightly curvilinear, may indicate some reluctance to rate exertion in accordance with the physiological stress. Data also suggest that the controls perceived each level of exercise to be more difficult than did the runners. When RPE ratings were plotted against the percentage of the HR max, some of the observed differences were diminished. This is consistent with the findings of Bar-Or, Skinner, Buskirk, and Borg (1972).

When RPE was plotted against $\dot{V}O_2$, similar results were obtained. The data appear linear, but at distinctly different levels, with the exception of the male controls where the mean $\dot{V}O_2$ was elevated at the second level of exercise. As expected, the controls perceived each level of exercise to be more difficult than did the runners. When RPE was plotted against the percentage of $\dot{V}O_{2\ max}$ to adjust for differences in the level of physical training between the groups, the groups looked much more alike than different. These findings are again consistent with the work of Bar-Or et al. (1972).

It appears from these data that both male and female trained and untrained children can subjectively evaluate the intensity of their exertion in a fairly consistent manner.

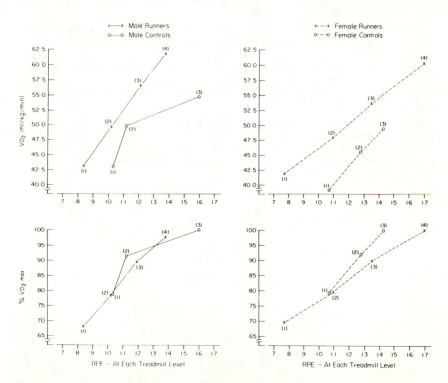

Figure 6.   The relationship of RPE to oxygen uptake and the percent of maximum oxygen uptake in male and female runners and control subjects following graded intermittent work to exhaustion (the numbers in parenthesis indicate work level).

References

Bar-Or, O., Skinner, J.S., Buskirk, E.R., & Borg, G. (1972). Physiological and perceptual indicators of physical stress in 41- to 60-year-old men who vary in conditioning level and in body fat. *Medicine and Science of Sports,* **4**, 96–100.

Burke, E.Y., & Brush, F.C. (1979). Physiological and anthropometric assessment of successful teenage female distance runners. *Research Quarterly,* **50**, 180–187.

Butts, N.K. (1982). Physiological profiles of high school female cross-country runners. *Research Quarterly for Exercise and Sports,* **53**, 180–187.

Eriksson, B.O. (1972). Physical Training, oxygen supply and muscle metabolism in 11- to 13-year-old boys. *Acta Physiologica Scandinavica,* (Suppl. 290).

Lehmann, M., Keul, J., & Hesse, A. (1982). Zur zeroben und anaeroben kapazitat sowie catecholaminexkretion von kindern und jugendlichen wahrend langdauernder submaximaler korperarbeit. *European Journal of Applied Physiology,* **48**, 135–145.

Lusier, L., & Buskirk, E.R. (1977). Effects of an endurance training regimen on assessment of work capacity in prepubertal children. *Annals New York Academy of Science,* **301**, 734–747.

Mayers, M., & Gutin, B. (1979). Physiological characteristics of elite prepubertal cross-country runners. *Medicine and Science of Sports,* **11**, 172–176.

Palgi, Y., Gutin, B., Young, J., & Wejandro, D. (1984). Physiologic and anthropometric factors underlying endurance performance in children. *International Journal of Sports Medicine,* **5**, 67–73.

Pandolf, K. (1983). Advances in the study and application of perceived exertion. In R.L. Terjung (Ed.), *Exercise and Sport Sciences Reviews* (pp. 118–158). New York: Academic Press.

Rutenfranz, J., Anderson, K.L., Seliger, V., Ilmarin, J., Klimmer, F., Kylian, H., Rutenfranz, M., & Ruppel, M. (1982). Maximal aerobic power affected by maturation and body growth during childhood and adolescence. *European Journal of Pediatrics,* **139**, 196–112.

Stewart, K.J., & Gutin, B. (1976). Effects of physical training on cardiorespiratory fitness in children. *Research Quarterly,* **47**, 110–120.

Sundberg, S., & Elovainio, R. (1982). Cardiorespiratory function in competitive endurance runners aged 12–16 years compared with ordinary boys. *Acta Paediatrica Scandinavica,* **71**, 987–992.

32

Anthropometric Assessment of Body Size and Shape of Young Runners and Control Subjects

Vern Seefeldt, John Haubenstricker, Crystal Branta, and Douglas McKeag
MICHIGAN STATE UNIVERSITY
EAST LANSING, MICHIGAN, USA

The influence of strenuous athletic competition on the biological growth of children and youth has been a concern to educators, parents, and physicians for several decades (Adams, 1965; Malina, 1979; Rarick, 1973; Rowe, 1934; Schuck, 1962). Anxiety about the possible detrimental effects of highly competitive sports on children seems to increase in direct proportion to the increase in training intensities and competitive events available to them. One of the most frequently mentioned sources of controversy in sports for children is that of long-distance running and the concomitant training that underlies the ability to participate in such events (Abramowicz, 1979; Mirkin, 1981; O'Connell, 1979; Olsen, 1982). Running has been identified as potentially injurious to children because of its repetitive demands for weight-bearing by the joints of the lower extremity.

The interrelationship of physical activity, growth, and biological maturation has been addressed in a series of excellent reviews (Malina, 1969, 1982; Parizkova, 1973; Rarick, 1974; Shephard, 1982). Other investigators have reported relative changes in physical dimensions over periods of time (Åstrand et al., 1963; Daniels & Oldridge, 1971; Ekblom, 1969; Parizkova, 1968). These reports confirm that the cause-effect relationship between activity and growth can only be determined by longitudinal studies. Comparing a homogeneous group of athletes with an available sample of control subjects simply provides data about the relative size of the two groups; such studies do not provide information about the extent to which activity influenced the growth of either group. In addition, any study which purports to demonstrate the influence of physical activity on biological growth and maturation must begin with evidence of the growth and maturational trajectories of the subjects prior to the time when training and competition, the independent variables, were introduced.

Data from which trends in growth can be established are especially valuable during circumpuberty, when great variation in the genetically controlled advent and rate of accelerated growth are evident in children of the same chronological age. The propensity toward linearity in body build of distance runners is well known; therefore, investigators must be certain that the body types that permit individuals to perform successfully as runners are not attributed to the training effects of the activity unless these changes occurred during the course of training.

The careful assessment of size and shape throughout the growing years is essential if a more accurate assignment of attributions to variables that are either genetic or environmental is an objective of the investigation. These data, representing the first year of a longitudinal study, are a source of comparisons in bodily lengths, girths, circumferences, and skinfolds of boys and girls classified as runners and controls.

Method

Subjects and Assessment Procedures

Twenty-six boys (13 runners and 13 controls) and 27 girls (15 runners and 12 controls) between the ages of 9 and 15 years served as subjects. A detailed description of the subjects' characteristics is provided in the introduction to this series of papers (Seefeldt, 1985). Anthropometric values were taken between early morning and midafternoon, depending on the random assignment of the subjects to this measurement station. The degree to which diurnal variation and exposure to other tests in the battery affected the anthropometric data is unknown. All 47 assessments of size and shape (see Table 1) were taken on the same day, but testing of the 53 subjects encompassed a 4-month period. All measures were part of a standard battery that had been used previously to assess the growth of children and young athletes. Two anthropometrists, experienced in the procedures used, conducted all of the assessments.

Measures

Anthropometric assessments included 10 skinfolds taken with the Lange caliper; 15 measures of girth, taken with a metal tape; 11 measures of length, taken with a bow caliper and an anthropometer; and 11 measures of breadth, taken with a bow caliper and an anthropometer. A complete list of the anthropometric assessments with means and standard deviations of the four subcategories is shown in Table 1. Protocols for each of the measures are available from the authors.

Table 1. Means and standard deviations for four subcategories of anthropometric assessments of young runners and control subjects

| Variable | Runners (N = 28) | | | | Controls (N = 25) | | | |
| | Boys (N = 13) | | Girls (N = 15) | | Boys (N = 13) | | Girls (N = 12) | |
	M	SD	M	SD	M	SD	M	SD
				Lengths				
Brachium	28.40	2.15	29.40	2.69	29.63	2.48	30.38	2.27
Forearm	24.24	2.45	24.41	2.14	25.40	1.74	25.28	2.05
Hand	16.36	1.56	16.37	0.96	16.98	0.99	16.95	1.11
Foot	23.01	1.70	22.81	1.38	24.31	1.32	23.59	1.36
Thigh	33.54	3.28	34.75	3.22	36.25	3.60	36.48	3.24
Leg	37.57	2.97	38.03	3.63	36.42	2.41	35.91	2.60
Upper extremity	64.33	5.58	62.86	9.16	67.15	4.60	67.59	5.14
Standing height	149.30	11.98	152.71	10.13	155.96	10.30	155.44	10.56
Trochanteric height	77.12	5.82	78.35	6.51	78.95	5.91	77.98	6.08
Seventh cervical height	126.23	10.26	129.13	9.03	131.15	11.17	129.07	10.05
Sitting height	78.79	6.39	80.77	4.61	82.72	4.21	83.08	5.37
				Breadths				
Biacromial	32.25	2.72	32.87	1.96	33.98	2.51	34.70	2.83
Biiliac	22.55	1.81	23.90	2.03	24.11	2.25	24.77	2.33
Bitrochanteric	25.40	2.58	27.07	2.69	27.09	2.55	27.96	2.75
Humerus	5.88	0.46	5.83	0.37	6.24	0.45	5.78	0.51
Wrist	4.57	0.40	4.61	0.23	5.09	0.29	4.71	0.52
Chest (max)	23.81	1.93	23.79	1.85	25.23	2.24	24.30	2.48
Chest (min)	21.98	1.81	21.88	1.65	24.24	3.56	22.61	2.22
Femur	8.62	0.52	8.29	0.40	9.16	0.43	8.42	0.56
Bideltoid	35.42	3.45	35.76	2.96	36.44	2.78	37.59	3.06
Knee	8.45	0.53	8.29	0.40	9.21	0.45	8.40	0.78
Ankle	6.37	0.38	6.17	0.26	7.02	0.36	6.27	0.40
				Girths				
Neck	29.26	2.11	28.23	1.79	32.35	2.11	30.08	2.25
Shoulder	85.82	8.24	86.82	5.16	91.45	6.13	91.43	8.57
Chest	69.12	5.72	72.11	7.17	74.71	4.82	78.70	10.06
Abdominal-1	61.63	5.33	59.78	3.93	67.89	3.75	63.15	5.75
Abdominal-2	61.12	5.30	59.31	4.60	67.45	5.79	62.85	5.55
Hip	72.64	6.89	75.08	6.31	80.56	6.33	81.51	7.87
Thigh	41.49	3.72	43.52	4.85	47.41	4.11	48.10	4.34
Knee	30.58	2.00	30.91	1.89	34.12	2.28	32.91	2.64
Calf	29.10	2.40	29.75	2.48	32.67	3.71	31.82	3.16
Ankle	19.02	1.25	20.10	2.40	21.18	0.93	20.17	1.49
Deltoid	26.87	4.47	27.10	2.35	32.88	6.52	29.26	3.21
Biceps (ext)	19.74	1.87	20.12	2.41	22.78	1.97	21.53	2.61
Biceps (flx)	22.11	2.19	21.86	1.84	24.92	2.21	23.55	2.73
Forearm	20.89	1.52	20.48	1.28	22.97	1.31	21.63	1.91
Wrist	13.89	1.28	13.73	0.36	15.25	0.66	14.38	0.89

(Cont.)

Table 1. (cont.) Means and standard deviations for four subcategories of anthropometric assessments of young runners and control subjects

Variable	Runners (N = 28)				Controls (N = 25)			
	Boys (N = 13)		Girls (N = 15)		Boys (N = 13)		Girls (N = 12)	
	M	SD	M	SD	M	SD	M	SD
			Skinfolds					
Subscapular	5.85	1.56	6.07	1.39	7.85	1.95	8.83	2.92
Triceps	7.92	2.41	9.10	2.30	12.08	3.07	12.46	3.86
Biceps	4.73	1.88	5.03	1.01	7.08	2.55	6.12	1.86
Chest	4.73	1.20	4.00	1.16	5.31	2.24	4.13	0.57
Mid-axillary	4.15	1.42	5.03	2.19	5.96	2.38	6.92	3.33
Supra-iliac	5.85	4.10	4.90	1.65	8.95	3.83	7.83	2.99
Abdominal	6.38	3.08	5.47	1.56	10.42	4.94	7.83	2.33
Thigh	11.96	3.61	13.00	3.45	15.54	5.81	14.67	5.02
Knee	5.08	1.30	5.10	0.99	6.85	1.74	7.33	1.61
Calf	6.38	2.03	7.87	2.74	10.19	3.67	10.71	2.61

Results and Discussion

The four subcategories of assessments were separately subjected to multiple analysis of variance (MANOVA) to determine if differences existed between the four groups (runners, controls, boys, girls). Multivariate effects were interpreted with the assistance of univariate Fs and discriminant analysis. Significance levels were set at .05.

Lengths

Results of the MANOVA demonstrated significant group differences for measures of length, $F(11,40) = 8.50$, $p < .001$, but gender effects were not evident. Univariate Fs reached significance for 3 of 11 variables (foot length, upper extremity length, and sitting height). Variables that most clearly distinguished the runners from the control subjects in the discriminant analysis were leg length (-4.177), trochanteric height (2.144), and thigh length (-1.430) (see Table 2). Thus, the greatest weightings were associated with measures of the lower extremity. This distinguishing feature is remarkable because the control subjects had greater values for standing height, (see Table 1), of which leg length is a function. Clearly, this group of young runners had a greater proportion of their total height made up of lower limb length than the control subjects.

Breadths

Significant group, $F(11,40) = 2.44$, $p < .020$, and gender, $F(11,40) = 7.62$, $p < .001$, effects resulted from the MANOVA of breadths. Univariate Fs for the group effects were significant for all variables except bitrochanteric, humerus, and maximum chest widths.

Table 2. Standardized discriminant function coefficients for lengths

Variable	Function 1 (Group)
Brachium	.380
Forearm	1.159
Hand	− .437
Foot	1.037
Thigh	−1.430
Leg	−4.177
Upper extremity	.583
Standing height	.781
Trochanteric height	2.144
Seventh cervical height	.891
Sitting height	− .927
Eigenvalue	2.857
Canonical correlation	.861
Chi square	81.350
Significance (DF)	> .001 (33)

Significant univariate Fs for gender included humerus, femur, ankle, and knee widths. The greatest weightings in function 1 (gender) of the discriminate analysis were for ankle width (.695) bitrochanteric width (− .666) and femur width (.625) (see Table 3 for the relative weightings of the remaining variables).

Reference to the means of Table 1 indicates that control boys and girls had greater breadths than the runners, except for the femur, knee, and ankle, where the male runners had larger values than the female runners and controls. This linearity of skeletal structure, especially in the trunk and upper extremities, is a well-known characteristic of adult distance runners, but these data indicate that such a selection process is already in effect at a younger age.

Table 3. Standardized discriminant function coefficients for breadths

Variable	Function 1 (Group)
Biacromial	− .436
Biiliac	− .181
Bitrochanteric	− .666
Humerus width	.470
Chest (max)	.013
Chest (min)	.557
Femur width	.625
Bideltoid	− .497
Knee width	.016
Ankle width	.695
Wrist width	.005
Eigenvalue	2.372
Canonical correlation	.839
Chi square	83.333
Significance (DF)	.001 (33)

Girths

Multivariate analysis of the girth measures demonstrated significant main effects for group, $F(11,37) = 5.35$, $p < .001$, and gender, $F(14,37) = 17.56$, $p < .001$, and an interaction, $F(14,37) = 1.99$, $p < .048$. Univariate main effects for group included significant F values in all 14 variables. Significant univariate Fs for gender included neck, abdomen, forearm, and wrist girths. Discriminant analyses identified five variables that clearly distinguished boys from girls. They were shoulder (-2.395), neck (2.308), knee (1.925), abdomen (1.829), and chest (-1.601). The relative distinctions of all girth assessments are shown in Table 4.

Mean values on Table 1 indicate that the greatest girths were recorded for the control subjects. In circumferences that customarily serve as fat depots (chest, hip, thigh) the values of the control girls exceeded those of all other groups. On all of the remaining measures, the control boys had the largest values. In 9 of 13 variables, the male runners had the smallest values. Thus, the significant group effect was expected, due to the larger size of both male and female controls. Significant effects for gender are probably due to the relatively small values of the male runners on most of the variables.

Skinfolds

Multivariate analysis for the skinfolds demonstrated significant main effects for group, $F(10,41) = 5.68$, $p < .001$, and gender, $F(10,41) = 2.23$, $p < .035$. Univariate main effects for group included significant Fs for all variables except chest and thigh. Gender effects produced only one of 10 variables with

Table 4. Standardized discriminant function coefficients for girths

Variable	Function 1 (Group)
Neck	2.308
Shoulder	−2.395
Chest	−1.601
Abdominal-1	1.829
Abdominal-2	− .925
Hip	− .208
Thigh	− .780
Knee	1.925
Calf	−1.197
Ankle	− .390
Deltoid	.489
Biceps (ext)	.025
Biceps (flx)	.655
Forearm	.484
Wrist	− .113
Eigenvalue	7.877
Canonical correlation	.942
Chi square	133.970
Significance (DF)	> .001 (45)

Table 5. Standardized discriminant function coefficients for skinfolds

Variable	Function 1 (Group)
Subscapular	.103
Triceps	.687
Biceps	-.167
Chest	-.544
Mid-axillary	.436
Supra-iliac	-.610
Abdominal	.359
Thigh	-.790
Knee	.740
Calf	.640
Eigenvalue	1.617
Canonical correlation	.786
Chi square	65.233
Significance (DF)	.0002 (30)

a significant F, that being chest skinfold. Discriminate analyses identified the thigh, knee, calf, triceps, and suprailiac skinfolds as those making the clearest distinctions between runners and controls (see Table 5). Mean values for all skinfolds (see Table 1) indicate that the control boys or girls had the largest values of all 10 sites.

The results of analyses for skinfold assessments confirmed the hypothesis that had been formulated on observational evidence. Although the control boys and girls were physically active, they did not engage in the extensive aerobic activity of the runners. In skinfold values, the runners were similar, regardless of gender. This was also true of the controls.

In summary, the anthropometric assessments confirmed that these young runners were distinctly different from their peers in bodily size and shape. Specifically, they were shorter in stature, but their leg length made up a greater absolute and relative amount of their total height than was the case for the control group. Runners also had significantly smaller values in girths and skinfolds. In these variables, the female runners were more similar to the male runners than to the control females. The association between body size and running was clearly apparent from the anthropometric data available on these subjects.

References

Abramowicz, M. (1979, April). Adverse effects of running. *The Medical Letter*, pp. 1–3.

Adams, J. (1965). Injury to the throwing arm. *California medicine*, **102**, 127–132.

Åstrand, P., Engström, L., Eriksson, B., Karlberg, P., Nylander, I., Saltin, B., & Thoren, C. (1963). Girl swimmers. With special reference to respiratory and circulatory adaptation and gynecological and psychiatric aspects. *Acta Paediatrica*, (Suppl.147), 1–75.

Daniels, J., & Oldridge, N. (1971). Changes in oxygen consumption of young boys during growth and running training. *Medicine and Science in Sports, 3,* 161–165.

Ekblom, B. (1969). Effect of physical training in adolescent boys. *Journal of Applied Physiology, 27,* 350–355.

Malina, R. (1969). Exercise as an influence upon growth. *Clinical Pediatrics, 8,* 16–26.

Malina, R. (1979). The effects of exercise on specific tissues, dimensions and functions during growth. *Studies in Physical Anthropology, 5,* 12–52.

Malina, R. (1982). Physical growth and maturity characteristics of young athletes. In R. Magill, M. Ash, & F. Smoll (Eds.), *Children in sport* (pp. 73–96). Champaign, IL: Human Kinetics.

Mayers, N., & Gutin, B. (1979). Physiological characteristics of elite prepubertal cross-country runners. *Medicine and Science in Sports, 11,* 172–176.

Mirkin, G. (1981). Marathon kids. *Health, 13,* 8–10.

O'Connell, E. (1979, March). Runner's World Editorial. *Runner's World* 14(12), 5-6.

Olsen, E. (1982, November). Children and running. *The Runner,* pp. 35–44.

Parízková, J. (1968). Longitudinal study of development of body composition and body build in boys of various physical activity. *Human Biology, 40,* 212–225.

Parízková, J. (1973). Body composition and exercise during growth and development. In G. Rarick (Ed.), *Physical activity: Human growth and development* (pp. 98-124). New York: Academic Press.

Rarick, G. (1973). Competitive sports in childhood and early adolescence. In G. Rarick (Ed.), *Physical activity: Human growth and development* (pp. 364–368). New York: Academic Press.

Rarick, G. (1974). Exercise and growth. In W. Johnson & E. Buskirk (Eds.), *Science and medicine of exercise and sport* (2nd ed.). New York: Harper and Row.

Rowe, F. (1934). Growth comparison of athletes and nonathletes. *Research Quarterly, 4,* 108–116.

Schuck, G. (1962). Effects of athletic competition on growth and development of junior high school boys. *Research Quarterly, 33,* 288–298.

Seefeldt, V. (1986). Introduction to an interdisciplinary assessment of competition on elite young distance runners. In M.R. Weiss and D. Gould (Eds.), *Sport for children and youths* (pp. 213-217). Champaign, IL: Human Kinetics.

Shephard, R. (1982). *Physical activity and growth.* Chicago: Year Book Medical Publishers.

33

Serum Alkaline Phosphatase in Young Runners

John R. Downs, Kenneth E. Stephens, and Richard G. Kimball
MICHIGAN STATE UNIVERSITY
EAST LANSING, MICHIGAN, USA

Alkaline phosphatase (AP) activity has been found to be closely related to human growth. Clark and Beck (1950), for example, reported that AP levels were high in the first year of infancy, dropped by the second year of life, and rose again during puberty. Similarly, Krabbe, Christiansen, Rodbra, and Tramsbol (1980) found that AP activity increased with age; that is, AP levels increased up to age 14 in males and age 11 in females and then showed declines before reaching adult levels at age 20 in males and age 18 in females. Males were also found to have significantly higher AP levels than females.

Experimental evidence also suggests that AP is related to growth through its association with rate of bone growth (Farley, Chesnet, & Boyli, 1981). Specifically, Schiede, Henry, Hitz, and Petitclerc (1981) found that age and sex hormonal state (i.e., puberty and menopause) were the main factors which modify plasma AP levels. In addition, it was concluded that bone enzyme was mainly responsible for the variation associated with sex, age, and puberty. Post menarchal females, for instance, reported higher AP plasma levels than females of the same age not experiencing menarche. AP levels in males were also found to be generally stable until age 10, reaching a maximum at age 15, with adult values reached by age 20. Highest AP levels were reached for females at age 12 with adult values obtained by age 17 or 18.

Not only has AP activity been associated with growth, but elevated AP levels have been shown to be related to a wide range of disease conditions. Specifically, in a review of the literature, Maltz and Menarcih (1980) have reported that elevated AP levels are associated with the following conditions: hyperparathyroidism, Paget's disease, healing fractures, osteoblastic tumors (primary or metastatic), osteogenesis imperfecta, familial osteoctasia, osteomalacia, rickets, polyostotic fibrous dysplasia, histiocytosis X, sarciodosis, leukemia, trimethoprin, sulfamethoxazide, hyperthyroidism, systematic infection, ankylosing spondylitis, inherited genetic elevation, and periodontal disease.

Thus, given the demonstrated relationships between AP activity and both bone growth and disease, alkaline phosphatase is an important topic of concern for those studying the biological foundations of growth in children. A special need exists to examine the relationship between AP activity and long-term physical activity levels because the only previous study in the area (King, Statland, & Savory, 1976) examined AP levels in young men engaged in explosive power activity. This segment of the elite young runners study was, therefore, designed to examine AP levels in male and female elite young runners and matched control subjects.

Method

Fasting venous blood samples were obtained from 27 young elite runners and 21 control subjects ranging in age from 9 to 15 years. Automated KDA profiles were performed on the samples. The kinetic alkaline phosphatase assay is based on the method of utilizing p-nitrophenylphosphate as the substrate in a diethanolamine-succinate buffer. The rate of appearance of p-nitrophenol (quantitated photometrically) is directly proportional to the amount of alkaline phosphatase activity present in the original.

Results

The mean alkaline phosphatase activity for all groups ($M = 725.1$ mg/kl, elite females; $M = 424.6$, control females; $M = 598.8$, elite males; $M = 549.1$, control males) was computed. All four groups exhibited elevated AP levels above the upper limits of the normal range (279 mg/kl). The results of a 2 × 2 (groups by gender) ANOVA indicated a significant group main effects (elite vs. control), $F(1,44) = 5.67$, $p < .022$. The main effects for gender and the interaction of group by gender were not significant, however.

Discussion

All group means showed elevations of AP activity, thus confirming the findings of most previous researchers. The significant group main effect also revealed that the elite runners showed marked elevation of activity over nonrunning control children. Moreover, an inspection of the individual group means shows that the marked elevation in AP levels for the elite young runners resulted primarily from the high AP activity in the female runners. These results suggest a rapid bone turnover in the young female runners. Correlation with injury data, menarch onset, and other factors would be of interest and should be pursued in future studies.

References

Clark, L.L., & Beck, E. (1950). Serum alkaline phosphatase and growth in adolescent children. *Journal of Pediatrics, 36*, 335–341.

Farley, J.R., Chesnet, C.H., & Boyli, P.J. (1981). Improved method for quantitative determination in serum alkaline phosphatase of skeletal origin. *Clinical Chemistry, 12*, 2002–2007.

King, S.W., Statland, B.E., & Savory, J. (1976). The effect of a short burst of exercise or activity on values of enzymes in sera of healthy young men. *Clinical Chemistry. Acta, 72*, 211–218.

Krabbe, S., Christiansen, C., Rodbra, P., & Tramsbol, L. (1980). Pubertal growth as reflected by simultaneous changes in bone mineral content and serum alkaline phosphatase. *Acta Paediatrica Scandinavica, 09*(11), 49–52.

Maltz, J., & Menarcih, J.R. (1980). Elevated alkaline phosphatase: An interesting cause. *Maryland State Medical Journal, 12*, 34.

Schiede, F., Henny, J., Hitz, J., & Petitclerc, C. (1981). Total bone and liver alkaline phosphatase in plasma: Biological variations and reference limits. *Clinical Chemistry, 29*(4), 634–641.

34

Temporal and Kinematic Characteristics of the Gait Patterns of Youth Distance Runners During an Intermittent Treadmill Stress Test

Eugene W. Brown, Dianne Ulibarri, Kaveh Abani, Michael Marrone, and Sharon Evans
MICHIGAN STATE UNIVERSITY
EAST LANSING, MICHIGAN, USA

Historically, running has been the focus of many biomechanics investigations (Miller, 1978). The mechanics of running, as performed by adults (often elite athletes), encompass the preponderance of these studies. During the past 25 years, however, researchers also have studied the influence of physical development on the kinematic and kinetic characteristics of running patterns of children (Beck, 1966; Brown, 1978; Clouse, 1959; Dittmer, 1962; Fortney, 1964; Mersereau, 1974; Wickstrom, 1977). More recently, the adult fitness boom and accompanying running activities have caused several biomechanists to direct their attention to the analysis of various aspects of distance running (Adrian & Kreighbaum, 1973; Cavanagh, Pollock & Landa, 1977; Gregor & Kirkendall, 1978; Nelson & Gregor, 1976) including the influence of fatigue (Elliot & Roberts, 1980) and changes in running speed and grade of running surface (Hoshikowa, Matsui, & Miyashita, 1973; Ito, Komi, Sjodin, & Bosco, 1983; Nelson & Osterhaodt, 1971) on the mechanics of performance.

The purported benefits of aerobic activity have influenced many parents to involve their children in recreational and competitive distance running. These young athletes, then, join adults in exposing themselves to overuse injuries associated with the repetitive absorption of force. Potential risks of epiphyseal growth plate damage, exposure to hypothermic and hyperthermic environmental extremes during training, and psychological stress versus fitness benefits to prepubertal and pubertal children participating in distance running has prompted considerable debate (American Academy of Pediatrics, 1982; Caldwell, 1982; International Athletes Association, 1982; Mirkin, 1981; O'Connell, 1979; Olsen, 1982; Sheehan, 1983). However, there is a paucity of research evidence to support either side of this issue. In particular, research on the kinematic and kinetic characteristics of the running patterns of youth distance runners was not found in the literature. This study represented an initial attempt to describe the movement patterns of youth distance runners. It was conducted as part of the elite young runners study with the purpose of describing temporal and kinematic characteristics associated with changes in speed and grade of treadmill running and in level of subject fatigue.

Method

The subjects for this study were 13 male and 15 female elite distance runners. At the time of data collection, the mean ages for the male and female groups were 148.2 ($SD = 18.9$) and 154.9 ($SD = 18.8$) months, respectively.

Stress Test

A stress test was administered to each of the subjects as part of a battery of tests chosen for the study. The stress test protocol consisted of alternating 3 min of running on a treadmill and 3 min of rest. During each rest interval, the treadmill speed and grade were systematically increased: Level 1, 2.68 m/s at 0% grade; Level 2, 2.68 m/s at 5% grade; Level 3, 3.13 m/s at 6% grade; Level 4, 3.58 m/s at 7% grade; Level 5, 4.02 m/s at 8% grade; and Level 6, 4.47 m/s at 9% grade. Subjects tested with this protocol were asked to run to exhaustion. Therefore, the total amount of exercise varied with each subject's physical condition and perception of exhaustion. Each subject was familiarized with running on the treadmill prior to participating in the stress test.

Limitations

Data on the mechanics of running were collected simultaneously with the administration of the treadmill stress test. Therefore, the scope of this study was limited to the analysis of running patterns exhibited under the constraints of the stress test protocol.

Are the mechanics of running on a treadmill similar to overground running? This question has been investigated by several researchers (Davies, 1980; Elliott & Blanksby, 1976; Frishberg, 1983; Nelson, Dillman, Lagasse & Bickett, 1972; Norman, Sharratt, Pezzack & Noble, 1976; Van Ingen Schenau, 1980). Nelson et al. (1972), for example, reported no significant differences in stride length and stride rate between overground and treadmill running in adult male experienced runners at velocities below 6.4 m/s on horizontal and uphill gradients (+10%). On a +10% gradient at 3.35 and 4.88 m/s, significantly shorter nonsupport times were recorded for treadmill running. Similarly, Elliott and Blanksby (1976) studied the running patterns of college age male and female joggers and found no significant differences in their stride length, stride rate, support phase time, and nonsupport phase time between horizontal overground and treadmill running at velocities of 4.8 m/s and slower. Whether nonsignificant differences existed between overground and treadmill running patterns in the subjects who participated in the present study was not determined.

Cinematographic Data Collection

Standard cinematograhic procedures, using a 16mm LOCAM camera, were employed to record the runners' movements in the sagittal plane. Commencing at the middle of the 3rd min (150 s) into each complete exercise level, cinematographic records of three or more strides were obtained at 100 frames per second on each subject. During the exercise level in which exhaustion was predicted to occur, an attempt was made to record three or more strides of the runners' gait patterns at the middle of the 1st, 2nd, and 3rd min (beginning at 30, 90, and 150 s, respectively). If a subject failed to complete an exercise level in which exhaustion was predicted to occur, less than three records of that level may have been collected.

Data Analysis

A Vanguard Motion Analyzer was used to project the processed film images onto a screen surface. Data analyzed in this study consisted of temporal and kinematic characteristics of each subject's running strides as recorded on film during their intermittent treadmill stress test. Prior to descriptive and statistical analysis, the data was categorized into nonfatigue and fatigue conditions. Data from the 3rd min of each level was included in the nonfatigue condition only if the subject ran in a subsequent level. For the fatigue condition, the running patterns were analyzed only for the exercise level in which exhaustion occurred and only if the subject completed a minimum of approximately 90 s (two filmings) of running during that level.

Temporal Analysis

Time intervals for support, nonsupport, forward swing, and stride were determined from the timing lights included in the film images. Two support, nonsupport, and forward swing intervals are included in a stride. The data used to represent each of these three intervals were the means of the two values within a stride. Forward swing was defined according to James and Slocum (1968) as the interval following toe off, beginning with the forward rotation of the thigh and ending at maximum hip flexion. Time intervals were also computed as a percentage of the total stride time. Separate 2×4 (sex by level) MANOVAs were conducted for each of the four dependent time measures collected under the nonfatigue condition. These were conducted separately because some of the dependent measures were linear components of others. Fatigue was treated as occurring at a single level. Therefore, MANOVAs could not be conducted on the fatigue condition.

Kinematic Analysis

The analysis of the mechanics of performance was limited to a description of the angular orientation of the left shank and thigh throughout the stride and a statistical comparison of stride length. The angular position of the shank and thigh were determined by digitizing projected film images of the stride on-line to a Cyber 750 main frame computer. Joint markers placed on the centers of the left ankle, knee, and hip joints prior to filming, served as targets for obtaining Cartesian coordinates. Raw data angles for the two body segments were measured at the distal joint of each segment relative to the right horizontal. The arrays of raw data were smoothed using a 4th order Butterworth filter.

Stride length was calculated from the Cartesian coordinates of the left heel from the first to the second heel strike. Because of anthropometric length variations among subjects, a standardized stride length was determined for each subject by dividing stride length by the standing height of his or her trochanter above the ground. Separate 2 × 4 (sex by level) MANOVAs were computed for these two dependent variables under the nonfatigue condition.

Results

Separate 2 × 4 (sex by level) MANOVA treatments using repeated measures on four dependent time measures for the nonfatigue condition resulted in 6 females and 10 males being included in the analysis. Others were excluded because they did not run into the 4th or 5th level. The results of this statistical analysis demonstrated significant level main effects on all of the dependent measures (see Table 1).

Specifically, increased level was associated with decreased support, forward swing, and stride time and with increased nonsupport time. A sex main effect was noted for the nonsupport phase: Males had significantly shorter nonsupport times than females. A significant sex by level interaction also occurred for the forward swing time interval. Similar results were evidenced (see Figure 1) when comparing the means of all subjects under nonfatigue conditions (n = 13, 13, 13, 10, 1 for males for Levels 1 through 5, respectively; n = 15, 15, 13, 6 for females for Levels 1 through 4, respectively). An evaluation of the temporal characteristics of treadmill running under fatigue conditions did not result in well-defined trends within the intervals in which exhaustion occurred.

Separate 2 × 4 (sex by level) MANOVAs, using repeated measures, were also conducted on stride length and on standardized stride length data for the nonfatigue condition. Significant level main effects were computed for each of the two dependent distance measures (see Table 2).

Increased stride length and standardized stride length were associated with increased level. Mean values computed for all subjects under nonfatigue conditions were in accord with the MANOVA results (see Table 3). Stride length

Table 1. Summary table of sex by level MANOVAs for temporal dependent measures under nonfatigue conditions

Source	df	F
Support		
Sex[a]	1,14	0.16
Level	3,12	65.15*
Interaction	3,12	3.16
Nonsupport		
Sex	1,14	6.27*
Level	3,12	5.73*
Interaction	3,12	2.64
Forward Swing		
Sex	1,14	3.73
Level	3,12	6.39*
Interaction	3,12	4.49*
Stride		
Sex	1,14	2.15
Level	3,12	11.84*
Interaction	3,12	2.10

[a] n = 6 females and 10 males.
*$p < .05$.

and standardized stride length under fatigue conditions did not result in well-defined trends within the intervals in which fatigue occurred.

The orientation of the left shank and thigh relative to the right horizontal was determined throughout the stride for each subject under both the fatigue and nonfatigue conditions. Figure 2 shows a typical plot of the nonfatigue results. In general, an increase in range of movement was associated with increased level. The indirect relationship between stride time and level could also be seen in these plots. Patterns associated with fatigue conditions were not easily discerned.

Table 2. Summary table of sex by level MANOVAs for stride and standardized stride length under nonfatigue conditions

Source	df	F
Stride Length		
Sex[a]	1,14	4.00
Level	3,12	80.92*
Interaction	3,12	2.66
Standardized Stride Length		
Sex	1,14	0.55
Level	3,12	156.60*
Interaction	3,12	2.28

[a] n = 6 females and 10 males.
*$p < .05$.

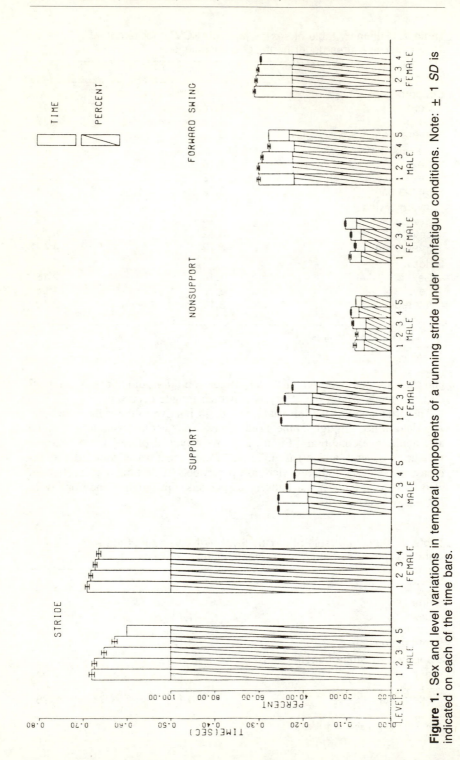

Figure 1. Sex and level variations in temporal components of a running stride under nonfatigue conditions. Note: ± 1 *SD* is indicated on each of the time bars.

Discussion

The results from the temporal and kinematic analysis of running revealed significant decreases in support, forward swing, and stride time and increases in nonsupport time, stride length, and standardized stride length with simultaneous increases in treadmill speed and grade. These results on elite youth distance runners are somewhat similar to previous findings on adults. Nelson & Osterhoudt (1971) reported an increase in stride length and stride rate and a decrease in support time with increases in speed of running (3.35, 4.88, and 6.40 m/s). With increases in grade (from 0 to 10%), they found a decrease in support time. These findings are in agreement with the present study. However, their finding of decreased stride length is contrary to the present findings. This disagreement may be due to a dominant influence of changes in speed of running over changes in grade when simultaneously altered. Hoshikawa, Matsui, and Miyashita (1973) studied the pattern of the ankle, knee, and hip accompanying increases in velocity (3.33, 4.17, 5.00, 5.83, 6.67, 7.50, and 8.33 m/s) in horizontal overground running. They reported increased displacements with increased speeds, which is in general agreement with the present findings.

What influence does fatigue have on the movement patterns of the shank and thigh during running? In the present study, temporal and kinematic differences were not predictably altered by changes in fatigue. Elliot and Ackland (1981) reported significant decreases in velocity and stride length in adults with increased fatigue in overground running. These changes were accompanied by slight changes in the angle of the thigh and shank at foot strike with the onset of fatigue. Whether or not these changes were related to the velocity

Table 3. Mean values for stride length and standardized stride length under nonfatigue conditions

Level	1	2	3	4	5
			Males		
n	13	13	13	10	1
Stride Length (m)					
M	1.83	1.81	2.04	2.01	2.42
SD	0.17	0.15	0.18	0.65	0.00
Standardized Stride Length					
M	2.37	2.35	2.65	2.89	3.04
SD	0.19	0.15	0.14	0.16	0.00
			Females		
n	15	15	13	6	0
Stride Length (m)					
M	1.85	1.83	2.10	2.37	
SD	0.13	0.12	0.14	0.18	
Standardized Stride Length					
M	2.38	2.34	2.66	2.96	
SD	0.18	0.16	0.16	0.23	

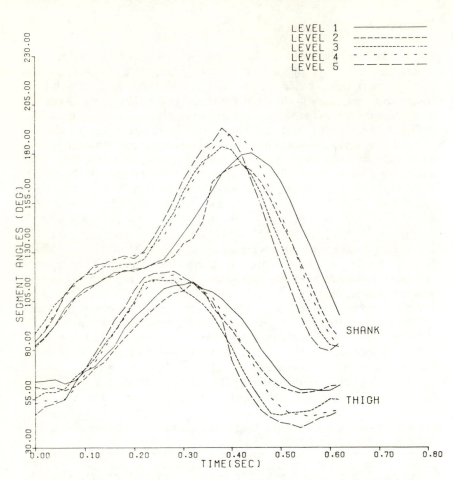

Figure 2. Typical angular orientation pattern of the shank and thigh for a complete stride, beginning and ending with left foot strike.

changes was not determined. In the present study, the subjects could not drastically alter their running velocity in a given level and still remain on the treadmill. Therefore, the limits placed upon velocity changes within a given level of treadmill running may have confined variability in other temporal and kinematic parameters.

References

Adrian, M., & Kreighbaum, E. (1973). Mechanics of distance running during competition. In S. Cerquiglini, A. Venerando, & J. Wartenweiler (Eds.), *Biomechanics III* (pp. 345–358). Basel, Switzerland: S. Karger AG.

American Academy of Pediatrics. (1982). *News and Comment,* **33**(6), 11.

Beck, M.C. (1966). *The path of the center of gravity during running in boys, grades one to six.* Unpublished doctoral dissertation, University of Wisconsin, Madison.

Brown, E.W. (1978). *Biomechanical analysis of the running patterns of girls 3 to 10 years of age.* Unpublished doctoral dissertation, University of Oregon, Eugene.

Caldwell, F. (1982). Physician urges caution for child marathoners. *Physician and Sportsmedicine,* **10**(6), 26.

Cavanagh, P.R., Pollock, M.L., & Landa, J. (1977). A biomechanical comparison of elite and good distance runners. *Annals of the New York Academy of Sciences,* **301**, 328–345.

Clouse, F.C. (1959). *A kinematic analysis of the development of the running pattern of preschool boys.* Unpublished doctoral dissertation, University of Wisconsin, Madison.

Davies, C.T.M. (1980). Effects of wind assistance and resistance on the forward motion of a runner. *Journal of Applied Physiology,* **48**, 702–709.

Dittmer, J. (1962). *A kinematic analysis of the development of the running pattern of grade school girls and certain factors which distinguish good and poor performance at the observed ages.* Unpublished master's thesis, University of Wisconsin, Madison.

Elliott, B.C., & Blanksby, B.A. (1976). Cinematographic analysis of overground and treadmill running by males and females. *Medicine and Science in Sports,* **8**(2), 84–87.

Elliott, B.C., & Roberts, A.D. (1980). A biomechanical evaluation of the role of fatigue in middle-distance running. *Canadian Journal of Applied Sport Science,* **5**(4), 203–207.

Fortney, V.L. (1964). *The swinging limb in running of boys ages 7 through 11.* Unpublished master's thesis, University of Wisconsin, Madison.

Frishberg, B.A. (1983). An analysis of overground and treadmill sprinting. *Medicine and Science in Sports and Exercise,* **15**(6), 478–485.

Gregor, R.T., & Kirkendall, D. (1978). Performance efficiency of world class female marathon runners. In E. Asmussen & K. Jorgensen (Eds.), *Biomechanics VI-B* (pp. 40–45). Baltimore: University Park Press.

Hoshikawa, T., Matsui, H., & Miyashita, M. (1973). Analysis of running pattern in relation to speed. In S. Cerquiglini, A. Venerando, & J. Wartenweiler (Eds.), *Biomechanics III* (pp. 342–348). Basel, Switzerland: S. Karger AG.

International Athletics Association Federation. (1982). Long-distance training and competition for young children—Is it harmful? *IAAF Bulletin,* **82**.

Ito, A., Komi, P.V., Sjodin, B., & Bosco, C. (1983). Mechanical efficiency of positive work in running at different speeds. *Medicine and Science in Sports and Exercise,* **15**(4), 299–308.

James, S.L., & Slocum, D.B. (1968). Biomechanics of running. *Journal of the American Medical Association,* **205**(11), 97–101.

Mersereau, M.R. (1974). *A cinematographic analysis of the development of the running pattern of female infants at 22 and 25 months of age.* Unpublished master's thesis, Purdue University, Lafayette, IN.

Miller, D. (1978). Biomechanics of running—What should the future hold? *Canadian Journal of Sports Science,* **3**, 229–236.

Mirkin, G. (1981). Marathon kids—What really happens to the littlest runners? *Health,* **13**, 8–10.

Nelson, R.C., Dillman, C.J., Lagasse, P., & Bickett, P. (1972). Biomechanics of overground versus treadmill running. *Medicine and Science in Sports,* **4**(4), 233–240.

Nelson, R.C., & Gregor, R.T. (1976). Biomechanics of distance running: A longitudinal study. *Research Quarterly,* **47**(3), 417–428.

Nelson, R.C., & Osterhoudt, R.G. (1971). In J. Vredenbregt & J. Wartenweiler (Eds.), *Biomechanics II* (pp. 220–224). Basel, Switzerland: S. Karger AG.

Norman, R.W., Sharratt, M.T., Pezzack, J.C., & Noble, E.G. (1976). Reexamination of the mechanical efficiency of horizontal treadmill running. In P.V. Komi (Ed.), *Biomechanics V-B* (pp. 87–93). Baltimore: University Park Press.

O'Connell, E. (1979, March). Age group records. *Runner's World*, pp. 5–6.

Olsen, E. (1982, November). The experts' view—Kids stuff. *The Runner*, pp. 36–45.

Sheehan, G. (1983, January). Children running? Why not? *The Physician and Sportsmedicine, 11*(1), 51.

Van Ingen Schenau, G.J. (1980). Some fundamental aspects of the biomechanics of overground versus treadmill locomotion. *Medicine and Science in Sports and Exercise, 12*(4), 257–261.

Wickstrom, R.L. (1977). *Fundamental motor patterns* (2nd ed.). Philadelphia: Lea & Febiger.

35

Serum Lipid and Lipoprotein Profiles in Elite Age-Group Runners

Bryan W. Smith, William P. Metheny, and Albert W. Sparrow
MICHIGAN STATE UNIVERSITY
EAST LANSING, MICHIGAN, USA

Coronary Artery Disease (CAD) is one of the most highly reported diseases in adults today. Severe atherosclerosis has been described in over 90% of cases of clinical CAD. There is also strong support to indicate that atherosclerosis starts to develop during childhood. In studies by Ibsen, Lous, and Anderson (1982) and Pometta, Micheli, Raymond, Oberhaensli, and Suenram (1980), for instance, decreased high-density lipoprotein cholesterol (HDL-C) and hyperlipidemia were the only risk factors that exhibited a high frequency in the progeny of CAD patients.

Physical activity in the form of aerobic exercise has been implicated as the primary factor responsible for increasing both the total amount and the percentage of HDL-C in the serum. Unfortunately, the research on physical activity and its effects on serum lipids and lipoproteins has focused almost exclusively on adults. The few studies reporting children's lipid profiles attempted to correlate only general physical activity or short-term exercise programs with HDL-C levels. Because habitual endurance exercise in adults is associated with a reduced serum lipid risk for atherosclerosis, this aspect of the young runners study examined the effect of habitual endurance exercise on serum lipids and lipoproteins in elite age-group endurance runners.

Method

Twenty-eight runners, 15 girls and 13 boys ranging in age from 9.5 to 15 years, were invited to participate in the study. Each runner had been in training for at least 2 years with 16 runners in training for 4 years or more. The control group consisted of 24 subjects, 11 girls and 13 boys, who were active participants in various other organized physical activities. All subjects were in good health and were taking no medications.

As reported by Vogel (1986) earlier in this volume, each subject was instructed to complete a detailed activity history questionnaire. The parents completed a family health history prior to their child's test date. Blood was drawn from an antecubital vein after a 12-hour fast during which no strenuous exercise occurred. Lipid analyses were performed according to the procedures described by the Lipid Research Centers. Adiposity of the participants was determined by using skinfold measurements (see Seefeldt, Haubenstricker, Branta & McKeag, 1986). Blood pressure and heart rate were recorded in the resting state. Work capacity was measured in terms of maximal oxygen uptake using a discontinuous treadmill protocol. Each subject was instructed, prior to the test date, to complete a 24-hour diet diary as reported by Schemmel, Stone, & Conn (1986). These diaries were coded for 57 nutrients using the Michigan State University Nutrient Data Bank. Total caloric intake, total cholesterol ingested, and percentages of caloric intake from fat, protein, and carbohydrate were computed for each individual.

Results and Discussion

Activity questionnaires collected and reported earlier by Vogel (1986) ascertained the number of years of participation in the past 5 years separately for the runners and control groups. Participation in activity is comparable, the runners averaging 3.7 years with a range of 2 to 5 years and controls averaging 3.5 years with a range 0 to 5 years. The number of weeks of participation per year, however, are quite different in the two groups with the runners' activity averaging two times that of the controls. In 1982, runners participated 43 weeks per year with a range of 30 to 50 weeks while controls participated in activity 23 weeks per year with a range of 0 to 47 weeks. Thus the controls are seen to be active/sedentary children but far less active than the elite age-group endurance runners.

Finally, we can look at activity in terms of runners' participation in miles run per week and controls' participation in days per week and/or minutes per day. Again the progression of activity from 1978 to 1982 is seen with the runners in 1982 averaging 27 miles per week, ranging from 7 to 49 miles per week. Controls average activity was 3 days per week with a range of 0 to 6 days per week with an average of 75 min per day. Again, we can conjecture that the work output of the runners exceeds that of the controls, yet the latter far exceeds that of the sedentary child.

With these activity data in mind we now look at blood pressure and resting heart rate in the runners and controls. Significant differences were demonstrated in all three variables: systolic blood pressures averaging 111 mm Hg in runners versus 123 ml Hg in controls; diastolic pressures 68 versus 77 mm Hg respectively; and resting heart rates of 65 versus 81 bpm. All show differences significant at the .01 level.

Cardiorespiratory fitness is assessed by maximal oxygen uptake (max VO_2) during the treadmill testing. The specifics of these data are reported in Van Huss et al. (1986). The different mean values for max VO_2 for runners (62.7 ml/kg/min) and controls (51.4 ml/kg/min) substantiates our classification of the participants as elite runners and physically active controls. Aerobic exercise training probably also accounts for the runners' significantly decreased adiposity as shown by body composition measurements using skinfold measurements.

The lipoprotein analysis was conducted using a 2 × 2 (group by gender) MANOVA with four dependent measures: (a) total cholesterol (TC), (b) high-density lipoprotein (HDL-C), (c) low-density lipoprotein (LDL-C), and (d) triglycerides (TG). The results of the MANOVA revealed a significant group effect, $F(4,47) = 6.46$, $p < .001$. Univariate F tests indicated no differences in total cholesterol (TC) between the two groups but a significant difference existed in the fractional distribution of high-density lipoprotein (HDL-C), $F(1,50) = 21.76$, $p < .0002$, and low-density lipoprotein cholesterol (LDL-C), $F(1,50) = 4.44$, $p < .04$. The HDL-C of the runners was approximately 32% higher than the controls (70 mg/dl vs. 53 mg/dl). The runners' LDL-C exhibited a concomitant decrease of 13.8% (98 mg/dl vs. 114 mg/dl). Triglycerides (TG) were also significantly different between the two groups, $F(1,50) = 4.54$, $p < .04$. Runners had lower triglyceride levels ($M = 68.25$) than controls ($M = 94.38$). These changes have not been shown previously in children.

We investigated the possibility that the serum lipid and lipoprotein differences between groups were exercise dose-dependent. Using Pearson product correlations of work capacity of both groups versus serum lipid and lipoprotein variables, a modest positive correlation ($r = .39$) existed between work capacity and high-density lipoprotein cholesterol. As expected, negative correlations are shown for triglycerides ($r = -.33$) and low-density lipoprotein cholesterol ($r = -.18$), respectively.

The lipid profiles of these youth age-group distance runners parallel the lipid profiles of elite adult distance runners studied by Martin, Haskell and Wood (1977). These lipid trends are further supported by similar findings in marathon runners and highly physically active adult men (Adner & Castelli, 1980; Hartung, Foreyt, Mitchell, Vlasek, & Gotto, 1980; Hartung & Squires, 1980; Lehtonen & Viikari, 1978). Our results are in disagreement, however, with work on children which shows no change in lipoproteins after exercise programs of 4 weeks (Linder, DuRant, Gray, & Harkness, 1979) and 8 weeks (Linder, DuRant, & Mahoney, 1983), respectively. The results support the work of Thorland and Gilliam (1981), who reported that physical activity in children decreased TG and the TC/HDL-C ratio and had no effect on TC. However, our results disagree with Thorland and Gilliam's (1981) findings of no change in HDL-C and LDL-C when comparing low physically active children. These disparate results are best explained by varying levels and duration of exercise programs—the extreme differences in level and duration of activity in our study groups predictably produced the greatest variance from control lipid levels.

Dietary analysis as reported by Schemmel, Stone, and Conn (1986) showed no significant differences between groups in total caloric intake. The runners consumed fewer total calories; yet slightly more calories/kg were consumed by runners who compared to the controls. After analyzing dietary intake, no difference was demonstrated in runners versus controls in terms of percent of calories from fat, proteins, or carbohydrates. Neither was there a significant difference in the amount of cholesterol ingested per day.

Conclusions

We conclude that habitual aerobic training as performed by elite age-group runners is associated with significant changes in serum lipids and lipoproteins. We do not believe these changes are related to dietary intake as we demonstrated no differences in control/athlete intake dietary analysis. We propose the changes are exercise dose-dependent and that even greater differences will be shown when the elite athletes and control active children are compared with random control children and/or inactive children. Finally, we propose that physical activity in children may be important in terms of cardiovascular risk for later life as has been shown in numerous adult studies correlating vigorous continuing exercise programs with similar lipoprotein changes, and correlating the latter with improved cardiovascular risk status and increased longevity.

An additional but unrelated important outcome of this study demands that we point out the futility of the current widespread use of serum total cholesterol as a screening procedure for lipid extremes, especially in children. Note that total cholesterol is the *only* lipid measurement showing virtually *no* difference between elite athlete and control levels. This is, of course, a function of the extreme difference in HDL-C levels between the two groups and, to a lesser extent, the difference in LDL-C levels. The use of serum total cholesterol as a screening procedure for lipid extremes in children is of no value. The single most important lipoprotein screening assessment in children is HDL-C.

References

Adner, M.M, & Castelli, W.P. (1980). Elevated high-density lipoprotein levels in marathon runners. *Journal of the American Medical Association, 243*, 534–536.

Hartung, G.H., Foreyt, J.P., Mitchell, R.E., Vlasek, I., & Gotto, A.M. (1980). Relation of diet to high-density lipoprotein cholesterol in middle-aged marathon runners, joggers, and inactive men. *New England Journal of Medicine, 302*, 357–361.

Hartung, G.H., & Squires, W.G. (1980). Exercise and HDL cholesterol in middle-aged men. *Physician and Sportsmedicine, 8*, 74–79.

Ibsen, K.K., Lous, P., & Anderson, G.E. (1982). Coronary heart risk factors in 177 children and young adults whose fathers died from ischemic heart disease before age 45. *Acta Paediatrica Scandinvica, 71*, 609–613.

Lehtonen, A., & Viikari, J. (1978). Serum triglycerides and cholesterol and serum high-density lipoprotein cholesterol in highly physically active men. *Acta Physiologia Scandinvica*, **204**, 111-114.

Linder, C.W., DuRant, R.H., Gray, R.G., & Harkness, J.W. (1979). The effects of exercise on serum lipid levels in children. *Clinical Research, 27*, 797.

Linder, C.W., DuRant, R.H. & Mahoney, O.H. (1983). The effect of physical conditioning on serum lipids and lipoproteins in white male adolescents. *Medicine and Science in Sports and Exercise, 15*, 237-242.

Martin, R.P., Haskell, W.L., & Wood, P.D. (1977). Blood chemistry and lipid profiles of elite distance runners. *Annals of the New York Academy of Science*, **301**, 346-360.

Pometta, D., Micheli, H., Raymond, L., Oberhaensli, I., & Suenram, A. (1980). Decreased HDL cholesterol in prepubertal and pubertal children of CHD patients. *Atherosclerosis, 36*, 101-109.

Schemmel, R.A., Stone, M., & Conn, C. (1986). Comparison of dietary habits and nutrient intake of competitive runners with age/gender matched controls. In M. Weiss & D. Gould (Eds.), *Sport for children and youths* (pp. 231-238). Champaign, IL: Human Kinetics.

Seefeldt, V., Haubenstricker, J., Branta, C., & McKeag, D. (1986). Anthropometric assessment of body size and shape of young runners and control subjects. In M. Weiss & D. Gould (Eds.), *Sport for children and youths* (pp. 247-254). Champaign, IL: Human Kinetics.

Thorland, W.G., & Gilliam, T.B. (1981). Comparison of serum lipids between habitually high and low active pre-adolescent males. *Medicine and Science in Sports and Exercise, 13*, 316-321.

Van Huss, W.D., Stephens, K.E., Vogel, P., Anderson, P., Kurowski, T., Janes, J.A., & Fitzgerald, C. (1986). Physiological and perceptual responses of elite age-group distance runners during progressive intermittent work to exhaustion. In M. Weiss & D. Gould (Eds.), *Sport for children and youths* (pp. 239-246). Champaign, IL: Human Kinetics.

Vogel, P.G. (1986). Training and racing involvement of elite young runners. In M. Weiss & D. Gould (Eds.), *Sport for children and youths* (pp. 219-224). Champaign, IL: Human Kinetics.

36

The Performance of Young Runners and Control Subjects on Reaction Time, Movement Time, and Selected Motor Skills

John L. Haubenstricker, Ardavan E-Lotfalian, Crystal F. Branta, Joy E. Kiger, and Sharon E. Culliton
MICHIGAN STATE UNIVERSITY
EAST LANSING, MICHIGAN, USA

A basic issue confronting researchers in youth sport has been the examination of the effects of early sport specialization on various physical, physiological, social, and motoric parameters of young athletes. More specifically, do athletes such as young distance runners differ in physical characteristics and basic motor abilities from sedentary peers or from age mates who participate in a variety of sport activities? and If so, do these differences become magnified across time as specialized training continues?

A second issue is the possibility of differential gender effects resulting from intensive and extended training in a sport during the growing years. For example, does early specialization in running affect boys and girls differently? Do prepubertal boys and girls respond physiologically in the same way to the same training regimen?

The purpose of this study was twofold: (a) to determine if elite young runners differ from a group of control subjects on measures of reaction time, movement time, and motor skill performance, and (b) to determine if gender differences in performance on these measures exist among the young runners and control subjects.

It was hypothesized that because the ability to react and perform short movements quickly does not appear to be a critical element in long-distance running, the reaction time and movement time performance of the runners and control subjects should not differ significantly.

However, it also was hypothesized that significant performance differences favoring the runners would occur on motor skills that require muscular endurance or flexibility. Gender differences were hypothesized to favor males on reaction time, movement time, power, muscular endurance, and agility measures, and to favor females on balance and flexibility measures.

Methods

The sample consisted of 27 elite young runners (12 males, 15 females) and 24 control subjects (13 males, 11 females). The subjects ranged in age from 9 to 15 years with a mean age of 12.68 years ($SD = 1.64$ years). The sample is described in detail by Seefeldt (1986) earlier in this volume.

Measures

Fractionated reaction time and movement time measures were obtained according to procedures outlined by E-Lotfalian (1981). Premotor time (PMT), motor time (MT), total reaction time (TRT), and movement time (MVT) scores were collected for the hand and foot under conditions of simple and choice responses.

A battery of eight motor tests designed to assess various abilities underlying gross motor behavior was administered to each of the subjects. The modified sideward leap (Scott & French, 1959) was administered to assess dynamic balance. Agility was assessed with the quadrant jump (Johnson & Nelson, 1969) and the figure eight run, a modification of the dodging run developed by Gates and Sheffield (1940). The former tested the ability of the subject to change body position rapidly by jumping; the latter tested the ability of the subject to change direction while running.

Leg power was determined through the vertical jump (Johnson & Nelson, 1969) and the standing long jump (AAHPERD, 1976). Muscular strength and endurance were assessed via the flexed arm hang (Branta, Haubenstricker, & Seefeldt, 1984) and the modified sit-ups test (AAHPERD, 1980). Flexibility of the lower back and posterior thighs was evaluated with the sit and reach test (AAHPERD, 1980).

Procedure

The subjects were tested individually on all of the tests. The order of the response conditions for the reaction time and movement time tests was foot-simple, foot-choice, hand-simple, and hand-choice. For the motor tests, the subjects progressed through a circuit of stations established to minimize fatigue in specific muscle groups. All tests were administered on the same day.

Results and Discussion

Multivariate analysis of variance (MANOVA) and multiple discriminant function analysis were used to examine differences between the runners and control subjects and between males and females. Because of the high intercorrelations among reaction time components, separate MANOVAs were carried out for PMT, MT, TRT, MVT as well as for the motor skills test battery. Significance level for the MANOVAs was set at .01 to minimize alpha error. The descriptive statistics for all the dependent variables are available upon request from the principal author.

No significant differences were found between the runners and control subjects or between the males and females on any of the fractionated reaction time and movement time measures (see Table 1). The lack of significant differences between the runners and the controls on these measures is not surprising and supports the outcomes hypothesized. A task analysis of distance running suggests that reaction time is not a critical factor in determining success and

Table 1. Summary of multivariate statistics for the reaction time, movement time, and motor skill performance of young runners and control subjects

Source of variation	Approx. F	df	Sig. of F
Premotor time			
Group	.399	2,4	.808
Gender	.064	2,4	.992
Interaction	.697	2,4	.598
Motor time			
Group	.871	2,4	.489
Gender	1.623	2,4	.186
Interaction	.758	2,4	.558
Total reaction time			
Group	1.151	2,4	.345
Gender	.207	2,4	.933
Interaction	1.599	2,4	.192
Movement time			
Group	1.613	2,4	.188
Gender	.349	2,4	.843
Interaction	.274	2,4	.893
Motor skills			
Group	5.604	2,8	<.001
Gender	5.179	2,8	<.001
Interaction	1.053	2,8	.414

that other variables such as cardiorespiratory and muscular endurance are of much greater importance.

The failure to obtain gender differences on the reaction time measures with young subjects is not consistent with results reported in the literature. Young males generally exhibit faster reaction times than young females (Eckert & Eichorn, 1977; Goodenough, 1935; Hodgens, 1963; Noble, Baker, & Jones, 1964; Thomas, Gallagher, & Purvis, 1981), although not in all instances (Fulton & Hubbard, 1975). Male superiority in reacting to stimuli is not as consistent at adult age levels (Henry, 1961; Klimovitch, 1977; Kroll, 1974; Yandell & Spirduso, 1981).

Significant group and gender differences were obtained for the motor skills battery. However, there was no interaction between these two independent variables (see Table 1). The absence of an interaction effect was interpreted to mean that participation in distance running provided no particular advantage (or disadvantage) to young males or females in their performance on the eight-item battery of motor tasks. Therefore, separate multiple discriminant function analyses were undertaken to determine which of the motor tasks contributed significantly ($p < .05$) to the group and gender differences (see Table 2).

Five of the eight variables contributed significantly to the function that discriminated the runners from the control subjects. In order of their weightings, these were the modified sit-ups test, the flexed arm hang, the standing long jump, the sideward leap, and the sit and reach (see Table 2). Two of the variables not included in the function, the figure eight run and vertical jump, were related to the standing long jump and may have been disregarded by the analysis for this reason. The runners were more proficient than the controls on the modified sit-ups, flexed arm hang, and the sit and reach. The control subjects scored better on the sideward leap and the standing long jump. These outcomes were hypothesized because the sit-up and flexed arm hang are considered measures of muscular endurance and the sit and reach a measure of flexibility (or extensibility) of the lower back, hips and posterior thighs

Table 2. Standardized discriminant function coefficients

Variable	Runners/ Controls Function 1	Males/ Females Function 1
Sideward leap	−.367	*
Quadrant jump	*	.249
Flexed arm hang	.597	*
Standing long jump	−.536	−.488
Figure eight run	*	*
Sit and reach	.345	1.049
Modified sit-ups	.766	*
Vertical jump	*	*
Eigenvalue	1.011	.760
Canonical correlation	.709	.657
Chi square	32.493	26.839
Significance (df)	<.001(5)	<.001(3)

*Did not contribute.

(AAHPERD, 1980). Muscular endurance and flexibility are regarded as vital to successful distance running (Daniels, Fitts, & Sheehan, 1978).

The fact that the runners did not perform as well as the controls on the long jump is not surprising because jumping, a power event, is dependent on different muscle fibers than distance running, an endurance task. In a study by Komi (cited by Komi, 1984), muscle fiber composition in the vastus lateralis muscle of various athletic groups and a control group was examined. Biopsy samples from endurance runners contained nearly 80% slow twitch (ST) fibers, whereas those from jumpers and the control subjects contained less than 40% and 50% ST fibers, respectively. Thus, distance runners may have as much as 30% fewer fast twitch (FT) fibers available for use in jumping than control subjects. A similar argument can be made for performance on the sideward leap test. A leap followed by an attempt to balance on the landing foot for a period of 5 s appears to require FT fibers rather than ST fibers. However, such postulation needs to be verfied.

The discriminant function for males and females contained only three significant variables. The most powerful of these was the sit and reach task, followed by the standing long jump and the quadrant jump (see Table 2). Males performed better than the females on the standing long jump, but the females were superior on both the sit and reach and the quadrant jump. These outcomes were in the predicted direction, except for performance on the quadrant jump. In the age range of 9 to 15 years, males generally outperform females on tasks of power such as the standing long jump (AAHPERD, 1976; Branta et al., 1984), and females exhibit greater flexibility than males (AAHPERD, 1980; Branta et al., 1984). The superior performance of the females on the quadrant jump was not expected, although in retrospect it is understandable. Males usually score slightly better than females on agility tasks that include running (AAHPERD, 1976) or rapid changes in body position, such as the squat thrust (Johnson & Nelson, 1969) and the gross body agility task (Cratty & Martin, 1969). However, the quadrant jump requires rapid changes of the legs and feet not unlike some of the movements required to play hop-scotch and to jump rope, activities engaged in more frequently by females. Johnson and Nelson (1969) found that college women scored better than college males on this task.

The lack of gender differences on the flexed arm hang, the modified sit-up, and the vertical jump is inconsistent with results reported in the literature. The review by Branta et al., (1984) shows that males generally exhibit higher performace levels than females on all of these tasks. The fact that the vertical jump (and the figure eight run) correlates well with the standing long jump may have produced a nonsignificant result as an artifact of the statistical procedure used. A partial explanation for the sit-up results may be found by examining the mean values for the subjects. Although the means for the control subjects are in the direction anticipated, they are reversed for the runners and have the effect of cancelling out potential gender differences. The pooled sample thus may not be representative of a larger general population due to the inclusion of a specific performance group whose female members may possess unique characteristics (perhaps in terms of body size, shape, or composition) that permit them to perform as well as or better than their male counterparts. For example, the median number of sit-ups for 13-year-old females is 35 (AAHPERD, 1980), which is comparable to the mean of 34.82 for the female controls, but substantially less than the mean of 45.33 for the distance runners. The female runners' mean is also larger than the median of 41 sit-ups for 13-year-old males (AAHPERD, 1980). Similarly, the average flexed arm hang time of the female runners (33.97 s) is much greater than that of 13-year-old females (18.95 s) and males (24.69 s) participating in the Motor Performance Study at Michigan State University (Branta et al., 1984). No explanations, other than possible sampling bias, is available to account for the lack of gender differences on the sideward leap task.

The effectiveness of a discriminant function also can be determined by examining its ability to correctly assign subjects within their actual groups. On this criterion, the discriminant function was very effective. Overall, 90.2% of the cases were correctly classified. Only 3 of the runners and 2 of the control subjects were incorrectly assigned. Predicted group membership was accurate for 80.4% of the males and females. Only 5 of 24 males and 5 of 27 females were assigned to the opposite gender group on the basis of their performance on three of the eight motor skill tests.

In summary, the results of this study indicate that young runners and control subjects are similar in their performance on fractionated reaction time and movement time tasks, but differ on motor tasks selected to evaluate balance, muscular endurance, leg power, and flexibility. The performance of the males was superior to that of the females on the standing long jump, while the females excelled on the quadrant jump and the sit and reach. There were no gender differences on the tests of balance, muscular endurance, reaction time, and speed of limb movements.

References

AAHPERD. (1976). *Youth fitness test manual* (rev. ed.). Washington, DC: American Alliance for Health, Physical Education, Recreation and Dance.

AAHPERD. (1980). *Health related physical fitness test manual*. Reston, VA: American Alliance for Health, Physical Education, Recreation, and Dance.

Branta, C.F., Haubenstricker, J.L., & Seefeldt, V. (1984). Age changes in motor skills during childhood and adolescence. In R.L. Terjung (Ed.), *Exercise and sport science reviews*, vol. 12. Lexington, MA: Collamore Press.

Cratty, J.B., & Martin, M.M. (1969). *Perceptual-motor development in children*. Philadelphia: Lea & Febiger.

Daniels, J., Fitts, R., & Sheehan, G. (1978). *Conditioning for distance running*. New York: John Wiley & Sons.

Eckert, H.M., & Eichorn, D.H. (1977). Developmental variability in reaction time. *Child Development*, **48**, 452–458.

E-Lotfalian, A. (1981). *A comparison of fractionated reaction time and movement time in males across selected age and activity levels*. Unpublished doctoral dissertation, Michigan State University, East Lansing, MI.

Fulton, C.D., & Hubbard, A.W. (1975). Effect of puberty on reaction and movement time. *Research Quarterly*, **46**, 335–344.

Gates, D.P., & Sheffield, R.P. (1940). Tests of change of direction as measurement of different kinds of motor ability in boys of the 7th, 8th, and 9th grades. *Research Quarterly*, **11**, 136–147.

Goodenough, F.L. (1935). The development of the reactive process from early childhood to maturity. *Journal of Experimental Psychology, 18*, 431–450.

Henry, F. (1961). Stimulus complexity, movement complexity, age, and sex in relation to reaction latency and speed in limb movements. *Research Quarterly, 32*, 353–366.

Hodgens, J. (1963). Reaction time and speed of movement in males and females of various ages. *Research Quarterly, 34*, 335-343.

Johnson, B.L., & Nelson, J.K. (1969). *Practical measurements for evaluation in physical education*. Minneapolis: Burgess.

Klimovitch, G. (1977). Startle response and muscular fatigue effects upon fractionated hand grip reaction time. *Journal of Motor Behavior, 9*, 285-292.

Komi, P.V. (1984). Physiological and biomechanical correlations of muscle function: Effects of muscle structure and stretch-shortening cycle on force and speed. In R.L. Terjung (Ed.), *Exercise and sport sciences reviews*, vol. 12. Lexington, MA: Collamore Press.

Kroll, W. (1974). Fractionated reaction and reflex time before and after fatiguing isotonic exercise. *Medicine and Science in Sports, 6*, 260-266.

Noble, C.E., Baker, B.L., & Jones, T.A. (1964). Age and sex parameters in psychomotor learning. *Perceptual and Motor Skills, 19*, 935-945.

Scott, M.G., & French, E. (1959). *Measurement and evaluation in physical education*. Dubuque, IA: W.C. Brown.

Seefeldt, V. (1986). Introduction to an interdisciplinary assessment of competition on elite young distance runners. In M. Weiss & D. Gould (Eds.), *Sport for children and youths* (pp. 213-217). Champaign, IL: Human Kinetics.

Thomas, J.R., Gallagher, J.D., & Purvis, G.J. (1981). Reaction time and anticipation time: Effects of development. *Research Quarterly for Exercise and Sport, 52*, 359-367.

Yandell, K.M., & Spirduso, W.W. (1981). Sex and athletic status as factors in reaction latency and movement time. *Research Quarterly for Exercise and Sport, 52*, 495-504.

37

Summary of the Interdisciplinary Assessment of Competition on Young Elite Runners

Vern Seefeldt
MICHIGAN STATE UNIVERSITY
EAST LANSING, MICHIGAN, USA

The influence of competitive long-distance running on the welfare of 28 highly successful runners was ascertained via a comprehensive battery of tests. Twelve boys and 15 girls between the ages of 9 and 15 years were selected as subjects because of their ability to finish within the top five contestants for their age group in races of 10K or longer. Control subjects from the Lansing metropolitan area were matched with the runners by chronological age, height, and gender. All subjects received the identical battery of tests under controlled laboratory conditions. The following results represent the first collection of data in a 5-year study.

The runners' involvement in training increased as age advanced. Duration of training encompassed a mean of 13 weeks per year for the youngest boys (7 to 8 years) to 43 weeks per year for the 13 to 15 year old girls. Distances run per year ranged from an average of 78 km for the youngest boys to 1,859 km for the oldest girls. Female runners were more committed than males to running, trained more days per week, ran more miles per week, and entered more races. The girls' commitment to running may explain some of their values in performance and body build, which frequently were more similar to those of the male runners than to those of the female or male controls.

The aerobic characteristics of running resulted in high maximum oxygen uptake values for both male and female runners. Cardiac efficiency, as reflected by lower heart rates during work, rest, and recovery from a treadmill run in the runners, was distinctly different from values obtained from the controls.

Analysis of lipoproteins showed no significant differences between runners and controls, but fractionation of high- (HDL-C) and low- (LDL-C) density lipoproteins revealed significantly higher levels of HDL-C and lower levels of LDL-C in the runners. Serum lipid and lipoprotein differences were dose-dependent, with a positive association between work capacity and HDL-C and a negative relationship between triglycerides and LDL-C. The female runners had markedly elevated alkaline phosphatase levels, but levels for male runners and controls were also high.

The young runners were shorter in stature than the control subjects, but had longer lower extremities. Bodily circumferences and breadths of the runners were smaller and all mean values of skinfolds were significantly smaller than those of male and female control subjects. The diets of the runners and controls were not significantly different, although the males consumed more kilocalories, total fat, protein, and carbohydrates than the females.

Runners and controls did not differ in fractionated reaction and movement times, but there were differences in balance, agility, and power, favoring the controls, and in muscular endurance and flexibility, favoring the runners.

Results of these analyses indicate that the young runners differed significantly on many of the parameters from the control subjects who were matched by gender, age, and height. At this writing, attributions to genetic endowment, predisposition to running, or to the effects of training are all plausible. Continued attention to these variables during the course of the longitudinal study may provide more definitive answers.